Gould and Davis h........................e run! I predict
that this will be one of the very best in the Counterpoints series. The
introduction and conclusion by Gould and Davis are helpful, informa-
tive, and very interesting. And, wow, did they pick great representatives
of each view or what? Oppy is, in my view, the top philosophical atheist
writing today. And McGrew and Moser are not only household names in
the field but top representatives of very important and distinctive views.
And Oliphint is among a very small handful of top Reformed apologists.
But what is really shocking about this treasure is that these high-level
thinkers have managed to write chapters that are understandable to a
nonspecialist. Christian philosophy is on the rise, and believers need
to think through its role in Christianity. This book is the place to start
that journey.

J. P. Moreland, Distinguished Professor of Philosophy
and author of *Love Your God with All Your Mind,*
Talbot School of Theology, Biola University

Drs. Paul Gould and Richard Davis have put together a "must-have" book
on a topic of critical importance to the Christian community. Far from
little-known scholars, their lineup of participants includes some of the
most well-known and well-respected philosophers in the field. *Four Views
on Christianity and Philosophy* will serve as an engaging text for courses
at the college, university, or seminary levels. It is smoothly written, easily
understood, and features a spectacular clash of ideas from philosophers of
diverse perspectives. Students will love it. This volume ranks among the
very best of Zondervan's wide array of Counterpoints books.

Gary Habermas, Distinguished Research Professor; Chair
of Philosophy, Liberty Baptist Theological Seminary

Gould and Davis have performed a great service. They have orchestrated an important and much-needed conversation on the relationship between the Christian faith and philosophy, and they have selected as dialogue partners truly excellent representatives of the respective "four views." This volume will serve as a superb resource for years to come.

Paul Copan, author of *A Little Book for New Philosophers,* and Pledger Family Chair of Philosophy and Ethics, Palm Beach Atlantic University in West Palm Beach, Florida

Despite the resurgence of Christian philosophy during the past several decades, many Christians, as well as others, are dubious that there is any sort of positive relationship between Christianity and philosophy. In this volume, four accomplished practitioners of philosophy with very different views of how it relates to Christianity debate this fundamental question. This is a valuable resource for persons on all sides of this fascinating and vital issue.

Jerry L. Walls, Scholar in Residence and Professor of Philosophy, Houston Baptist University

In addition to learning about different views relating philosophy to Christianity, readers will see how these distinctive approaches are put into practice with the dynamic interaction from the four principal contributors. Both newcomers and seasoned scholars will find many ideas in this book worthy of serious thought and reflection.

John M. DePoe, Associate Professor of Philosophy, Marywood University

"What has Jerusalem to do with Athens?" Tertullian's famous question about the relationship between Christianity and philosophy has been variously answered by thinkers throughout the centuries. Some, like Tertullian, have believed that philosophy is incompatible with Christian faith. Others, like Augustine and Aquinas, have seen them as compatible yet in different ways and to varying degrees. *Four Views on Christianity and Philosophy* explores this topic of perennial concern, utilizing the skill of some of the best philosophers in the field. Each contributor addresses the nature and methods of philosophy, the nature of Christian commitment, the relationship between faith and reason, and the value and extent of evidence for and against the Christian worldview. Ideal for classroom use or personal study, for anyone interested in answering Tertullian's famous question, this book is the place to start.

Steven B. Cowan, Associate Professor of Philosophy and Religion, Lincoln Memorial University

I'm a big fan of the Counterpoints series by Zondervan. And this is one of my favorites. The expert will find insight and clarification, and the novice will learn the scope of the debate. All will walk away with an appreciation of how important it is to wrestle with the relationship between philosophy and Christianity.

Sean McDowell, Assistant Professor of Apologetics, Biola University, and author of *A New Kind of Apologist.*

Books in the Counterpoints Series

Church Life

Bible and Theology

FOUR
VIEWS
ON
CHRISTIANITY
AND PHILOSOPHY

Graham Oppy

K. Scott Oliphint

Timothy McGrew

Paul K. Moser

Paul M. Gould and Richard Brian Davis, general editors
Stanley N. Gundry, series editor

COUNTERPOINTS
BIBLE & THEOLOGY

ZONDERVAN®

ZONDERVAN

Four Views on Christianity and Philosophy
Copyright © 2016 by Paul K. Moser, K. Scott Oliphint, Timothy McGrew, Graham Oppy, Richard
Brian Davis, Paul M. Gould

This title is also available as a Zondervan ebook.

Requests for information should be addressed to:
Zondervan, 3900 Sparks Dr. SE, Grand Rapids, Michigan 49546

Library of Congress Cataloging-in-Publication Data

Names: Oppy, Graham, 1960- author.
Title: Four views on Christianity and philosophy / Graham Oppy, K. Scott Oliphint, Timothy
    McGrew, Paul K. Moser ; Paul M. Gould and Richard Brian Davis, general editors.
Description: Grand Rapids : Zondervan, 2016. | Series: Counterpoints: Bible and theology |
    Includes bibliographical references and index.
Identifiers: LCCN 2016015701 | ISBN 9780310521143 (softcover)
Subjects: LCSH: Philosophy and religion. | Christian philosophy.
Classification: LCC BR100 .F6717 2016 | DDC 261.5/1—dc23 LC record available at https://lccn.
    loc.gov/2016015701

Cover design: Tammy Johnson
Cover art: © Jesus Among the Doctors by Paolo Veronese
Interior design: Kait Lamphere

Printed in the United States of America

16 17 18 19 20 21 22 23 24 25 26 /DHV/ 15 14 13 12 11 10 9 8 7 6 5 4 3 2 1

CONTENTS

ABOUT THE EDITORS AND CONTRIBUTORS ▬▬▬

Richard Brian Davis is Professor of Philosophy at Tyndale University in Toronto, Canada. He is the author or editor of four books, including *Loving God with Your Mind: Essays in Honor of J. P. Moreland*. He has published thirty book chapters or articles in such places as *Australasian Journal of Philosophy*, *Religious Studies*, *Acta Analytica*, *Philo*, *The Modern Schoolman*, *Philosophia Christi*, *Heythrop Journal*, *The Journal of Medicine and Philosophy*, and *Axiomathes*. Rich blogs at: tyndalephilosophy.com.

Paul M. Gould is Assistant Professor of Philosophy and Christian Apologetics at Southwestern Baptist Theological Seminary in Fort Worth, Texas. He is the author of *The Outrageous Idea of the Missional Professor*, editor of *Beyond the Control of God? Six Views on the Problem of God and Abstract Objects*, and coeditor of *The Two Tasks of the Christian Scholar: Redeeming the Soul, Redeeming the Mind*; *Loving God with Your Mind: Essays in Honor of J. P. Moreland*; and *Is Faith in God Reasonable? Debates in Philosophy, Science, and Rhetoric*. Paul blogs at: www.paul-gould.com.

Timothy McGrew is Professor and Chairman of the Department of Philosophy at Western Michigan University. He specializes in theory of knowledge, logic, probability theory, and the history and philosophy of science. He has published in numerous journals including *Mind*, *The Monist*, *Analysis*, *Erkenntnis*, *British Journal for the Philosophy of Science*, and *Philosophia Christi*. His recent publications include the article on "Evidence" in *The Routledge Companion to Epistemology*, coauthorship of *The Philosophy of Science: An Historical Anthology*, coauthorship (with Lydia McGrew) of the article on "The Argument from Miracles" in *The Blackwell Companion to Natural Theology*, and the article on "Miracles" for *The Stanford Encyclopedia of Philosophy*.

Paul K. Moser is Professor of Philosophy at Loyola University in Chicago, as well as past editor of *American Philosophical Quarterly*. He has authored over one hundred articles and authored or edited over twenty books. Some of his books include: *Empirical Justification*; *Knowledge and Evidence*; *Philosophy after Objectivity*; *Morality and the Good Life*; *The Theory of Knowledge: A Thematic Introduction*; *Moral Relativism*; *Oxford Handbook of Epistemology*; *Divine Hiddenness: New Essays*; *The Rationality of Theism*; *The Elusive God: Reorienting Religious Epistemology*; *Jesus and Philosophy: New Essays*; *The Evidence for God: Religious Knowledge Reexamined*; *The Wisdom of the Christian Faith*; and *The Severity of God: Religion and Philosophy Reconceived*.

K. Scott Oliphint is Professor of Apologetics and Systematic Theology at Westminster Theological Seminary in Philadelphia and is the author of numerous articles and books, including "Is There a Reformed Objection to Natural Theology?: A Review Article," "Using Reason by Faith," "Bavinck's Realism, the Logos Principle and Sola Scriptura," "Something Much Too Plain to Say," "Epistemology and Christian Belief," and "Plantinga on Warrant." His books include *The Battle Belongs to the Lord*; *Reasons for Faith: Philosophy in the Service of Theology*; *God with Us: Divine Condescension and the Attributes of God*; and his most recent book, *Covenantal Apologetics*. He is also the coeditor of the two-volume *Christian Apologetics Past and Present: A Primary Source Reader* and *Revelation and Reason: New Essays in Reformed Apologetics*.

Graham Oppy is Professor of Philosophy at Monash University. He is author of *Ontological Arguments and Belief in God*; *Philosophical Perspectives on Infinity*; *Arguing about Gods*; *Reading Philosophy of Religion* (with Michael Scott); *The Best Argument against God*; *Reinventing Philosophy of Religion: An Opinionated Introduction*; and *Describing Gods: An Investigation of Divine Attributes*. He is editor of *The Routledge Handbook of Contemporary Philosophy of Religion* and (with Nick Trakakis) *The History of Western Philosophy of Religion*.

INTRODUCTION TO CHRISTIANITY AND PHILOSOPHY: FOUR VIEWS

PAUL M. GOULD AND RICHARD BRIAN DAVIS

What is the relationship between Christianity and philosophy? This is not an easy question to answer, not least because it is difficult to specify in terms agreeable to all. For example, how do you define philosophy? Is philosophical thinking, as contemporary philosopher Allen Wood puts it, "simply the human mind in operation, unaided by anything supernatural and unfettered by any human authority or any procedure for reaching some pre-given end"?[1] If so, there is little hope for a positive working relationship between Christianity and philosophy. Or, in defining Christianity, do we accept that it intends to "[teach] that unquestioned faith is a virtue"?[2] If so, then once again there is little hope for a positive relationship between Christianity and philosophy.

While contemporary philosophers in the West rightly see themselves as building on a Greek heritage, other sources are significant as well, including Judeo-Christian sources. The question of Christianity's relationship to philosophy cannot be dismissed at the outset via sterile definitions of philosophy or religion. The fact that there has been an ongoing conversation over centuries and perhaps a positive relationship requires—at minimum—deeper reflection. In addition, there is a natural affinity between philosophical reflection and the religious instinct that is suggestive. To understand this natural affinity, let us consider the concept of wonder as it is employed in philosophy and Christianity.

In Plato's *Theaetetus*, Socrates asserts that philosophy begins in wonder.[3] Certainly wonder includes unfettered curiosity and the asking of questions, often of the form, "What is X?" where X may stand for "justice," "knowledge," "man," or "God," for example. Moreover, as

---

1. Allen Wood, "Philosophy—What Is To Be Done?" *Topoi* 25 (2006): 133.
2. Richard Dawkins, *The God Delusion* (New York: First Mariners Books, 2008), 346.
3. 155d. Aristotle also argues for this in Book One of *Metaphysics*.

these examples indicate, philosophical wonderment is most appropriately understood in terms of fundamental questions about reality.[4] But wonder is more than mere unfettered curiosity. It also hints at a sense of awe, astonishment, and passion regarding the object in question and a transformation of the one who asks.[5]

Textbooks tell us that philosophy is the love of wisdom. Plato (427–347 BC) says so himself (*Republic* 475b–c), and the etymology suggests as much. The Greek prefix *philo-* refers to love, while *sophia* signifies wisdom; thus *philo-* plus *sophia* comes out to mean "the love of wisdom." This is a good start. Yet for Plato, it is better to say—and this sounds scandalous—that he was a lover of wisdom, or even wisdom's lover. Wisdom moved him. He sought it with all of his being, toiled to obtain it, and followed the lonely path to find it, realizing it was worth the effort.

Yet a word of caution is in order here. Paul, the "apostle to the (Greek-speaking) Gentiles" (Gal 2:8) warns us that this love of wisdom can become distorted and even an impediment to our knowing God through Christ. Paul stresses that his mandate is "to preach the gospel," but "not with wisdom and eloquence, lest the cross of Christ be emptied of its power" (1 Cor 1:17). If we're not careful, our love of wisdom can putrefy into a base desire to be *publicly recognized as wise*, say, by way of demonstrating our philosophical prowess. When *that* assumes center stage, "the message of the cross" (1 Cor 1:18)—the gospel's content and power—takes a backseat to *how* it is communicated. The emphasis becomes the philosopher—the messenger—and not the message. Our attention is arrested upon the speaker and their eloquence, rhetorical skill, and sheer force of presence. Invariably this leads to a rank ordering of personalities inside the guild. Thus, even in Paul's day, one faction in the church at Corinth followed Apollos

---

4. Wonder is often taken to mean merely unfettered curiosity. For example, the statesman Charles Malik wrote, "The Greeks, more than any other people, displayed an irrepressible and unbounded passion for the exercise of reason and an incredible curiosity to investigate and know everything" (Charles Malik, *A Christian Critique of the University* [Waterloo, CA: North Waterloo Academic Press, 1987], 17). We do not deny that it is unfettered curiosity. We will deny that it is merely such.

5. Compare Herman E. Stark: "Wonder is the metaphysical condition evoked and sustained by philosophical asking. The phenomenon, in other words, seeps into one's being and thereby alters who one is" ("Philosophy as Wonder," *Dialogue and Universalism* 1–2 [2005]: 135). See also Bertrand Russell (*The Problems of Philosophy* [Oxford: Oxford University Press, 1997], chapter 15), who argues that the chief value of philosophy is the personal enrichment that comes by the very act of questioning.

(1 Cor 1:12), no doubt because—as Luke tells us—he was "a learned man" who "vigorously refuted his Jewish opponents in public debate, proving from the Scriptures that Jesus was the Messiah" (Acts 18:24, 28). If he had a Twitter account, its followers would have been through the roof in numbers.

By contrast, although he had seen the risen Lord and shown "the marks of a true apostle, including signs, wonders and miracles" (2 Cor 12:12), the Corinthians *still* complained of Paul: "His letters are weighty and forceful, but in person he is unimpressive and his speaking amounts to nothing" (2 Cor 10:10). Notice the total disregard of truth. They admit Paul's letters are "weighty," but then promptly dismiss what he says. They do this not because the ideas are erroneous or lack divine confirmation but simply because the one penning them isn't impressive in person. Knowing their obsession with philosophical celebrity, Paul wisely (and strategically) adopts a wholly *alethic* stance: "My message and my preaching were not with wise and persuasive words, but with a demonstration of the Spirit's power" (1 Cor 2:4). Why so? It is "so that your faith might not rest on human wisdom, but on God's power" (1 Cor 2:5). Paul's concern is to lay a solid epistemic foundation for Christianity. He has no interest whatever in playing to the shallow and superficial whims of the cultural intelligentsia.

There is a tradition going back to at least Epicurus that views fear as the beginning of religion. But there is another tradition—going back to Plato himself—which identifies the supreme object of wonder as the transcendent good that is God.[6] If so, it means that philosophy and religion spring from the same source, and in this we find justification for exploring the question of Christianity's relationship to philosophy. According to Christianity, God is absolute perfection, the greatest possible being who is *the* perpetual novelty that forever fills the human heart with a sense of awe and wonder. Augustine, building upon Plato, would later put it this way: "You stir man to take pleasure in praising you, because you have made us for yourself, and our heart is restless until it rests in you."[7]

---

6. Douglas Hedley, "Forms of Reflection, Imagination, and the Love of Wisdom," *Metaphilosophy* 43.1–2 (2012): 123.

7. Augustine, *Confessions*, trans. Henry Chadwick (Oxford: Oxford University Press, 2008), 1.1.

From Athens to Jerusalem and Back Again

While the Greeks started a *wisdom movement*, roughly characterized in terms of the pursuit of happiness (*eudaimonia*) via intellectual and moral virtue, the movement Jesus and his followers inaugurated appears to be substantially different.[8] From the first public words of his ministry (Matt 4:17) to his last (Acts 1:8), Jesus was concerned with the progress of the gospel—the good news that the kingdom of God was at hand. The coming of Jesus alerts us that something new is taking place in human history. The world is not the way it's supposed to be—it is cracked, violated, and fallen—yet God in love sent his Son to die on a cross to bring redemption to humanity and ultimately to restore all creation. A new *power* was available that offered people spiritual, moral, and even bodily redemption by God. It could be said that Jesus started a *shalom movement*, roughly characterized in terms of God's renewal of sinful humanity through faith in Jesus, and ultimately—when the kingdom of God is consummated—a full restoration of the world to its original state of goodness, delight, and flourishing.

The central question when we journey from Athens to Jerusalem is *cognitive*: How can we *know* that the claims of Christianity—the movement inaugurated by Jesus and his followers—are true? But the central question in the journey from Jerusalem to Athens is *volitional*: Are we humans willing to locate our lives within God's story, giving up our self-focus and self-salvation plans for the sake of the love of God and humanity?[9] Both questions were front and center when the apostle Paul found himself in Athens in the spring of AD 51.

In this great city—the city of Socrates, Plato, Aristotle, Epicurus, and Zeno—Paul was distressed to see Athens full of idols (Acts 17:16), and he began to publicly share the good news of Jesus.[10] As he reasoned in the synagogue and in the marketplace, a group of Epicurean and Stoic philosophers engaged in argument with Paul (17:18). The reaction to Paul in the "marketplace of ideas" was not noticeably positive. Some

---

8. Paul K. Moser, "Introduction: Jesus and Philosophy," in *Jesus and Philosophy: New Essays*, ed. Paul K. Moser (Cambridge: Cambridge University Press, 2009), 2.

9. Moser, "Introduction," 6.

10. In fact, the pagan writer Petronius sarcastically quipped that it was easier to find a god in Athens than a man. See R. C. H. Lenski, *The Interpretation of the Acts of the Apostles* (Minneapolis: Augsburg, 1961), 708.

asked what this "babbler" wished to say, while others suggested that Paul seemed to be a purveyor of "foreign gods" (17:18). The former term is derogatory—conveying the sense that Paul was a kind of dilettante. The second complaint, however, was more dangerous—the charge of being a herald of foreign or strange gods is the very same charge that led to the demise of Socrates.[11] They took Paul and brought him to the Areopagus to have him present his case before the council, saying, "May we know what this new teaching is that you are presenting? You are bringing some strange ideas to our ears, and we would like to know what they mean" (17:19–20). The men of Athens wanted to assess the meaning and truth of Paul's claims. Paul stood up in their midst and delivered his answer by arguing that the unknown god worshipped by the Athenians was in fact *the* true God (17:22–28). Humanity's fundamental questions don't find their answers in water (Thales), or change (Heraclitus), or the impossibility of change (Parmenides), but in the God in whom "we live and move and have our being" (17:28).

Once Paul answers Athens's question to Jerusalem, he then asks Jerusalem's question to Athens. Paul moves the discussion from what was familiar to the Greek mind into a distinctly Judeo-Christian worldview by introducing the concept of personal moral accountability and guilt before God and the requirement of personal repentance (17:30). Then he introduces his hearers to him who was crucified and raised from the dead (17:31). This latter claim is all the more startling given the location of its utterance, for at the mythical founding of the Areopagus, the god Apollo emphatically stated, "Once the dust drinks down a man's blood, he is gone, once for all. No rising back, no spell sung over the grave can sing him back."[12] As a result of Paul's speech, some mocked, some wanted to hear more, and others believed and became followers of Jesus (17:32–24).

Standing on that hill, Paul began the "great conversation" that continues to this day between the philosophers and Jesus and his followers.[13] Very early in the history of the Christian church, Christianity

---

11. Ben Witherington III, *The Acts of the Apostles: A Socio-Rhetorical Commentary* (Grand Rapids: Eerdmans, 1998), 515.

12. The quote is from the Greek poet Aeschylus and his play *Eumenides*, written and performed almost five hundred years before Paul arrived in Athens. See Aeschylus, *The Oresteia*, trans. Robert Fagles (New York: Penguin, 1979), 260.

13. One writer goes so far as to say that Mars Hill is the birthplace of Christendom, where Christendom is to be understood as "the culture of Christians after Jesus' life, death and

and philosophy became partners. While some—such as Tertullian (AD 160–225)—rejected this partnership, others couldn't conceive of Christianity apart from Greek moorings.[14] For example, Origen (AD 184–253) often pinned his understanding of Scripture more on his Neoplatonism than on the clear meaning of the biblical text. Still, most Christians found a middle way between these extremes, bringing philosophy and Christianity into conversation in order to understand truth and live the good life.

Augustine (AD 354–430) as a young man was awakened by a genuine love and passion to seek the truth by reading Cicero's *Hortensius*. Eventually, after his conversion to Christ, he concluded that the mind is weak and needs the guidance of divine authority to find the truth.[15] Still, Augustine believed that Christianity and philosophy were significant conversation partners. Augustine appropriated much of Plato and Neoplatonism into service in explicating and defending Christian theology.

Aquinas (AD 1225–1274) continued on this path, pressing Aristotelian philosophy into service in explicating and defending the Christian faith. According to Aristotle (384–322 BC), the goal of philosophy is found in the knowledge of first principles and causes. In his *Summa contra Gentiles*, Aquinas picks up this Aristotelian thread, saying that it is the role of the wise to seek the truth about things' highest causes and last ends, and then at once adds, "Divine Wisdom testifies that He has assumed flesh and come into the world in order to make the truth known."[16] Thus, divine truth is a person—the person of Christ—and philosophy seeks *inter alia* knowledge of Christ, even if the philosopher is unaware. Moreover, for Aquinas, since God's nature determines all necessary truths, including the true nature of things, all knowledge is bound up within the nature of the Christian God.[17] Here of course Aquinas

---

resurrection" (John Mark Reynolds, *When Athens Met Jerusalem* [Downers Grove: InterVarsity Press, 2009], 14).

14. While Tertullian is famous for his desire to keep the church pure by rejecting "secular learning," his own writings echoed Greek philosophy on nearly every page. See Reynolds, *When Athens Met Jerusalem*, 17.

15. John Rist, "Faith and Reason," in *The Cambridge Companion to Augustine*, ed. Eleonore Stump and Norman Kretzmann (Cambridge: Cambridge University Press, 2001), 28.

16. Thomas Aquinas, *Summa contra Gentiles*, trans. Anton C. Pegis (Notre Dame: University of Notre Dame Press, 1975), 60.

17. Brian Leftow, "Jesus and Aquinas," in *Jesus and Philosophy: New Essays*, ed. Paul K. Moser (Cambridge: Cambridge University Press, 2009), 125, 128–29.

was doing no more than echoing the great apostle, who prayed that the Colossians might "have the full riches of complete understanding"—an understanding ultimately to be found in Christ, "in whom are hidden all the treasures of wisdom and knowledge" (Col 2:2–3).

When we consider the modern and contemporary periods of philosophy, we find a radical departure from these approaches. No longer do we find the pursuit of wisdom in Christ. For the most part, philosophy is no longer seen as the handmaiden to Christianity but instead something magisterial and autonomous. Philosophy answers only to itself (and possibly science), but certainly not to Scripture, the creeds, or the church. The foundational tenets of Christianity—the incarnation, resurrection, and atonement—if they are to be judged true and reasonable, must pass the bar of cutting-edge academic philosophy, which is by no means an unchanging plumb line. Thus, René Descartes (AD 1596–1650) tells us that knowledge requires certainty and indubitability. We can know that we exist, for example, and whatever we can manage to deduce therefrom. But from the fact that we exist, how does it even remotely follow "that God was reconciling the world to himself in Christ" (2 Cor 5:19)?

Or consider Kant (AD 1724–1804) and his philosophical system. On his view, we know nothing of the way things really are (*noumena*). Instead, what we know is the *phenomena*: the way things appear to us after the mind has shaped and formed the unstructured data of sensation. *Existence, space, time, object, property, cause* and *effect*—all of these are just patterned ways the mind processes reality. Reality, whatever it is, doesn't contain any of these things. Rather, we humans now play the role of God, constructing the world of objects and their properties in space and time. Obviously, this way of thinking is incompatible with biblical Christianity.

Things do not improve when we examine the currently fashionable postmodern position. The French philosopher Jacques Derrida (AD 1930–2004) famously said that "there is nothing outside of the text."[18] According to James K. A. Smith, this implies that even "the world is a kind of text [story] requiring interpretation."[19] Sadly, due to our

---

18. Jacques Derrida, *Of Grammatology*, trans. Gayatri Chakravorty Spivak (Baltimore: John Hopkins University Press, 1976), 158.

19. James K. A. Smith, "Who's Afraid of Postmodernism? A Response to the 'Biola School,'" in *Christianity and the Postmodern Turn: Six Views*, ed. Myron B. Penner (Grand Rapids: Brazos, 2005), 225.

situatedness (ethnic, historical, and otherwise), we never really get at that world. Smith writes, "So we never get past texts and interpretations to things 'simply as they are' in any kind of unmediated fashion . . . rather, we move from interpretation to interpretation. The entire world is a text. Thus, 'there is nothing outside of the text.'"[20]

This means we can never know the world of the Nazarene, the world in which he carried out his ministry of miracle working and exorcisms, where he was crucified, buried, and then raised on the third day. We're stuck with the various interpretations of it. We are told that Jesus's disciples didn't proclaim the facts about his resurrection. That wasn't possible. They simply did the best they could. They told their story—an interpretation for which, in principle, there can be no objective evidence. Indeed, how could there be, if there is *nothing* outside of interpretations?

With all of these conflicting approaches to philosophical inquiry, what is God to do? Should he accommodate himself to this or that philosophical system? If so, which one? Should he reveal himself in Christ *through* Aristotelianism, or Thomism, or Cartesianism? Should he seek preapproval from us philosophers before he does anything with epistemic import? One thing is perhaps clear: God hasn't chosen to do any of these things. Indeed, it might be said that he has done precisely the opposite. Thus, Paul asks:

> Where is the wise person? Where is the teacher of the law? Where is the philosopher of this age? Has not God made foolish the wisdom of the world? For since in the wisdom of God the world through its wisdom did not know him, God was pleased through the foolishness of what was preached to save those who believe. (1 Cor 1:20–21)

But why does God reveal himself in this way? From a Christian perspective, the answer is that you cannot deduce "the message of the cross" (1 Cor 1:18) from "the wisdom of the world" (1 Cor 1:20). The gospel doesn't stoop to "the wisdom of the wise" (1 Cor 1:19) before making itself known. Christianity concerns the *salvation* of human beings—not from themselves, or their sin, or their bad choices, but from the wrath of a just and holy God. It is hardly surprising that the intellectual systems

---

20. Smith, "Who's Afraid of Postmodernism?," 225.

erected by sinful and self-serving philosophers would downplay these truths considerably.

This shows us that in some significant ways Christianity and worldly or non-Christian philosophy are at odds. Yet it doesn't spell out how they *are* to be related. Paul tells us that we are to avoid "hollow and deceptive" philosophy because it depends on "the basic principles of the world rather than on Christ" (Col 2:8). But this seems to assume that there could be a philosophy *based on Christ*. Is that really possible? What might it look like?

In this Counterpoints volume, four distinct explanations of Christianity's relationship to philosophy are set out and defended. Graham Oppy defends the *Conflict* view, arguing that philosophy is vastly superior as a way to truth and a way of life, and thus trumps Christianity. Scott Oliphint defends the *Covenant* view, arguing in the opposite direction that Christianity, and not philosophy, has pride of place in epistemic and practical matters—Christianity trumps philosophy. Timothy McGrew advocates for the *Convergence* view that philosophy confirms Christianity and Christianity completes philosophy. Finally, Paul Moser defends the *Conformation* view, reconceiving philosophy in Christ-shaped terms.

Each contributor's essay will be followed by brief responses from the other contributors, putting into dialogue these four important views on the relationship between Christianity and philosophy in a way that will better help you—our reader—to understand and assess the relative merits of each position.

CONFLICT MODEL

GRAHAM OPPY

I have been assigned the task of defending a *conflict* view of the relationship between Christianity and philosophy. At the outset, I should note that I am a metaphysical naturalist. My metaphysical naturalism is—on a great many points—inconsistent with Christian worldviews. In this essay, I shall do my best to sketch a case for saying that metaphysical naturalism trumps Christianity. In the end, I do not think that the case yields a *persuasive* argument; nonetheless, I think that it is a case that deserves serious consideration.

I am also a philosophical neutralist. My philosophical neutralism is, I think, consistent with both metaphysical naturalism and Christianity. I shall do my best to defend the conception of philosophy that I favour. One question that I shall leave unresolved is whether there is ultimately compelling reason to adopt philosophical neutralism.

I shall spend quite a bit of time developing a framework for presenting and discussing worldview disagreements. I shall suggest that, while there are Christian and naturalistic worldviews, there are no merely philosophical worldviews. This conclusion is of a piece with my philosophical neutralism.

Christianity

Christianity is a *religion*. While it is controversial exactly what religions are, we don't go too far wrong if we follow Atran and Norenzayan in supposing that religions are something like forms of social organization that regulate passionate, communal displays of costly commitments to nonnatural agents. (I would modify what they say by also allowing for commitments to nonnatural superstructures of reality, e.g., cycles of reincarnation, reward, and punishment. However, in the interests of brevity, I shall follow their simpler formulation.) Atran and Norenzayan argue that in almost all human societies we find

1. widespread belief in gods, ancestor spirits, and other nonnatural agents;
2. hard-to-fake public expressions of costly material commitments to those nonnatural agents in the form of offerings or sacrifices of goods, property, time, and perhaps even life;
3. mastering of people's existential anxieties concerning death, deception, disease, catastrophe, pain, loneliness, injustice, want, and loss, by these costly commitments to nonnatural agents;
4. ritualized, rhythmic, sensory coordinations of items 1, 2, and 3 in communion, congregation, and intimate fellowship; and
5. evolutionary canalization and convergence of items 1, 2, 3, and 4 that tend toward passionate, communal displays of costly commitments to supernatural agents.

Christianity certainly fits this account. In Christian societies, we plainly observe: (1) widespread belief in God; (2) hard-to-fake public expressions of costly material commitments—offerings and sacrifices of goods, property, time, and sometimes even life—to God; (3) mastering of people's existential anxieties—death, deception, disease, catastrophe, pain, loneliness, injustice, want, and loss—by these costly commitments to God; and (4) ritualized, rhythmic, sensory coordinations of (1), (2), and (3) in communion (congregation, intimate fellowship, and so forth).

Christian religion has many dimensions, including symbols, creeds, scriptures, sacraments, rituals, music, buildings, institutions, populations, history, theology, and so forth. For many of these dimensions of Christian religion, there is enormous variation. Different Christian groups in different times and places are distinguished from one another by their—sometimes very different—symbols, creeds, sacraments, rituals, music, theology, and so forth. But all Christian groups share an early—if contested—history, almost all share the same Scripture, and most have considerable overlap in their core beliefs about, for example, the significance of the life and teachings of Christ as recounted in the canonical gospels.

Philosophy

Philosophy is, I think, primarily a *domain of inquiry*. But even to say this much about philosophy is controversial. Some suppose that philosophy is primarily an *activity*: the pursuit of wisdom or the pursuit of certain kinds of knowledge. Others suppose that philosophy is primarily a *way of life* that accords primary importance to certain kinds of intellectual virtues. Yet others suppose that philosophy is primarily a *systematic body of doctrines* concerning the nature of things and the proper conduct of life.

I suggest that philosophy is the discipline that addresses questions for which we do not yet know how to produce—and perhaps cannot even imagine how to produce—agreed answers using the methods of other established disciplines. One consequence of this way of thinking about philosophy is that whether or not given questions are philosophical depends upon the state of other disciplines of inquiry. For example, many questions that are now clearly questions of physics were once questions of philosophy. Another consequence of this way of thinking about philosophy is that, for almost all other disciplines, there are borderline questions for which it is not currently clear whether those questions will—in time—be given agreed answers, using what will then be established methods of those disciplines. Thus, for almost any discipline, there is also the subfield of philosophy that is the *philosophy of* that discipline. A third consequence of this way of thinking about philosophy is that in those subdisciplines that currently belong to philosophy—metaphysics, epistemology, philosophy of mind, of logic, of language, of science, of ethics, of aesthetics, political philosophy, and so forth—there are no agreed answers to the questions that are addressed in those subdisciplines, and there are no agreed methods for resolving disagreements about the answers to those questions.

Given that Christianity is a religion and that philosophy is a domain of inquiry, it is not immediately clear that there are questions of interest concerning the relation of each to the other. True enough, it is obvious that one might seek to address questions about Christianity, for which we do not yet know how to produce agreed answers, using any of the other disciplines that might be used in studying Christianity (e.g., sociology, demography, anthropology, human geography, or religious studies). If one were to do this, perhaps one might be described as engaging in the *philosophy of Christianity*. But this plainly fails to suggest anything particularly challenging for either Christians or non-Christians.

Perhaps you might be inclined to suggest that one could bring a Christian perspective—a bunch of Christian presuppositions—to philosophy. If one were to do this, would that not be properly described as engaging in *Christian philosophy*? I'm inclined to think not. But it will take some work to bring out the difficulties that arise at this point.

Worldviews

It is natural, I think, to take Christianity to encompass a family of greatly overlapping *worldviews*, that is, a family of greatly overlapping *comprehensive* accounts of our world and our place within that world.

In principle, worldviews are comprehensive normative and descriptive theories. In principle, worldviews are descriptively, explanatorily, ontologically, normatively, methodologically, epistemologically, axiologically, and etiologically complete. In practice, however, what we call "worldviews" are none of these things. In practice, worldviews fall far short of descriptive, explanatory, ontological, normative, methodological, epistemological, axiological, and etiological completeness. However, it remains the case that what we call worldviews involve fundamental descriptive, explanatory, ontological, normative, methodological, epistemological, axiological, and etiological principles. It also remains the case that competing worldviews typically disagree about these very same fundamental principles. What goes for worldviews in general goes for Christian worldviews in particular. Christian worldviews involve fundamental descriptive, explanatory, ontological, normative, methodological, epistemological, axiological, and etiological principles, but they fall well short of descriptive, explanatory, ontological, normative, methodological, epistemological, axiological, and etiological completeness.

One of the most important tasks for philosophy is comparison and adjudication of worldviews. Given our account of worldviews, assessment of competing worldviews must do at least the following three things: (1) it must assess and compare the *descriptive* components of the competing worldviews; (2) it must assess and compare the *normative* components of the competing worldviews; and (3) it must assess and compare the fit between descriptive and normative components in the competing worldviews. Some of the components of worldviews have both descriptive and normative components (e.g., epistemology); other components of worldviews are exclusively descriptive (e.g., explanation and ontology).

Two-Person Worldview Disagreement

Given our account of worldviews, it is appropriate to model worldviews as sets of propositions—i.e., as theories. When we assess and compare the descriptive components of worldviews, we assess those components in terms of familiar theoretical virtues: simplicity, fit with data, explanatory depth, explanatory breadth, and so forth. When we assess and compare the normative components of worldviews, we also assess those components in terms of familiar theoretical virtues: simplicity, explanatory depth, explanatory breadth, and so forth. However, in the case of comparison of normative components of worldviews, it is not immediately clear that there is anything that plays the role of data. Some say that we can and should treat intuitions—intuitive judgments—as data when we compare the normative components of worldviews; others say that it is inappropriate to treat intuitions as data.

I think that it is helpful to start by considering the case of two-person worldview disagreement. If S1 and S2 disagree in their worldviews, then there will be a collection of propositions Wi about which they explicitly disagree—that is, for each of the Wi, one of them believes Wi and the other believes not-Wi—and there will also be a collection of propositions Xi about which they explicitly agree—that is, for each of the Xi, one of them believes that Xi if and only if the other also believes that Xi. For notational simplicity, I shall represent S1 as believing all of the Wi, S2 as believing all of the not-Wi, and both as believing all of the Xi. Under this notation, the theory to which S1 is committed is the logical closure of {Wi, Xi}; the theory to which S2 is committed is the logical closure of {not-Wi, Xi}.

Of course, this representation of the worldview disagreement between S1 and S2 is too simple. In practice, there will be propositions Yi which one party explicitly believes but about which the other party suspends judgment. Moreover, in practice, there will be propositions Zi to which one party has an explicit attitude, but to which the other party has no attitude (perhaps because they have never even entertained those propositions). For notational simplicity, I shall stipulate (1) that the propositions that S1 believes but on which S2 suspends judgment are the Yi; (2) that the propositions that S2 believes but on which S1 suspends judgment are the not-Yi; (3) that the propositions that S1 believes but which S2 has not even considered are the Zi; and (4) the propositions that S2 believes but which S1 has not even considered are the not-Zi. Under this notation, the theory to which S1 is committed is the logical closure of {Wi, Xi, Yi, Zi}, and the theory to which S2 is committed is the logical closure of {not-Wi, Xi, not-Yi, not-Zi}.

There is another respect in which our representation of the worldview disagreement between S1 and S2 may be too simple. As things stand, our representation of the worldview disagreement between S1 and S2 makes it the case that each proposition that either believes is relevant to their worldview disagreement. If we suppose that the parties to a worldview disagreement have beliefs that are simply irrelevant to that disagreement, then we shall need to add further complications to our representation of their disagreement. Since the relevant adjustments are both tedious and complicated—and since they make no difference to the subsequent discussion—I shall simply omit them.

Assessment

Assessment of theories weighs the virtues of theories under assessment. Given competing theories T1 = {Wi, Xi, Yi, Zi} and T2 = {not-Wi, Xi, not-Yi, not-Zi}, there is a three-stage process of assessment to be followed.

The first—and most important—stage is the *articulation* of the theories. If we genuinely want to compare two theories, then we need to make sure that we give accurate articulations of both theories. In practice, it may well be that we can only ever give partial articulations of theories to which we are committed. But even if that is so, we can certainly give articulations of competing theories to the same level of detail and with the same accuracy of formulation. It should go without saying that if we do not make a proper undertaking of this first stage, then there is no point in moving on to subsequent stages. After all, it is almost certain that if you compare your carefully and lovingly articulated theory with a hasty straw articulation of a competing theory, you'll get out the result that yours is the superior theory. But that result will not be of any interest or value to anyone.

At the second—*internal*—stage, we consider whether either of the theories fails on its own terms. Here, the important question is whether either theory is inconsistent. If we stipulate that the Xi are the data against which the theories are assessed, then it may be that a theory is inconsistent in its purely theoretical part—in the case of T1, {Wi, Yi, Zi}; in the case of T2, {not-Wi, not-Yi, not-Zi}. Or it may be that a theory is only inconsistent when data is taken into account. Either way, in order to substantiate the claim that a theory is inconsistent, one needs to be able to explicitly derive a contradiction from claims all of which belong to the theory in question.

At the third—*external*—stage, we consider the theoretical virtues of the two theories. The most important considerations to be weighed together are simplicity, explanatory depth, and explanatory breadth. Simplicity is a matter of ontological and ideological commitments: the leaner the ontology and ideology, the better. Explanatory depth and breadth are matters of goodness of explanation: the more that pure theory explains, and the more that pure theory provides a unified explanation of data, the better. In general, decisions between theories require trade-offs between simplicity and goodness of explanation. Of course, it can be that one theory *trumps* a second. This occurs if a theory does better than the second on one dimension of assessment, and no worse than the second on the other dimension of assessment. However, where it is not the case that one theory trumps a second, we may be unable to determine whether—or to reach stable agreement that—one theory is better than the other. In those circumstances where there is disagreement about how the weighing of the virtues comes out, perhaps all we can reasonably do is agree to disagree.

So far in this discussion of the assessment of theories, I have made no distinction between the descriptive and normative components of theories. If we suppose that we need to consider the descriptive and normative components of theories separately, then—as I noted above—there will be a further three-stage process in the evaluation of competing worldviews. For now—at least in the interests of simplicity—I shall suppose that we can weigh theories in a single process, without distinguishing between descriptive and normative components.

Idealized Worldview Disagreement

Two-person worldview disagreements are idiosyncratic: they turn on the particular beliefs and capacities of the people involved. Moreover, the same is true if we simply add more people to the mix: n-person disagreements are idiosyncratic, no matter how large n happens to be.

In order to apply the preceding discussion to the kind of worldview disagreement that is of interest to philosophers, we need to introduce some kind of idealization. The most obvious thought is that, when we come to compare worldviews, we should focus on *best* versions of worldviews. This takes us back to the first stage of assessment. What we really most want is to give a careful articulation of best versions of competing worldviews. Of course, we should not suppose that, for example, there is just one best Christian worldview. At least at the outset of inquiry, we are free to suppose that there may be many equally good—but competing—Christian worldviews.

Here is one possible characterization of Christian belief:

> There is an immaterial, omnipotent, omniscient, wholly good creator (*ex nihilo*) and sustainer of all things who is three persons in one substance, with one of these three persons being numerically identical to a human being who died to atone for human sins; who exercises providential control over free human beings; who will bring about the bodily resurrection of all to eternal life; who allows some lives to lead to eternal bliss and other lives to lead to eternal torment; and who is the author of authoritative (and perhaps inerrant) scripture, viz. the Christian *Bible*.

Of course, not all Christians believe all of this; indeed, some Christians reject a great deal of it. However, I do not think that anything I say in what follows will depend upon the controversial elements in this characterization.

Within the framework that is provided by this characterization of Christian belief, we can mark out further distinctive features of a Christian worldview. Perhaps what is most important to note here is that embracing a Christian worldview requires not only that you hold Christian beliefs but also that you act upon your Christian beliefs. In part, this is a matter of public affirmation of belief and public commitment of goods, time, and so forth. But, at root, what really matters is that having Christian eschatological, soteriological, and Christological beliefs inevitably influences what you do and what you suppose that you—and everyone else—ought to do.

Naturalism

If we are to compare Christian worldviews with something else, then, as I have already argued, it will not be that we compare Christian worldviews with philosophy. Whatever philosophy may be, it is clear that it is not a worldview. However, we are not short of alternative proposals.

Some might think that we ought to compare Christian worldviews with *philosophical* worldviews. But—apart from anything else—that proposal seems to suggest that Christian worldviews are not philosophical worldviews. Perhaps we might instead suggest that we compare Christian worldviews with *other* philosophical worldviews. But—apart from anything else—that proposal presupposes that Christian worldviews are philosophical worldviews!

Some might think that we ought to compare Christian worldviews with *non-Christian* worldviews. In a certain sense, that's clearly right. But non-Christian worldviews do not form an interesting kind: there is nothing that non-Christian worldviews have in common apart from their rejection of Christianity.

Some might think that we ought to compare Christian worldviews with *atheistic* worldviews. Again, there is a sense in which that appears likely to be productive. But again, the difficulty is that atheistic worldviews do not form an interesting kind: there is nothing that atheistic worldviews have in common apart from their rejection of theism.

I think that in the twenty-first century perhaps the most obvious comparators for Christian worldviews—at least in Western secular democracies—are *naturalistic* worldviews. Of course, there are many different naturalistic worldviews, just as there are many different Christian worldviews. But we can certainly hope to articulate best versions of Christian and naturalist worldviews, and then weigh them against one another.

As a starting point, we may take it that a naturalist is committed to the following three claims: (1) there are none but natural causes involving none but natural entities; (2) the distribution of minds in the universe is late and local: only recently evolved creatures have minds and mental properties, and those minds and mental properties are tied to relatively complex biological structures of the evolved creatures in question; and (3) there is nothing that is divine, or sacred, or worthy of worship. If you are inclined to give a rather different characterization of naturalism, then you may treat this definition as stipulative: what it picks out is the kind of worldview that I want to pit against Christian worldviews.

While I think that most naturalists will be happy with (1)–(3), there is very little agreement among naturalists about foundational normative questions (e.g., foundational questions about morality, meaning, and value). At least for the sake of having an account, I will suppose that naturalists follow Aristotle in supposing the following things. Flourishing human beings

1. are flourishing members of flourishing communities;
2. exercise moral and intellectual virtues;
3. have genuine friendships;
4. exercise both theoretical and practical wisdom;
5. act with a range of virtues in the pursuit of valuable individual and collective ends;
6. are not subject to certain kinds of liabilities: they are not impoverished, or unhealthy, or severely traumatized, or the like.

Moreover, for the sake of having an account, I shall further suppose that human beings can only be flourishing members of flourishing communities if there is mutual recognition of rights and obligations among the members of those communities. Our moral rights and moral obligations in respect of one another are grounded in requirements for our individual and collective flourishing.

Two Worldviews Compared

I think that it is obvious that no one has yet shown that there are no consistent Christian worldviews and that no one has yet shown that there are no consistent naturalist worldviews. One way of seeing that this *is* obvious is to note that there are intelligent, thoughtful, well-informed Christians and intelligent, thoughtful, well-informed naturalists. If there were an available demonstration of the inconsistency of Christian worldviews, then there would not be any intelligent, thoughtful, well-informed Christians. And if there were an available demonstration of the inconsistency of naturalist worldviews, then there would not be any intelligent, thoughtful, well-informed naturalists. Another way of reaching the same conclusion is to work your way through the purported demonstrations of the inconsistency of best Christian—or best naturalist—worldviews, bearing in mind the requirement that the claims allegedly shown to be jointly inconsistent must both really be inconsistent and really all belong to the targeted worldview. In several decades of examining purported demonstrations of the inconsistency of best Christian—or best naturalistic—worldviews, I have yet to find a demonstration that meets that requirement.

I think that it is also obvious that naturalistic worldviews are simpler than Christian worldviews. At a first pass, we can put the comparison between the two kinds of worldviews in the following terms. Naturalists suppose that causal reality just is natural reality, whereas Christians suppose that—in addition to natural reality—there is a further, nonnatural causal reality (involving at least God, and perhaps also angels and other nonnatural entities). In addition, naturalists suppose that causal properties are just natural properties, whereas Christians suppose that—in addition to natural causal properties—there are also nonnatural causal properties (e.g., divine causal properties, angelic causal properties). In short, the ontology of naturalism is a subset of the ontology of theism, and the ideology of naturalism is a subset of the ideology of theism.

This first pass is crude and not exactly right. There are disputes about ontology and ideology amongst Christians as well as amongst naturalists. Suppose that N and N' are two naturalist theories that differ in their ontology and ideology. Suppose further that T is a theistic theory that embeds the ontology and ideology of N, and that T' is a theistic theory that embeds the ontology and ideology of N'. By construction, the ontology and ideology of N is not a subset of the ontology and ideology of T', and the ontology and ideology of N' is not a subset of the ontology and ideology of T.

Perhaps it might be said in reply that, since we are only considering *best* versions of theism and naturalism, we can reasonably expect that whatever account of the natural world—in terms of natural entities, properties, and laws—is embedded in a best version of theism, it will coincide with an account of the natural world—in terms of natural entities, properties, and laws—provided by one of the best versions of naturalism. If we find ourselves wishing to compare N and T', we do best to start by comparing {N, N'} with {T, T'}. For then we can note that the ontology of N is a subset of the ontology of T, the ontology of N' is a subset of the ontology of T', the ideology of N is a subset of the ideology of T, and the ideology of N' is a subset of the ideology of T'.

Given that Christian worldviews have additional investments in ontology and ideology, the most important question to consider is whether those additional investments allow greater explanatory breadth and depth: Does the additional ontology and ideology of Christianity make for better explanations of data? If there is no better explanation of data afforded by additional Christian ontology and ideology, then— given our account of theoretical virtue—we are bound to conclude that naturalism is the better worldview. On the other hand, if there is better explanation of data afforded by additional Christian ontology and ideology, then there are several ways that things might pan out: (a) if the better explanations are sufficiently good, then we will be bound to conclude that Christianity is the better worldview; (b) if the better explanations are only moderately better, then we will be bound to con- clude that our methods do not enable us to decide between the two worldviews; and (c) if the better explanations provide only a sufficiently small improvement, then we will bound to conclude that naturalism is the better worldview.

Among the elements of ontology and ideology that feature in Christian worldviews but not in naturalist worldviews, there are all of the following: God, the Trinity, the incarnation, the resurrection, the atonement, miracles, afterlife, and God as Sustainer and Provider.

God

There is a significant amount of data that might be thought to be better explained on the hypothesis that God exists than on the competing naturalistic hypothesis. The list includes global causal structure, cosmic fine-tuning, the history of the earth, the history of humanity, *a priori* knowledge of logic, mathematics, and modality, as well as morality and human flourishing (including conscience, virtue, enforcement, and happiness). We can also add consciousness and reason, religious experience, scripture, authority, organization, tradition, and salvation, as well as meaning and purpose. I think in fact, however, that none of these are better explained on the hypothesis that God exists than on the competing naturalistic hypothesis. I argue for this claim in detail in *The Best Argument against God*, and I do not propose to repeat the details of that argument here.[1]

However, as an illustrative case, let me consider the first piece of data: global causal structure. There is a network of causal relations. But why is there a network of causal relations rather than complete absence of causal relations?

There are, I think, only two ways that one might think to answer this question. One answer that might be given is that it is impossible for there to be complete absence of causal relations. The other answer that might be given is that there is ultimately no reason why there is a network of causal relations rather than complete absence of causal relations.

Both of these answers are equally available to theists and naturalists. On the one hand, if a theist supposes that it was impossible for God to refrain from engaging in creative activity, then the theist will hold that it was impossible for there to be complete absence of causal relations. And, if a theist supposes that it was possible for God to refrain from engaging in creative activity, then the theist will maintain that there is nothing that explains why God actually did engage in creative activity (and so, ultimately, there is no reason why there is a network of causal relations rather than complete absence of causal relations). On the other hand, if a naturalist supposes that it was impossible for some initial part of the actual world not to exist, then the naturalist will hold that it was impossible for there to be complete absence of causal relations. And, if a naturalist supposes that it was possible for any initial part of the actual world not to exist—while also maintaining (with the theist) that any possible world must share an initial part with the actual world—then the naturalist will maintain that there is nothing that explains why any given initial part of the actual world exists (and so, ultimately, there is no reason why there is a network of causal relations rather than a complete absence of causal relations).

---

1. Graham Oppy, *The Best Argument against God* (New York: Palgrave-Macmillan, 2013).

Given that the same answers are available to theists and to naturalists—and that the ontological and ideological costs of purchasing those answers are the same in either case—the fact that there is a network of causal relations provides no reason to favour one kind of worldview over the other.[2]

Trinity and Incarnation

The Christian doctrine of the Trinity says that there is one God in three persons—the Father, the Son, and the Holy Spirit—who are distinguished by their relations to one another even though they are one substance or nature. Many, but not all, Christians also claim that God is simple, i.e., without parts of any kind.

Opponents of Christianity have often deemed the doctrine of the Trinity incoherent; Christians themselves have often claimed that the doctrine is a mystery that eludes human understanding, or that is not capable of explanation, or that is not able to be grasped by unaided human faculties.

When we compare naturalism with Christianity, it seems that the doctrine of the Trinity adds significantly to the ontological and ideological costs of Christianity without leading to any improvement in the explanation of data, that is, of claims that are held in common by naturalists and theists.

Perhaps it will be objected that we can explain the adoption of the doctrine of the Trinity—and the defeat of Adoptionism, Sabellianism, and Arianism—in terms of the truth of that doctrine. But naturalists can give exactly the same blow-by-blow account of the adoption of the doctrine of the Trinity without supposing that the doctrine is true, and hence without taking on the associated ontological and ideological costs.

Perhaps it will be objected that there is the evidence of Scripture, and in particular, the occasional uses of the combined expression, "Father, Son, and Holy Spirit." However, it is hardly controversial that there is no independent textual support for the doctrine on the Trinity in Scripture. As the previous paragraph has already suggested, we know on independent historical grounds that the doctrine of the Trinity did

---

2. If you would like to see a much fuller and more carefully spelled out version of this argument, please have a look at my chapter, "Ultimate Naturalistic Causal Explanations," in *The Puzzle of Existence*, ed. Tyron Goldschmidt (New York: Routledge, 2013), 46–63.

not receive a mature formulation until several hundred years after the relevant parts of Scripture were written.

Resurrection and Atonement

The Christian doctrine of the resurrection asserts that after Jesus was crucified for our sins, he rose again from the dead. According to the New Testament accounts, Jesus appeared to many people over a period of forty days following his resurrection and prior to his ascension to heaven. The significance of the doctrine of the resurrection to Christianity is hard to overstate. In 1 Corinthians 15:14, Paul writes: "If Christ has not been raised, our preaching is useless and so is your faith."

When we compare naturalism with Christianity, it seems that the doctrine of the resurrection adds significantly to the ontological and ideological costs of Christianity without leading to any improvement in the explanation of data. In particular, the claim that someone came back to life after being dead for three days is completely at odds with all of the other evidence that we have concerning life and death in our species and in relevantly similar species. In order for someone to come back to life after being dead for three days, they would have to be of a significantly different kind from the regular humans and related animals countenanced by naturalism. Moreover—and perhaps more importantly—a view according to which someone can be *crucified for the sins of others* clearly requires ontological and ideological commitments beyond those made available by naturalism.

Perhaps—echoing the second objection raised in connection with the Trinity—it will be said that there is evidence in Scripture that Jesus rose from the dead. This time, it can hardly be replied that there is not direct scriptural affirmation that Jesus rose from the dead. However, the crucial question to be asked is whether the evidence that we have justifies the ontological and ideological costs that Christianity incurs but naturalism does not.

What is our evidence? First, we have a modest number of Christian documents of uncertain pedigree. Almost all scholars agree that there are intermediaries between the Christian documents that we have and whatever the events were that ultimately led to their production. Some scholars advert to preceding oral tradition; some scholars advert to preceding written tradition; some scholars advert to both preceding oral tradition and (then) preceding written tradition. Given this state of affairs, it is hard to determine how many independent sources we have for the events described in the Christian documents that we have. Moreover, for the crucial events that are of interest to us—e.g., the resurrection—we have no independent archaeological evidence and no textual evidence from non-Christian sources that we know to be independent of the Christian documents that we have.

Second, we have the content of those Christian documents. For example, in 1 Corinthians 15 we are told that the risen Christ "appeared to Cephas, and then to the Twelve. After that, he appeared to more than five hundred of the brothers and sisters at the same time. . . . Then he appeared to James, then to all the apostles." This gives us that, according to Christian tradition, there were many appearances of the risen Christ; but, of course, it does not give us that there were many appearances of the risen Christ. One explanation of why Paul says that there were these many appearances is because there were these many appearances, and he was reliably informed of there being these many appearances. But another explanation of why Paul says that there were many appearances is because he was told that there were many appearances—even though, in fact, there were none appeared to by the risen Christ—and he believed what he was told.

Third—and most importantly—we have a massive amount of evidence that detailed beliefs with almost no foundation in fact can become widely accepted in very short timeframes by large numbers of people. Consider, for example, the John Frum cult that arose in Vanuatu—at that time the New Hebrides—in the first half of the twentieth century. In 1941, only a few years after the stories of John Frum began to circulate, believers disposed of all their money, quit their homes, and moved inland to join in feasts, dances, and rituals. Quite generally, we know that particularly in difficult and stressful times, people can come to share detailed and largely—although not perfectly—overlapping beliefs that have little or no foundation in fact, and that those beliefs help to explain why those people do quite extraordinary things.

Naturalists and theists agree about what to say in the case of the John Frum cult and in countless similar cases. Somehow—we know not how—stories began to circulate that ended up being accepted as truth by a significant number of people, even though much—if not all—of what is contained in those stories is not true. Naturalists can say much the same about the resurrection and the atonement. Somehow—we know not how—stories began to circulate that ended up being accepted as truth by a significant number of people, even though much—if not all—of what is contained in those stories is not true.

If we just focus on the first two parts of our evidence, it may seem that Christianity offers a better explanation of that evidence than does naturalism; moreover, it may also seem that the additional ontological and ideological costs that Christianity incurs are justified by this explanatory improvement. However, it is very important not to overlook the third part of our evidence. The naturalistic explanation is of a piece with the explanation that both Christians and naturalists want to offer in countless similar cases, whereas the Christian explanation is not. This discontinuity in the Christian explanation of the full range of our evidence overturns any judgment that we might be inclined to make about the explanatory advantages that accrue to Christianity.

Miracles

Christian tradition adverts to many miracles, including those associated with Jesus—his birth, his acts of healing, his death, and his resurrection—and those associated with subsequent events in various Christian churches. While some Christians treat all of these miracle reports—even including the resurrection—as myth, many Christians accept some or all of these miracle reports as literal and unvarnished truth.

There are many non-Christian sources for miraculous reports. Many of those non-Christian miracle reports are similar in style and content to Christian miracle reports.

Consider miraculous births. Alongside reports of the miraculous births of, for example, Isaac, Samson, Samuel, John the Baptist, and Jesus, we can set reports of the miraculous births of Buddha, Krishna, Karna, Kabir, Zoroaster, Marduk, Horus, Romulus, Asclepius, Oedipus, Augustus Caesar, Qi, Lao-tse, and others. While Christians have often been concerned to argue that the account of the birth of Jesus is unique—and that other alleged instances of *virgin* births are either inadequately detailed or else adapted from the Christian account of the birth of Jesus—concession on this point leaves untouched the many similarities between Christian miraculous births and miraculous births in other religions and traditions. Whereas naturalists uniformly discern mythic elements in all accounts of births to the virginal, the barren, the post-menopausal, and so forth, many Christians only discern mythic elements in the accounts of such births in *other* traditions. But, in all cases, we have no supporting evidence beyond the uncorroborated reports themselves.

Consider the miraculous healing of blindness. In the New Testament, there are four one-off reports of Jesus's restoring sight to the blind (Matt 9:27–30; Mark 8:22–25; 10:46–52; John 9). In his *Lives of the Caesars*, Suetonius provides a report that Emperor Vespasian restored sight to a blind man (*Vespasian* 7.2), corroborated by a similar report in Tacitus's *Annals* (4.81). Even if, as some have claimed, the report that Tacitus gives is ironic and sarcastic—suggesting that Tacitus himself supposed that Vespasian's restoration of sight to the blind man was stage managed—it would remain true that we have no more supporting evidence for the claims made in the New Testament than we do for the claims made by Suetonius. While naturalists insist that all of these claims fly in the face of what we know about the capacities of touch and spittle to heal blindness—and hence are evidently motivated by considerations other than concern for truth—those Christians who take the New Testament claims to be true only make these allegations against Suetonius (and perhaps Tacitus).

Consider astronomical miracles. Compare the failure of the light of the sun in Luke 23:45, or Joshua ordering the sun to be still (Josh 10:12–13), or the shadow going back on the dial of Ahaz (2 Kgs 20:8–11), or the star of Bethlehem (Matt 2:1–11) with the "splitting of the moon" in Quran 54:1–2 or the "darkening of the sun" at the execution of Ichadon according to Buddhist lore. If we suppose that we are to take Luke 23:45 to be saying that the light of the sun failed for several hours across the face of the earth at the time of the crucifixion, and that we are to take Quran 54:1–2 to be saying that the moon was literally sundered in the sky, then we have two one-off cases unsupported by any further evidence. While naturalists will ask why—given that they would have been visible across the globe—no one else recorded the occurrence of these celestial events, and while naturalists will also insist that the alleged events are simply impossible, given what we know about the sun and the moon, Christians who wish to take Luke 23:45 to be saying that the light of the sun failed for several hours across the face of the earth at the time of the crucifixion are obliged to give a quite different treatment of Quran 54:1–2. Yet in each case the evidence to be explained is a single, unsupported textual reference.

Afterlife

Christian teachings about the afterlife vary considerably in their details. Most Christians suppose that there is an afterlife; what we call "death" is not the endpoint of an individual's existence. Many Christians suppose further that what happens in the afterlife is not independent of what we make of our present life. For some Christians, the afterlife is a time of strict reckoning: rewards and punishments are conferred in the afterlife according to the demands of justice. For other Christians, the reckoning in the afterlife is leavened by divine mercy—perhaps to the extent that, eventually, all are reconciled to God.

When we compare naturalism to Christianity, we see that Christian teachings about the afterlife add significantly to the ontological and ideological costs of Christianity without leading to any improvement in the explanation of data, that is, of claims that are held in common by naturalists and theists. Depending upon the details of a particular Christian worldview, heaven, hell, resurrection bodies, souls, and so forth may all be items in that Christian worldview that have no counterpart in naturalistic worldviews.

Perhaps it might be objected that there is data that is best explained by heaven, hell, resurrection bodies, souls, and so forth. However, while it may be granted that scriptural references and other testimonial reports to heaven, hell, resurrection bodies, souls, and so forth *would be* explained by the existence of heaven, hell, resurrection bodies, souls, etc., it is clear that—for example—testimonial reports and references in the scriptures of Eastern religions to reincarnation, samsara, karma, nirvana, and so on are not well explained by the existence of heaven, hell, resurrection bodies, souls, and so forth. While naturalism provides a uniform explanation of the eschatological teachings of all of the religions of the world without any additional ontological and ideological costs, Christianity provides a non-uniform treatment that gives special place to Christian teachings at the cost of additional, uniquely Christian, ontology and ideology.

Sustainer and Provider

Many Christians suppose that God sustains the universe in existence, and that God provides for the creatures that inhabit the universe.

The claim that God sustains the universe in existence is pure ontological and ideological loss for Christianity in comparison to naturalism. Insofar as we are focused on the ultimate explanation of the fact of continuing existence, Christians and naturalists have the same options: either they shall say that the ultimate explanation of continuing existence lies in ultimately necessary existence—whether of God or of the universe—or else they shall say that, ultimately, there is no ultimate explanation of continuing existence. Just as Christians suppose that there is no need to invoke anything else that sustains God in existence, so naturalists suppose that there is no need to invoke anything else that sustains the universe in existence.

The claim that God provides for the creatures that inhabit the universe is also pure ontological and ideological loss for Christianity in comparison to naturalism. If we consider the distribution of flourishing among creatures across the history of life on earth, it is clear that an enormous number of creatures have not lived flourishing lives. While there is no additional ontology and ideology that needs to be invoked by naturalism in order to explain why it is that there have been creatures—and indeed, so many creatures—that have not lived flourishing lives, Christian responses to the widespread lack of flourishing invariably introduce new ontology and ideology in order to bring about a fit with this otherwise recalcitrant data. Some Christians appeal—at least in part—to the free, malicious actions of fallen angels and demons. Some Christians appeal—at least in part—to the collateral consequences of the actions of such angels and demons. Many Christians appeal to benefits that accrue to creatures in the next life. No matter which of these—or other—explanations is invoked, it is clear that the additional ontological and ideological costs do not purchase an explanation of the distribution of flourishing among creatures across the history of life on earth that is better than naturalistic explanations of the distribution of flourishing among creatures across the history of life on earth.

Interim Summary

If the kind of argument that I have been sketching in the last few sections could be made out, then we would have an argument for the conclusion that naturalism trumps Christianity. On the one hand, naturalism is ontologically and ideologically leaner; on the other hand, there is nothing that Christianity explains better than naturalism.

Of course, the claim that the argument I have been sketching in the last few sections *can* be made out is highly controversial. I certainly don't claim that I have successfully made out such an argument here. The broad brush strokes that I have presented leave a myriad of points of detail unexamined, both with respect to the topics that have been explicitly taken up and with respect to topics that have not been considered at all.

However, in the discussion to come, I shall not need the assumption that the considerations I have been developing in the last few sections eventually yield an argument that is ultimately successful. Rather, in order to respond to the questions that we have been asked to discuss in the present work, all I need to have done is to have conveyed something of the reasons I have for thinking that naturalism trumps theism. What is most important to understand is why I think that naturalism—or naturalistic worldviews—are proper and serious comparators to Christianity and Christian worldviews.

Common Goals

Christianity and naturalism share intellectual goals because both aspire to be—or to encompass—comprehensive worldviews. At least in principle, Christian and naturalistic worldviews both aim for descriptive, explanatory, ontological, normative, methodological, epistemological, axiological, and etiological completeness. In practice, Christian and naturalistic worldviews aim to do the best that they can in articulating foundational descriptive, explanatory, ontological, normative, methodological, epistemological, axiological, and etiological principles.

While philosophy may share *some* intellectual goals with Christianity and naturalism, philosophy is not a direct competitor with either. One of the primary goals—if not *the* primary goal—for philosophy is evaluation of worldviews. It is one of the jobs of philosophy to say what worldviews are and how they should be assessed. It is another of the jobs of philosophy to try to carry out the task of assessing worldviews and of saying whether *this* worldview is better than *that* worldview. Ultimately, one might hope that the task of assessing worldviews will tell us which is the best worldview, or at least which is the best worldview that we can formulate, or which is the best worldview among those that we have formulated to date.

Christianity and naturalism share *some* moral goals. Since Christian and naturalistic worldviews both aspire to normative and axiological completeness, Christian and naturalistic worldviews both aspire to give comprehensive moral theories. However, while Christian worldviews are embedded within Christian religion, naturalistic worldviews are not embedded in any wider framework that incorporates symbols, creeds, scriptures, sacraments, rituals, music, buildings, institutions, populations, mission, and the like. True enough, some naturalists aspire to have naturalistic worldviews embedded in wider frameworks that do incorporate such items; but—at least at present—those naturalists are very much in a minority. Consequently, while Christianity and naturalism share some goals with respect to moral *theory*, it is much less clear that they share goals with respect to what they take to be moral *action*.

Given the comments that I have already made, it should be clear that there is only an even more attenuated sense in which philosophy shares moral goals with Christianity and naturalism. Again, it is one of the jobs of philosophy to say what moral theories are and to determine how they should be assessed. It is another of the jobs of philosophy to try to carry out the task of assessing moral theories, of saying whether *this* moral theory is better than *that* moral theory. Ultimately, one might hope that the task of assessing moral theories will tell us which is the best moral theory, at least among those we have formulated to date. So philosophy shares some goals with Christianity and naturalism with respect to moral theory; but it is not at all clear that philosophy shares any goals with Christianity and naturalism with respect to moral action.

Common Means

It is clear that Christianity and naturalism share intellectual means to common intellectual goals. When it comes to the construction of worldviews, tools are shared in common between all would-be worldview builders. While I have not had much at all to say about the methods of worldview construction, it is clear that reason and imagination will both have significant roles to play.

Philosophy shares intellectual means to common intellectual goals with both Christianity and naturalism precisely to the extent that the tools for worldview evaluation are the same as the tools for worldview construction. What goes for worldview construction goes for worldview evaluation as well: there will be significant roles for reason and imagination in the evaluation of worldviews.

Given that the only moral goals that Christianity and naturalism share concern moral theory, it is not at all clear that there are—or could be—shared moral means to those shared moral goals. I am not inclined to accept that facility in moral theorizing is correlated with moral rectitude in action. Plato's authority notwithstanding, it is perfectly possible for people to know the good and yet to fail utterly to pursue it.

Given my previously evinced skepticism about whether philosophy shares any goals with Christianity and naturalism with respect to moral action, it should be clear that I am not at all inclined to accept the suggestion that there are moral means to moral goals that are shared by philosophy, Christianity, and naturalism.

Distinctions

Naturalism and Christianity are primarily distinguished by their ontology and ideology. As I noted above, naturalism is distinguished among worldviews by the sparseness of its ontological and ideological commitments. Other worldviews—including Christian worldviews—make ontological and ideological commitments in addition to the ontological and ideological commitments that are characteristic of naturalism.

Philosophy is distinguished from both naturalism and Christianity in that it is a discipline rather than a worldview, and so is not properly characterised in terms of ontological and ideological commitments. Philosophy provides the tools for weighing competing worldviews with competing ontological and ideological commitments; it does not itself have ontological and ideological commitments that might cause it to have common cause with some worldviews at the expense of others.

Central Questions

The central questions from philosophy to Christianity and naturalism concern the theoretical virtues of these competing worldviews. Is each internally consistent (both in the purely theoretical part and when conjoined with data)? Does one of these worldviews make a better *descriptive* trade-off—between minimizing ontological and ideological commitment, and maximizing explanation of data—than the other? Does one of these worldviews make a better *normative* trade-off—between minimizing ontological and ideological commitment, and maximizing explanation of data—than the other? Does one of these worldviews make a better *overall* trade-off—between minimizing ontological and ideological commitment, and maximizing explanation of data—than the other?

I do not think that there are questions from Christianity and naturalism to philosophy (unless we count the questions from philosophy to Christianity and naturalism as being equally questions from Christianity and naturalism to philosophy). As I noted much earlier, we can make sense of a "philosophy of Christianity" and we can similarly make sense of a "philosophy of naturalism." But there is nothing in either of these projects that calls philosophy into question or raises problems for philosophy itself.

Significance

I am inclined to deny that Christianity and naturalism make *disciplinary* differences to philosophy.

Part of the data we all bring to philosophy is that there is no expert agreement on the answers to philosophical questions. There is no agreement among intelligent, thoughtful, well-informed scholars who devote their lives to addressing those questions. If those scholars are to be in genuine conversation with one another, there must be a place—a discipline—where none of the claims upon which they disagree is on the "conversational scoreboard." Anyone who wants to make partial—parochial—insistence on the inclusion of particular claims on the "conversational scoreboard" simply fails to understand the nature of the philosophical enterprise. In particular, if there is to be a genuine conversation between Christians and naturalists, the only things that go onto the "conversational scoreboard" are things that I have been calling "data"—things upon which both parties agree.

While I deny that Christianity and naturalism make disciplinary differences to philosophy, I accept that philosophy does make practical differences to Christianity and naturalism because it has theoretical implications for Christianity and naturalism. In particular, I think reflection on the nature of philosophy teaches a certain kind of modesty in the way that we advance controversial opinions.

From the standpoint of philosophy, it is obvious that people have limited capacities when it comes to the construction of true and (moderately) comprehensive worldviews. To date, no (moderately) comprehensive worldview has been embraced by more than a small fraction of the population of the world; moreover, no (moderately) comprehensive worldview has been embraced by more than a small fraction of those philosophical experts who devote their lives to the assessment of worldviews.

The conclusion to draw from these considerations is that there is nothing currently available to us that ought to forge worldview consensus. If anything of this kind were currently available, there would already be worldview consensus, at least among those philosophical experts who devote their lives to the assessment of worldviews. Consequently, any worldview that maintains it already provides materials that ought to suffice to forge worldview consensus is shown to be mistaken on that point. Whatever materials it may have provided thus far are not up to the task. In particular, then, Christian and naturalistic worldviews that claim to provide materials that ought to suffice to bring everyone to accept them are shown to be mistaken by considerations available from the standpoint of philosophy.

Whether the considerations just advanced entail that philosophy makes a *religious* difference to Christianity may depend upon the way in which mission is conceived in Christianity. I suspect that most Christians are well aware that there simply isn't any set of considerations that ought to bring everyone to adopt a Christian worldview. If this is correct, then at the very least most Christians already accept that mission is much more an art than a science.

It may well be the case that there are other ways in which philosophy makes practical differences to Christianity and naturalism; however, I shall not attempt further to investigate that question here.

Conflict Resolution

Near the beginning of this chapter, I canvassed the possibility of *Christian philosophy*—philosophy based upon Christian presuppositions—and *naturalistic philosophy*—philosophy based upon naturalistic presuppositions. Why might we be uneasy with these labels?

If Christian philosophy is nothing more than development of Christian worldviews, and naturalistic philosophy is nothing more than development of naturalistic worldviews, then these are clearly respectable enterprises. While we might wonder whether we should locate the development of worldviews as a component of philosophy—rather than merely as a component of the project of inquiry more generally—we might accept that there is no particular problem that arises on this way of understanding "Christian philosophy" and "naturalistic philosophy." For similar reasons, we may also suppose that there is no particular problem that arises for the suggestion that there can be Christian and naturalistic approaches to metaphysics, epistemology, philosophy of mind, of logic, of language, of science, of ethics, of aesthetics, political philosophy, and so forth.

However, if we think that part of what philosophy must do is make provision for genuine conversation between proponents of competing worldviews, then we cannot also think that *that part* of philosophy is a place to which it is appropriate to bring presuppositions that belong to particular worldviews. After all, to bring presuppositions to an inquiry is precisely to insist that those presuppositions are on the "conversational scoreboard." If we insist on contested Christian presuppositions—or contested naturalistic presuppositions, or contested presuppositions from any other particular worldview—in that part of philosophy that aims to provide for genuine conversation between proponents of competing worldviews, then we make it impossible for genuine conversation to take place. In this sense, it is impossible for there to be Christian philosophy, or naturalistic philosophy, or the like. And of course this same point applies *mutatis mutandis* to those parts of metaphysics, epistemology, philosophy of mind, of logic, of language, of science, of ethics, of aesthetics, political philosophy, and so forth, that aim to provide for genuine conversation between proponents of competing worldviews.

Perhaps some will respond to the claims I have just made by saying:

so much the worse for the idea that part of the aim of philosophy is to provide for genuine conversation between proponents of competing worldviews. However, I cannot accept the implicit suggestion that philosophy ought properly to be the mouthpiece of dogmatism. Philosophy is a cooperative enterprise between all of the people on the planet. One minimal aim of that enterprise is to improve the worldview of each by allowing the worldview of each to be fairly tested against the worldviews of everyone else.

Concluding Remarks

In this chapter, I have sketched a case for the superiority of naturalism to Christianity, paying attention to particular Christian doctrines that—as I see it—bring with them ontological and ideological costs that are not justified in terms of accompanying explanatory benefits. I do not expect the other participants in this conversation to be persuaded by the considerations I have advanced, nor do I think that if I piled up more considerations of the same kind, they would be more likely to be persuaded. Moreover, I do not think it irrational to fail to be persuaded by the kinds of considerations I advance. It is plausible that at best we shall end up reasonably agreeing to disagree about the proper weighing of these kinds of considerations.

The other significant thing that I have done in this chapter is to advance a neutralist conception of philosophy which suggests that one of the most important tasks for philosophy is the assessment of competing worldviews. On this conception of philosophy, it is clear that contemporary philosophical practice fails most when it comes to the articulation of competing worldviews. The effort of imagination that is required to see another worldview from the inside is one that does not come naturally to any of us. Moreover, on this conception of philosophy, it is a mistake to think that we can bring presuppositions from a particular worldview to the philosophical enterprise. There is a central component of the philosophical endeavour that requires the setting aside of all disputed presuppositions.

RESPONSE FROM THE COVENANT MODEL

K. SCOTT OLIPHINT

I am grateful to Graham Oppy for the explanation that he gives of a "Conflict Model" of Christianity and philosophy. As a metaphysical naturalist whose impressive output is substantial, he is uniquely qualified to help us recognize some of the central tenets of his position.

In a response of this brief length, it will be impossible to address in adequate detail the significant concerns that a "Covenantal Model" will have with Oppy's position. We will need to limit ourselves to a couple minor points, each of which will be related to one major question in his essay. Perhaps, as he affirms about his own essay (p. 21), my response will fail to persuade (though my hope is that it will). At least, again to follow Oppy's lead (21), the concerns herein merit "serious consideration." I should also note that I am not assuming that Oppy has not addressed these questions. Given the sheer volume of his work, he has likely thought about my concerns. I am, however, contending that my proposals below should be seen as central to a "Covenantal Model" of Christianity and philosophy.

On one level, Oppy sees no real conflict or tension between Christianity or naturalism or any other worldview and philosophy. This point leads to my first minor concern. Oppy initially provides us with a sociological description of Christianity as a *religion*. That description may be accurate as far as it goes, but no serious Christian would want to see such a description as in any way adequate.

Having given a sociological description of religion, into which Christianity fits, Oppy goes on to aver that philosophy is a "domain of inquiry" (23). With these descriptions of Christianity and philosophy in place, Oppy then says:

Given that Christianity is a religion and that philosophy is a domain
of inquiry, it is not immediately clear that there are questions of
interest concerning the relation of each to the other. (23)

This, I think, is a fair point, given the way he has described Christianity
and philosophy. If it is the case that Christianity is a sociological
phenomenon and that philosophy's task is simply to inquire, then the
relationship between the two may be less than direct.

But there is *some kind of* relationship between the two, as Oppy himself recognizes. He goes on to note that Christianity, like naturalism,
is a worldview:

Christian worldviews involve fundamental descriptive, explanatory,
ontological, normative, methodological, epistemological, axiological, and etiological principles, but they fall well short of descriptive,
explanatory, ontological, normative, methodological, epistemological, axiological, and etiological completeness. (24)

Given this description, it seems to me that the relationship between
Christianity and philosophy, for Oppy, is not one of conflict. Instead,
perhaps Oppy's view should be the "counselor model," as philosophy's
task is to inquire and adjudicate as to a particular worldview's "fitness"
as a worldview.

But herein lies the problem. On what basis, we could ask, does
philosophy engage in its assessment and adjudication? To put it another
way, *how* might philosophy adjudicate what is "better" with respect to
competing worldviews?

Oppy thinks that philosophy's adjudications and assessments will be
based on questions that will show how different worldviews perform in
"minimizing ontological and ideological commitment, and maximizing
explanation of data" (44). But these criteria are themselves in need of
assessment and adjudication. They cannot stand on their own.

For example, what does it mean to "minimize ontological and ideological commitment," and why must that be seen as a virtue? For Oppy,
"minimizing" at least means that it is best not to add ideas, concepts,
terms, and notions that unduly complicate supposedly already-sufficient
ontological commitments.

If this is accurate, then it should be clear that the notion of simplicity—of "minimizing"—in this case is itself loaded with ontological presuppositions. In this particular instance, simplicity makes sense only in the context of naturalistic presuppositions.

Maybe an analogy will help clarify. Suppose a child, precocious beyond his years, in his first moment of self-consciousness, comes to the dinner table and finds a perfectly cooked, well-balanced meal at his place at the table. What might be the "best" way for him to "minimize" his ontological and ideological commitments about such a dinner? He may begin to reason that his dinner came about by conditions "internal" to each of the food items. The fish, over time, perished and began to decompose, and then to be prepared for consumption by natural causes. And, over time, it made its way to the plate on his table, perfectly prepared and ready to eat. So also for the broccoli, potatoes, and fruit. Each of these diverse elements were, by way of natural causes over a significant amount of time, presented to him in just this way at just the right time. This is a naturalistic view of the child's dinner. It minimizes ontological and ideological commitments with a view toward the virtue of simplicity.

But what kind of simplicity is this? It is a simplicity that requires an intellectually inordinate amount of undocumented conjecture, which itself is fraught with a complexity beyond credulity. So many basic and pressing questions would remain unanswered with such a "minimization" that ontological simplicity would be tantamount to absurdity.

As Oppy recognizes, "Decisions between theories require trade-offs between simplicity and goodness of explanation" (27). So perhaps one response to the above would be that the naturalistic simplicity I have proposed with respect to the child's dinner does a lackluster job of explaining the data. That, I think, is exactly right. Not only so, but it is the explanation of data that ought to determine to what degree "simplicity" of explanation or "minimizing" of ontological commitments is even warranted. So while it may "complicate" ontology to introduce another person—in this case, the child's mother who prepared the dinner—into the analogy above, such an introduction so "simplifies" the explanation of the data that a naturalistic ontology, though "simpler," renders that simplicity as virtually irrelevant.

I recognize that all analogies break down, but my point in the analogy is this: ontological simplicity is either minimally significant or irrelevant, given the explanation of data of the respective worldview. In light of our overall discussion in this volume, this means that the introduction of the Christian God to account for the intricacies of reality, in all of its complexity and design, is much "simpler" than an account that relies on virtually inconceivable and undocumentable naturalistic conjecture. The notion that mind came from non-mind, no matter how often repeated, is inconceivable; there are no data available to show how such a thing could happen. It is theoretically "simpler" in that it accounts for the existence of human minds to recognize that such minds came from the mind of the personal God of Christianity. With respect to "simplicity," mind from Mind wins over mind from non-mind. So also for the rest of human personality.

My second, more minor, concern will lead more directly to my major concern. When Oppy writes about explanation of "data" as to its breadth and depth, he writes as though the data out there are simply given, brute facts, which themselves need to be interpreted according to a particular worldview, which will then make better or worse "sense" of those data. But this view of "data" itself presupposes a naturalistic view of the world, which takes me to my overall concern with Oppy's position.

Oppy proposes a notion of "philosophical neutralism" which, he says, is "consistent with both metaphysical naturalism *and Christianity*" (21, my emphasis). Included in philosophical neutralism is the notion that the presuppositions of various worldviews are disallowed on the "conversational scoreboard" (46). If philosophy is to do its work according to Oppy, then there can be no presuppositional influence on the philosophical assessment of worldviews. He puts it this way:

> If we insist on contested Christian presuppositions—or contested naturalistic presuppositions, or contested presuppositions from any other particular worldview—in that part of philosophy that aims to provide for genuine conversation between proponents of competing worldviews, then we make it impossible for genuine conversation to take place. (46)

And, in conclusion, he says:

> There is a central component of the philosophical endeavour that requires the setting aside of all disputed presuppositions. (47)

To be fair, Oppy does say that he will leave aside the question of whether philosophical neutralism is worthy of adoption. I would propose that it is not, at least for the following reasons.

First, as I have noted in my two minor concerns, the very notions of ontological "simplicity" and "minimizing" depend themselves on a particular worldview in order to be understood and applied properly. Simplicity is a fluid and moving target, as is obvious in Oppy's application of it. Not only so, but the very notion of "explanatory data" is packed full of worldview presuppositions at the outset.

Second, Oppy says that he "cannot accept the implicit suggestion that philosophy ought properly to be the mouthpiece of dogmatism" (47). But Oppy's own criteria for philosophical neutralism is itself the "mouthpiece" of the dogmatism of naturalism; it dogmatically excludes Christianity at the outset since Christianity and its view of creation requires that all data are in the first place what God says they are.

Third, while I very much appreciate Oppy's summaries and brief explanations of certain Christian doctrines (e.g., God, the Trinity, the incarnation), what is missing from those explanations are the *principia* of Christianity *as principia*. That is, for Christians it is not the case that "God" or "the Trinity" are only doctrinal or creedal beliefs. For Christians, the triune God and his revelation are the ontological and epistemological foundations upon which everything else, even philosophy, depends. Given those *principia*, the "data" that are out there are not brute facts awaiting the best (as adjudicated by a neutral philosophy) worldview interpretation. Instead, the "data" are themselves revelatory of the God who created and sustains them. In that sense, they continually "speak" of what they are and of *whose* they are. Without such a presupposition, the data are assumed to be meaningless until and unless "fitted" with a particular worldview. But meaningless data do not exist; they can only be thought to be meaningless by way of naturalistic presuppositions. So, contrary to philosophical neutralism, presuppositions enter in *at the beginning* of the philosophical enterprise.

Fourth, as noted above, Oppy thinks the infringement of presuppositions on the philosophical enterprise renders genuine conversation impossible. But this is clearly false. Suppose, for example, Oppy and I are standing in front of a tree, and we both say together, "There is a tree." Oppy would see this as a part of his "Xi" component (25) in which there is a collection of propositions with which both of us, regardless of our presuppositions, can agree. The problem, however, is that the agreement can *only* be at the level of terms. As we have already seen, Oppy's understanding of the data of the tree presupposes his naturalism. The tree is simply there as a brute fact, to be understood and interpreted by us. My understanding of the tree is that it is both sustained by and revelatory of God. Thus, our presuppositions, automatically and inevitably, always and everywhere inform our understanding of the data.

But this in no way precludes the possibility of meaningful conversation and discussion. For such discussion to take place, what is needed is not necessarily *agreement* but *understanding*. Oppy's essay is a fine example of this. He in no way agrees with the notions of God, the Trinity, or the incarnation that he describes in his essay. But there is communication between us because we each understand what the other is saying. Oppy understands God, the Trinity, and the incarnation which he describes. To force agreement as a precondition of conversation is itself a naturalistic tenet that assumes a neutrality of data where none exists.

Of course, the only reason why there can be a mutual *understanding* is that Oppy and I are both made in God's image and, as such, retain certain mutual "image" capacities. The problem of our lack of *agreement*, however, cannot be overcome intellectually. All of us, since Adam, are intellectually corrupt; our minds do not function as they should (see, for example, Rom 8:4; 1 Cor 2:14; Col 3:10). As the apostle Paul reminded the philosophers at Athens, it is not possible for me or Oppy or anyone else to see the world for what it truly is except by an act of repentance and a turn from our naturalistic worldview to belief in Christ. At that point, the new worldview becomes the true worldview, and philosophy can be brought under the lordship of Christ.

TIMOTHY MCGREW

Of the contributors to this volume, Graham Oppy is the only one I have had the pleasure of meeting in person. On a summer afternoon at a conference in Leuven back in 2009, we had to scamper inside a cafe to escape a sudden rainstorm. Our conversation was irenic, and we did not (as I recall) try to hash out any of the big questions. Irenic exchange is still my goal. But this time, big questions are very much on the agenda.

Two fundamental commitments shape Oppy's approach to the relation of Christianity to philosophy: metaphysical naturalism and philosophical neutralism. What he means by "neutralism" is not altogether clear to me. At the end of his essay he suggests that at least one strand in it involves leaving out presuppositions from a particular worldview when doing philosophy, an act he glosses as "the setting aside of all disputed presuppositions." While I appreciate the motivation behind Oppy's desire to keep philosophy free from the dogmatic endorsement of particular worldviews, I do not see how this could possibly be done on the scale he seems to be suggesting. Is there a claim in the whole of philosophy that has not been challenged by someone or other? Oppy himself makes logical coherence a nonnegotiable desideratum in the construction of a worldview, though he is well aware that the law of non-contradiction itself has been challenged in certain quarters. We might more profitably approach the issue by making a distinction between reasonable and frivolous objections to presuppositions or a distinction between methodological and content presuppositions. But then someone would have to draw the relevant distinction; and though I would be happy to do so, I am guessing that this would not meet the standard of sociological neutrality Oppy wants to espouse.

Oppy considers favorably the idea that philosophy might play a role in conflict resolution, like an academic referee who makes sure that the proponents of different worldviews have a space for genuine conversations. He is aware that the suggestion has problems, for the very standards of fair testing and serious conversation form part of the territory disputed by philosophers. But he considers making philosophy the mouthpiece of dogmatism to be an even worse option. I wonder why these should be our only choices. Despite what some of its detractors would say, it seems to me that philosophy does make progress; and if that progress is slow these days, that is due in part to the sheer difficulty of the questions and in part to a misplaced egalitarianism that affords something like equal time to the sheer nonsense that passes for deep thought in certain quarters. I am all in favor of thoughtful, civil dialogue between people who differ widely on important issues; this volume itself is a venture in generating that kind of discussion. And I certainly agree that there ought to be some boundaries to those discussions—no blows below the belt, so to speak. But I am concerned lest neutralism come into conflict with our following the evidence wherever it leads.

Oppy's metaphysical naturalism looks much clearer to me. It entails at least three claims: (1) that the only causes are natural causes, involving only natural (physical?) entities; (2) that mental powers are lately arrived in the universe and are tied, in some manner left unspecified, to fairly complex biological structures of evolved creatures; and (3) that there is nothing that is divine, or sacred, or worthy of worship.

He offers a brief sketch of the way he would argue for the superiority of naturalism to Christianity. Granting for the sake of the argument that both Christianity and naturalism can be articulated in a coherent way, he defends two claims. First, naturalism is *ontologically leaner* than any interesting version of Christianity, that is to say, simpler, and therefore, all else being equal, more plausible. Second, there is nothing that Christianity *explains* better than naturalism does, nothing that might offset that initial plausibility deficit. Therefore, naturalism is at least somewhat preferable to Christianity—not, perhaps, so much as to make the latter an irrational position to hold, but enough to give philosophical naturalists assurance that they are, at any rate, not worse off than their Christian brethren.

I have much to say about both claims. First, appeals to simplicity as a ground for belief are not so straightforward as they are sometimes made to appear. To be sure, some cases are plain enough. The metaphysician who maintains two ontological commitments, A and B, is, *all else being equal*, claiming more than one who maintains only A.[1] There is, after all, more that can go wrong with the first metaphysician's view than there is with the second one's view; in probabilistic terms, when the assumption of A leaves B less than certain, it is a theorem that P(A&B) < P(A). But metaphysical naturalism is not simpler than Christianity in this sense. The naturalist is not someone who is merely agnostic about (or has never even considered) the additional commitments involved in B. Rather, he is someone who affirms A and also *actively denies* B. There is no simple and straightforward ordering of these two positions with respect to simplicity, just as there is no general inequality that holds between P(A&B) and P(A&~B). It seems to me, therefore, that in claiming that metaphysical naturalism has greater simplicity—and therefore greater initial plausibility—than Christian theism, Oppy has given his own view an illicit head start.

The natural response would be that we can see that affirming B—here, the existence of God and other commitments that come with it—is ontologically extravagant because the extra baggage bundled into the claim does no explanatory work. This response brings us to Oppy's second claim, that naturalism, suitably filled out, explains everything at least as well as Christianity does. Here we disagree very widely indeed, too widely even to lay out all of the disagreements in a short response essay. He has very candidly admitted that his sketch is not an argument that even he thinks should be rationally compelling. But there are issues well worth contesting even so. I will therefore focus on three points: the origin of Christianity, the extent and nature of miracle reports, and the particular evidence for the resurrection of Jesus.

In dealing with the origins of Christianity, Oppy makes much of the fact that, in his words, "detailed beliefs with almost no foundation in fact can become widely accepted in very short timeframes by large numbers of people" (36). No doubt they can. But he wants to make use of this entirely general platitude to explain (or explain away) a particular set of beliefs. Here we are within our rights in asking for a more detailed analysis, lest the skeptical miasma thus released should spread unchecked across other beliefs—including belief in metaphysical naturalism, for example.

Unfortunately, what we get instead of a detailed examination of the

---

1. For the sake of a simple illustration I am taking the obvious restrictions as read—that A does not entail B, for instance.

origin of Christianity is a gesture in the direction of the John Frum cult. Here I must enter a sharp demurrer. Christianity stands or falls on its own evidence; it cannot be tried by proxy. And these are not, despite what Oppy says, similar cases either in the structure of the beliefs or in the nature and quality of the evidence. The suggestion that the rise of a Melanesian cargo cult—its votaries unified by their return to native rituals and lured by the promise of physical goods to be brought in by airlift—bears any useful analogy to the rise of Christianity will appeal most to those who have made no serious study of either.

Oppy points out that miracle claims abound across many religions (37). I concur. But nothing of interest follows from this point. Counterfeit money abounds as well; that does not prove that all money is counterfeit. What we want is some touchstone, a way to distinguish the true, if there are any, from the fraudulent or muddled.

We can do some preliminary sorting with a few simple questions. Are the first reports widely separated from the events either in space or in time? Were the alleged miracles performed in defense of opinions already established, so that even if they were false they might have been suffered to pass without critical examination? Granting *arguendo* that events fell out just as described, is there an obvious and plausible natural explanation for them? Historical claims, even miracle claims, might fail to pass one or more of these filters and yet be true. But a failure at any of these points gives us a reason for doubt. Almost all of the miracle claims of antiquity stumble on criteria like these at multiple points. If anyone wishes to make a serious examination of the value of reported miracles as an argument for religious belief, the most reasonable place to start will be with the very few that pass.

This brings us to the third issue. Oppy claims that the evidence in the case of the miracles recorded in the New Testament is no better than that for the miraculous cures attributed to Vespasian in Alexandria (38). For some of the miracles of Jesus noted in passing in the Gospels, this claim might have some face of plausibility. But with respect to the resurrection of Jesus, the central miracle which casts a light back upon all other miracle reports, it will not survive even a cursory examination of the sources. The physicians who examined the two men reported that the blind man was not totally blind, nor the lame man totally lame (Tacitus, *Histories* 4.81). Serapis, in whose temple they had allegedly received the instruction to appeal to Vespasian, was the favored local deity, and a report of a miraculous cure would thus redound to the credit both of the pagan religious community in Alexandria and of Vespasian himself, who had just announced his aspirations to the imperial throne. And the physicians suggested a backup plan (blame the beggars) in case the attempted cure was unsuccessful. Here political, religious, and (for the beggars no doubt) financial motives all conspired together to create a pious and useful fraud. The contrast with the situation of the early Christians, who proclaimed the resurrection of Jesus at Jerusalem in the teeth of the opposition and endured labors, dangers, and sufferings for that proclamation, could scarcely be more marked.

Oppy says that

> the claim that someone came back to life after being dead for three days is completely at odds with all of the other evidence that we have concerning life and death in our species and in relevantly similar species. (35)

Therefore, he says, anyone who comes back from the dead must be a very different sort of creature from regular humans. Here it seems to me that he fundamentally misconceives the nature of a miracle claim. The traditional Christian view is not that medical science is mistaken and men who are really dead and buried just occasionally and randomly come back to life. It is that in the natural course of things, dead men *really do stay dead*, and therefore the resurrection of Jesus represents a break in the natural order.

Oppy complains that we have no textual evidence from non-Christian sources substantiating the resurrection (36). But what is he looking for? People who were persuaded of the resurrection of Jesus became Christians. From whom else should we expect such testimony?

Oppy extends an olive branch, born of his strong agnosticism, by granting that we might each be rational in our respective positions despite our disagreements. I would not wish to be thought ungrateful. But I cannot accept his offer, since I am persuaded that the public evidence points strongly to the truth of Christianity. All that I have to offer in return is my conviction that engaging with the public evidence, as he is doing, is the only way we can hope rationally to arrive at the truth. For that, despite our differences, he has my respect.

RESPONSE FROM THE CONFORMATION MODEL

PAUL K. MOSER

Graham Oppy aims "to sketch a case for saying that metaphysical naturalism trumps Christianity" (p. 21). His naturalism implies that "(1) there are none but natural causes involving none but natural entities; (2) the distribution of minds in the universe is late and local...; and (3) there is nothing that is divine, or sacred, or worthy of worship" (29–30). A Christian perspective affirms the existence of a God worthy of worship and denies that this God, being supernatural, is a "natural cause" in the relevant sense. So, Christianity and metaphysical naturalism cannot both be true.

In Oppy's language, one theory *trumps* another theory "if [the first] does better than the second on one dimension of assessment, and no worse than the second on the other dimension of assessment" (27). Assuming that metaphysical naturalism and Christianity can avoid internal inconsistency, we may introduce two dimensions of assessment used by Oppy: *simplicity* and *explanatory goodness*. He states: "Simplicity is a matter of ontological and ideological commitments: the leaner the ontology and ideology, the better. Explanatory depth and breadth are matters of goodness of explanation: the more that pure theory explains, and the more that pure theory provides a unified explanation of data, the better" (27). Oppy aims to reach his desired conclusion on this basis: "On the one hand, naturalism is ontologically and ideologically leaner; on the other hand, there is nothing that Christianity explains better than naturalism" (41). We shall see that his case fails owing to neglect of a crucial distinction.

Christianity does carry metaphysical baggage absent from metaphysical naturalism because it acknowledges the existence of God, whereas metaphysical naturalism does not. That baggage places a special epistemic, or evidential, burden on proponents of Christianity, and this should be no surprise or regret. Oppy puts a relevant question

59

as follows: "Does one of these worldviews [Christianity and metaphysical naturalism] make a better *overall* trade-off—between minimizing ontological and ideological commitment, and maximizing explanation of data—than the other?" (44). We need to attend to the relevant notion of *data*. Oppy holds that Christians and naturalists must "agree" upon any data relevant to this comparison. He states: "If there is to be a genuine conversation between Christians and naturalists, the only things that go onto the 'conversational scoreboard' are things that I have been calling 'data'—things upon which both parties agree" (p. 44–45). In his view, "contested presuppositions" from either Christians or naturalists would "make it impossible for genuine conversation to take place" (46).

We need to introduce a crucial distinction, inadequately handled by Oppy, between data *had by a person* and data *agreed upon by persons*. Suppose that I have data in my experience of feeling challenged by another person to change my selfish ways to unselfish ways. Suppose also that the person offering the challenge wants to keep this challenge confidential, just between the two of us, in order to discourage my blaming others for my selfishness. As a result, we may suppose, this person does not display to others his challenge to me, and I cannot reproduce for others his challenge to me in its original form. The original challenge to me comes from another person, after all, and not from me. I therefore could have data regarding such a challenge to me, even though the data would not be agreed upon by persons other than me and the source of the challenge.

Data can come in two forms: propositional and nonpropositional. Propositional data include a judgment, or a proposition; a (grounded) belief that I am now reading a book is a good example. Sensory data, in contrast, need not be propositional, even though they have (more or less) determinate qualitative features in one's experience. A bright red patch presented to me need not be a proposition or even commit me to a proposition. Even so, it can be a component of my empirical evidence in need of explanation; it thus can be part of my "data" figuring in what it is epistemically reasonable, or justified, for me to believe. The bright red patch does not need to be acknowledged (as existing) or even experienced by others for it to be relevant epistemic data *for me*. Others could be color blind in a way that blocks their experiencing a red patch, but this would not preclude its role in *my* experience and evidence.

We need to acknowledge a crucial distinction between one's *having* evidence or justification and one's *presenting*, or *giving*, evidence or justification to another person. Oppy's "conversational scoreboard," requiring agreement of participants on all relevant "data," fails to capture the importance of that distinction. I can have undefeated evidence (and hence epistemic justification) for a belief, but not be able to give that evidence to another person, at least in a way that persuades or compels agreement from that person. So, I could have an epistemically justified belief on the basis of evidence but lack the resources to convince another person of my belief. One's having evidence and epistemic justification, then, does not depend on socially shared agreement about data. Social conversation, therefore, is an inadequate model for one's having evidence and epistemic justification.

Neglecting our crucial distinction, Oppy blithely moves from considerations about his "conversational scoreboard" to considerations about evidence and justification. He states: "The crucial question to be asked is whether the evidence that we have justifies the ontological and ideological costs that Christianity incurs but naturalism does not" (35). Although appropriate, the question of whether one's evidence justifies ontological costs is more basic than, and hence differs from, Oppy's question about the epistemological import of data agreed upon by all inquirers in terms of a "conversational scoreboard." One's evidence could justify an ontological cost for oneself even though that evidence is not acknowledged or agreed upon by all relevant inquirers. Evidence and its justifying import, we might say, are "natural kinds" that do not depend on human agreement.

Oppy adds: "I have sketched a case for the superiority of naturalism to Christianity, paying attention to particular Christian doctrines that—as I see it—bring with them ontological and ideological costs that are not justified in terms of accompanying explanatory benefits" (47). Here again we find a use of "justified" that neglects our crucial distinction. Oppy's case rests on a requirement of social agreement on relevant data in a "conversational scoreboard," but justification in terms of explanatory benefits does not have that requirement. Such justification, as one's *having* justification, emerges from the evidence one has and its role in a best available explanation for one.[2] It does not depend on one's being restricted to "data" agreed upon by other inquirers, as if one's evidence or justification depended on one's being able to persuade other inquirers in a conversation. Otherwise, we would give conversation too much evidential significance. Oppy's case for naturalism faces that problem.

We still must ask whether, and if so how, a God worthy of worship could earn his keep from a human explanatory point of view. Everything depends on what we build into the standard of earning one's keep from a human explanatory point of view (and on what needs explanation for one). Consider a person's belief in the Christian God. This belief would be more than a belief *that* God exists because it would include trust in God. Even so, it could be based on undefeated evidence had by a person, and that evidence could have a *de re* component irreducible to a proposition. (Being *de re*, this component would concern a thing, and not a proposition or judgement that something is the case.) In particular, the evidence could include the person's having a *de re*, a direct-acquaintance relation with God. This relation would include the direct acquaintance of a human will with God's will. Part of God's will, if God is worthy of worship, would include unselfish love, and direct acquaintance with such love would be *de re*. More accurately, it would be *de te*, because it would be an I–*Thou* relation between a human and God (in the second person).

If God is worthy of worship and hence morally perfect independently, then God is in a distinctive category relative to our ordinary world. In particular, if monotheism is true, this God is *sui generis*, and the same is true of God's moral character. In addition, if God self-manifests aspects of this moral character, such as divine love, to some humans, then this self-manifestation will be irreducible to a belief and will supply unique evidence of God's reality to some humans. God would not be required to self-manifest to all humans by any particular time, because some humans may not be prepared to receive the self-manifestation in agreement with God's purpose for it. God thus could hide divine self-manifestation from some people, at least for a time. As a result,

2. For relevant details, see Paul K. Moser, *Knowledge and Evidence* (Cambridge: Cambridge University Press, 1989), and Moser, *The Elusive God* (Cambridge: Cambridge University Press, 2008).

we should not require that the "data" or evidence for God's reality be agreed upon by all inquirers about God. Even so, God could supply epistemic self-authentication via self-manifestation for humans who are suitably receptive. (This does not entail that any religious experience or document is self-authenticating.)[3]

The variability of the evidence for God among persons does not entail subjectivism or noncognitivism about God's reality. Indeed, if God has redemptive purposes for humans, we should expect that evidence to be variable, because people may be more or less prepared for it. Oppy remarks: "I suspect that most Christians are well aware that there simply isn't any set of considerations that ought to bring everyone to adopt a Christian worldview. If this is correct, then at the very least most Christians already accept that [their] mission is much more an art than a science" (45). I cannot tell what Oppy means by "art" or by "set of considerations." If he means by the latter phrase "what is in a person's actual evidence," I can agree. If some people are not ready to receive God as their Lord, God may postpone supplying salient evidence of God's reality for them. (Some Christian apologists miss this important lesson.) If Oppy means something stronger, we will have a different story. If by "art" he means something noncognitive, which does not entail truth or evidence, then his inference is doubtful. I suspect that by "science" he means a discipline whose "data" must be agreed upon by all relevant inquirers in terms of a "conversational scoreboard." I have no problem now if he prefers to use "science" in that manner, but in that case we should hesitate, unlike Oppy himself, to argue against Christian belief as if it aimed to be a "science" (in the sense indicated). I have offered a crucial distinction that easily frees grounded Christian belief from Oppy's science model for "trumping" positions.

Oppy seems driven to his conversational model by a concern about "dogmatism." He claims: "I cannot accept the implicit suggestion that philosophy ought properly to be the mouthpiece of dogmatism.... One minimal aim of that enterprise is to improve the worldview of each by allowing the worldview of each to be fairly tested against the worldviews of everyone else" (47). We should avoid any kind of dogmatism

3. For more on this approach, see Paul K. Moser, *The Severity of God* (Cambridge: Cambridge University Press, 2013), and Paul K. Moser, "God without Argument," in *Is Faith in God Reasonable?*, eds. Corey Miller and Paul Gould (New York: Routledge, 2014), 69–83.

that neglects relevant evidence, but Oppy goes social too fast and hence neglects our crucial distinction. The needed testing of one's having evidence for beliefs, whether religious or scientific, must begin with testing against *one's own evidence* and not "the worldviews of everyone else." If we neglect this order, we risk sacrificing to social agreement genuine evidence that an individual has. In that case, we risk neglecting evidence crucial to what a person epistemically should believe. Oppy's case for naturalism fails on this front.

GRAHAM OPPY

One important task for philosophy is comparison of worldview. One important goal of this important task is arriving at expert consensus: if we don't have expert consensus, then even the best among us have not collectively arrived at the truth. Note that I do not say that the important task I identify is the only important task; nor do I say that the important goal I identify is the only important goal. Indeed, in my initial essay, I note some important subsidiary tasks, including the task of articulating best worldviews. This task of articulation presupposes prior activity of developing and working out worldviews. And the task of developing and working out worldviews is both an individual project and a collective project.

The individual project of developing and working out worldviews is always a work in progress. Whether at any given time a particular person is making good progress with their personal project depends upon a range of factors, including their cognitive capacities, the information with which they are working, their application to the task, and what they make of their encounters with those who do not share their worldview. I have argued elsewhere that, on any standards that one might sensibly adopt, there is a wide range of worldviews rationally maintained in the face of acquaintance with other rationally maintained worldviews.

Against this background, it seems to me that Paul Moser's response does not engage with the view that I hold. I have never maintained that one's having evidence and epistemic justification depends upon socially shared agreement about data. I'm happy to allow that one need not be—and need not be deemed to be—irrational or lacking in doxastic justification merely in virtue of one's taking oneself to have *de re* direct acquaintance with God. But, for the purposes of the important task of trying to arrive at expert consensus, the data that we *collectively* have is only that some people take themselves to have *de re* direct acquaintance with God. (In other presentations of my framework, I define *data* as those claims that are held in common between the worldviews up for assessment; and I say that all the other claims that belong to those worldview are *theory*. A *fully* articulated worldview would include exactly one of p and ~p for each proposition that p. If—like McGrew—you feel the need to reckon with those who hold that there are true contradictions, then the requirement is more complicated: a fully articulated worldview includes at least one of p and ~p for each proposition that p where (p&~p) would not be a vicious contradiction; and it includes exactly one of p and ~p for each proposition that p where (p&~p) would be a vicious contradiction. Other departures from "classical logic" might require further adjustments.)

Given this characterization of my view, you might think that there is no prospect of arriving at expert worldview consensus: if I do take myself to have *de re* direct acquaintance with God, then I'll simply deem inadequate any inquiry that won't allow my *de re* direct acquaintance with God as data. I agree that there is no near prospect of expert worldview consensus. However, it is important to recognize that taking the data to be that some people take themselves to have *de re* direct acquaintance with God is perfectly consistent with arrival at expert consensus on the view that the reason why some people take themselves to have *de re* direct acquaintance with God is precisely that those people do have *de re* direct acquaintance with God. (Here I part company with Scott Oliphint, who thinks that it requires some kind of naturalistic presupposition to maintain that, in the context of the attempt to arrive at expert worldview consensus, we should accept that our relevant data is only that some people take themselves to have *de re* direct acquaintance with God.)

While there is no immediate prospect that my three-stage assessment—articulation, internal evaluation, external comparison—will be carried out, I think that it is clear that *trade-off* between minimizing ontological and ideological commitments and maximizing explanatory breadth and depth will be the most important consideration in any attempt to carry out external comparison. Oliphint and McGrew disagree. Oliphint first suggests that naturalists will seek to minimize ontological and ideological commitments come what may, and then suggests that we ought to maximize explanatory breadth and depth come what may. I think that both of these suggestions are mistaken. If we suppose that all that matters is minimizing ontological and ideological commitments, then we shall be nihilists: we shall suppose that there isn't anything at all. And if we suppose that all that matters is maximizing explanatory breadth and depth, then we shall commit ourselves to a profligate panoply of explainers for what we would otherwise take to be mere coincidences. McGrew suggests that the notion of minimization of ontological commitment is deeply problematic: "while . . . it is a theorem that $P(A\&B) < P(A)$ . . . there is no general inequality that holds between $P(A\&B)$ and $P(A\&\sim B)$" (56). But McGrew's criticism supposes that ontological commitments are propositions. This assumption is inconsistent with the standard Quinean conception of ontological commitment that my discussion takes for granted. (Here, Moser is right on the money: "Christianity does carry metaphysical baggage absent from metaphysical naturalism because it acknowledges the existence of God, whereas metaphysical naturalism does not" (59).

In my initial essay, I gave a very brief outline of a case for the conclusion that an application of my three-stage process of evaluation would lead to the conclusion that naturalism is a better worldview than theism. That sketch is very broad brush, and—as I explicitly noted—leaves lots of details unexamined. Since McGrew makes some critical observations about details, I shall try to give some brief responses on those points.

McGrew says that I claim that "the evidence in the case of the miracles recorded in the New Testament is no better than that for the miraculous cures attributed to Vespasian in Alexandria" (57). This is simply untrue. What I claimed is that we have no more supporting evidence *for the four cases of miraculous healing of blindness* in the New Testament than we do for the miraculous cure of blindness attributed to Vespasian *by Suetonius*. Each of the four reports in the New Testament is a one-off; none is supported by any other relevant evidence. Likewise, there is no other relevant supporting evidence for the claim made by Suetonius. True enough, as McGrew says, the account that Tacitus gives of Vespasian's miracle working clearly—and perhaps knowingly—reveals political, religious, and financial motives. But it is no less clear that there would have been political and religious motives to include the four cases of miraculous healing of blindness in the Gospels, whether or not those stories were true.

McGrew says that I suggest that the rise of the John Frum cult bears useful analogy to the rise of Christianity. This, too, is simply untrue. What I claimed is that the John Frum cult provides *one example* of a very widespread phenomenon: detailed beliefs with almost no foundation in fact becoming widely accepted in very short timeframes. And if—as many naturalists suppose—the naturalistically unacceptable details in the Gospels instance this phenomenon, then we have as complete an explanation of the presence of those details in the Gospels as we are ever likely to get. McGrew thinks that preliminary sorting will winnow out almost all other examples of this phenomenon, while leaving the Gospel stories in need of more careful examination. In particular, he claims that the first Gospel reports are not "widely separated" in time from the reported events. But the timeframes for the widespread phenomenon can be *very* short: a matter of months. There is plenty of time for all the naturalistically unacceptable details to be woven into whatever is the core true narrative.

McGrew says that I "fundamentally misconceive the nature of a miracle claim" (58). I'm not sure that's right. We agree that in the normal course of things the dead stay dead. Naturalists think that there is nothing but the normal course of things: (barring extraordinary advances in medical science) the dead always have, and always will, stay dead. McGrew thinks that there is a very important exception: the resurrection of Jesus. There is no evidence for the resurrection of Jesus apart from Christian writings. All the evidence we have is the contents of a modest number of documents of uncertain pedigree. Given the ontological and ideological commitments of Christian worldviews, it seems to me that the trade-off between commitment and explanation is best made on the naturalist's terms: the accounts of the resurrection of Jesus in Christian documents record detailed false beliefs that became widely accepted in the developing Christian community in a relatively short period of time. This kind of thing—detailed false beliefs becoming widely accepted in relevant communities in short periods of time—happens all the time, and we all typically rest content with just this level of explanation when we suppose that those detailed beliefs are false.

McGrew says that Christians are entitled to ask for "a more detailed analysis" in the case of the resurrection of Jesus "lest the skeptical miasma thus released should spread unchecked across other beliefs—including belief in metaphysical naturalism" (56). I think that Christians need not be irrational to believe in the resurrection of Jesus. So, I think that Christians can reasonably "ask for a more detailed analysis." After all, it would be inconsistent with Christian belief to suppose that the accounts of the resurrection of Jesus in Christian documents record detailed *false* beliefs that became widely accepted in the Christian community in a relatively short period of time. But, from the standpoint of worldview comparison, I think it is pretty clear that there is no skeptical threat *to naturalism* that arises from appeal to the same kind of explanation that we are all happy to accept in connection with a vast range of reports of naturalistically unacceptable phenomena.

McGrew claims that "nothing of interest" follows from the fact that false miracle claims abound in the religions of the world. I don't think that's right. Nor do I think that it's exactly right to say that we need "some touchstone . . . to distinguish the true [claims], if there are any, from the fraudulent or muddled" (57). It seems to me that we distinguish the true and the false by asking ourselves whether, in the light of everything else that we believe about the world, it is more likely that the testimony is true than false. That the earliest reports we have are widely separated from events in space or time, or that the earliest reports we have clearly serve the interests of established opinions, may sometimes be considerations that tell against particular testimonies to miracles. But—as the history of contemporary urban legends reveals—it often happens that detailed false beliefs become widely accepted in relevant communities in short periods of time, even though there are no "established opinions" that are served by the reporting of those beliefs, and even though the time it takes for the entrenchment of those reports is measured in months.

McGrew responds to my observation that we have no textual evidence for the resurrection from non-Christian sources that we know to be independent of the Christian documents we have with the claim that "people who were persuaded of the resurrection of Jesus became Christians. From whom else should we expect such testimony?" (58) I think that this response relies on a narrow conception of what could serve as textual evidence for the resurrection. Even if all the facts were as the Christian texts have them, the vast majority of people who heard stories about the resurrection of Jesus were not persuaded that those stories were true. If we had independent texts from the period 30–35 CE which made detailed references to the beliefs and assertions of Christians, written by people who thought that those beliefs and assertions were false, that evidence might *strengthen* the case for the resurrection. But we have no independent texts of this kind.

K. SCOTT OLIPHINT

> There are more things in heaven and earth, Horatio, than are
> dreamt of in your philosophy.
>
> —Hamlet to Horatio

My task in this chapter is to argue for a form of the "Christianity trumps philosophy" view by presenting what can be called a covenantal understanding of philosophy. In order to do that, it will be important to clarify what we're discussing. I would like, first and briefly, to set forth what is meant by "Christianity," then by "philosophy," and then to clarify what I mean by "trumps." I'll take the second one first.

By "philosophy" I mean the discipline that takes as its subject matter the nature of reality (including ultimate reality), the nature of knowledge (including the use and nature of logical thinking), and the nature of right and wrong. There are a number of specifics that can be included under these three general topics. Under "the nature of reality," for example, I mean to include such topics as the nature of being, of individuality, of necessity, of possibility, etc. As with the "nature of reality," so also with the "nature of knowledge" and the "nature of right and wrong": I mean to include any of the subtopics that can legitimately be listed under each general topic. So the general topics are not meant to exclude, but should happily include, all of their legitimate specifics.

I will also take for granted that philosophy is attempting to discover the truth about these matters and thus to provide a proper way of seeing and understanding each of them. I recognize that my description is inadequate in that it does not do justice to the intricate details of philosophical discussion or the usefulness of (some of) its conclusions, but it will do for our purposes in this essay.

By "Christianity" I mean something much more than "theism," and something more specific than a generic form of Christianity. By "Christianity" I mean the theology that came out of the Reformation (including the post-Reformation) era, as expressed in the creeds and confessions of that era. So, for example, while there are differences in the details of some of those creeds and confessions—such as the Belgic Confession, the Canons of Dordt, and the Westminster Confession of Faith—the *foundations* of the theology expressed in each of them is in agreement and unified. It is important to recognize also that those creeds and confessions were not written in a vacuum. They depend on earlier ecumenical creeds of the church in order to confess and affirm their particular theology. So there is significant historical weight in the position that I hope to describe. This historical dependence has two implications, both of which explain my use of the term "trumps."

The first implication, as just noted, is that my view is not simply *mine*, but it stands in a (relatively) long tradition. Given that the Reformation creeds and confessions rest on previous creeds of the church, my view is representative (though not the *only* representative) of the history of Christian thought. My intent in this essay is to remain within that tradition in order to affirm why it must be the case that the theological foundations that were reasserted during the time of the Reformation must be the starting point for philosophy (and for any other science). The bulk of what I argue in this essay, therefore, will be taken from that tradition. The second implication is that my argument will seek to affirm the *theological* necessity of any philosophical activity that aims at truth. These two implications explain what I mean by "trumps."

Foundations

In order to explain the relationship of Christianity to philosophy, and to highlight the historical precedence for this view, we need to look all too briefly at the notion of *principia*. The Latin term *principia* is one that has its roots in the Greek term *archē*, which means "a foundation, a beginning point, a source, or a first principle." Its theoretical roots go back at least as far as Aristotle. Aristotle argued that an *archē*, a first principle or beginning point, is "a common property . . . of all *archōn* (ἀρχῶν) to be the first thing from which something either *is* (ἔστιν) or *becomes* (γίγνεται) or becomes *known* (γιγνώσκεται)."[1] This concept of a beginning point, what some have called an Archimedean point, is a necessary and crucial aspect of *all* thinking and *all* existence. Aristotle understood this in his own way, and Christian theology has adapted and adopted it in order to show the necessity of *principia* in any and all disciplines.

The *principia* of theology are different from the *principia* of other disciplines. In theology, following the traditional philosophical usage of the term, two *principia* have been confessed, and they are mutually dependent (with respect to human beings). The *principium essendi* is the principle, source, or foundation of *existence* or of *being*. What is affirmed here is that there must be a *reason* why things exist; we recognize that the things that exist in the world are not self-generating; neither are they self-existent. The source of the existence we recognize and experience must be one in whom existence is intrinsic to his nature. Apart from such a foundation, existence can only take its place on the shifting sands of contingency, which is too unstable and inadequate to provide its own rationale.

The other *principium* that theology confesses is the *principium cognoscendi*, or the principle of *knowledge*. This *principium* affirms that the foundation of knowledge cannot be self-generated; knowledge needs a firm foundation upon which to begin and in which to operate. Without that foundation, knowledge can only take its place *within* each individual and—as the history of philosophy shows—will lose touch with any notion of a unified reality. Without these two foundations, in other words, explanations of existence and of knowledge will be "shots in the dark," i.e., empty and futile attempts to construct *de novo* the matters at hand. In this way, theology provides the *principia* for all other disciplines. Like the multiple floors of a high rise, without the first foundation (i.e., theology), the others will eventually give way.

With respect to the relation of the *principia* of theology to other

---

1. Gk.: πασῶν μὲν οὖν κοινὸν τῶν ἀρχῶν τὸ πρῶτον εἶναι ὅθεν ἢ ἔστιν ἢ γίγνεται ἢ γιγνώσκεται (Aristotle, *Metaphysics*, ed. W. D. Ross [Oxford: Clarendon, 1924], 1013a.15–19).

disciplines, the theologian Sibrandus Lubbertus (1555–1625), to use just one example, argued that all disciplines require *principia*, and that (following Aristotle) such *principia* partake of at least the following properties: (1) they are necessarily and immutably true, and (2) they must be known *per se*, that is, in themselves, as both immediate and indemonstrable.[2] By "immediate" is meant that the *status* of a *principium* is not taken from something external to it but is inherent in the thing itself. It does not mean, strictly speaking, that nothing *mediated* the truth therein, but rather that nothing *external* to the *principium* mediated that truth. By "indemonstrable" is meant that the *fact* of a *principium* is not proven by way of syllogism but is such that it provides the ground upon which any other fact or demonstration depends. It is, in that sense, a transcendental notion.

The relationship of theological *principia* to the *principia* of other sciences is summed up well by Philippe du Plessis-Mornay (1549–1623). Speaking of the discipline of theology, the so-called "Huguenot Pope" states:

> For if every science has its *principles*, which it is not lawful to remove, be it ever so little: much more reason is it that it should be so with that thing which hath the ground of all *principles* as its *principle*.[3]

What Mornay is saying here is not unique among theologians. Not only was he saying that theology has its own *principia*, but he was saying much more than that. He was also affirming that, whereas all disciplines have their own *principia*, theology's *principia* undergird and underlie any and all other *principia*. The *principia* of other disciplines are relative to those disciplines; the *principia* of theology are prior to any other *principia* of any and all other disciplines.[4] This is the case, not because theology is intrinsically *better* than other disciplines, but because the *principia* of

---

2. Richard A. Muller, *Post-Reformation Reformed Dogmatics: The Rise and Development of Reformed Orthodoxy; Volume 1: Prolegomena to Theology*, 2nd ed. (Grand Rapids: Baker Academic, 2003), 431.

3. Philippe du Plessis-Mornay, *A Worke Concerning the Trunesse of Christian Religion, Written in French: Against Atheists, Epicures, Paynims, Iewes, Mahumetists, and Other Infidels*, trans. Sir Philip Sidney Knight and Arthur Golding (London: George Potter, 1604), 2.

4. According to Muller, "Divinity alone begins with the absolute first principles of things which depend on no other matters; whereas the basic principles of the other sciences are only first relative to the science for which they provide the foundation, the basic principles of theology are prior to any other 'principle of Being' or 'principle of knowing'" (*Reformed Dogmatics*, 436).

theology come—as it were—from the outside, in. They come from a transcendent source and are not generated *within* the discipline itself.

An important and central point to notice in this discussion is that theological *principia* could never be located in the human self. The confession of theology is that neither the foundation of "being/existence" or of "knowledge" is, or can be, self-generated. They both rely on someone who transcends the existence and knowledge of a human being and who has existence and knowledge intrinsically. In order to provide proper parameters, as well as a true rationale, for progress made and for purpose to be had in any discipline, there must be an external foundation present.

Apart from theological *principia*, all that is available is contingent existence and relative "truth." To rely on the contingent and relative would lead to the kind of skepticism that followed, for example, in the wake of Cartesian philosophy. Instead, as Richard Muller notes,

> The classical philosophical language of *principia* was appropriated ... at a time and in a context where ... [it] served the needs both of the Reformation sense of the priority of Scripture and the Reformation assumptions concerning the ancillary status of philosophy and the weakness of human reason. By defining both Scripture and God as principial in the strictest sense—namely as true, immediate, necessary, and knowable ... —the early orthodox asserted the priority of Scripture over tradition and reason and gave conceptual status to the notion of its self-authenticating character in response to ... philosophical skeptics of the era.[5]

In *Metaphysics*, Aristotle notes that first principles, in order to be *first* principles, must themselves be most certain, indemonstrable, immediately evident, and *never* a postulate or hypothesis.[6] First principles are those which anyone must have when he comes to study anything at all. First principles, therefore, cannot be something that someone *demonstrates* as a result of one's reasoning or argument.[7]

---

5. *Reformed Dogmatics*, 432.

6. Gk.: βεβαιοτάτη δ' ἀρχὴ πασῶν περὶ ἣν διαψευσθῆναι ἀδύνατον·γνωριμωτάτην τε γὰρ ἀναγκαῖον εἶναι τὴν τοιαύτην (περὶ γὰρ ἃ μὴ γνωρίζουσιν ἀπατῶνται πάντες) καὶ ἀνυπόθετον (Aristotle, *Metaphysics*, 1005b.10–14).

7. In the words of Duns Scotus, "To demand the reasons and proof for all things is to be intellectually undisciplined. For proof is not identical with the principles of proof" (as quoted in Herman Bavinck, *Reformed Dogmatics: God and Creation*, vol. 2 of *Reformed Dogmatics*, ed. John Bolt, trans. John Vriend (Grand Rapids: Baker Academic, 2004), 235.

So the *principia* that form the foundation for everything else are themselves transcendental in nature. That is, they provide for the possibility of anything else; in a particular science or discipline—such as philosophy—they provide for the possibility of that science. The *principia* of theology provide those truths that are requisite for any other discipline, in that they provide the foundation for *all being* and for *all knowing*.

In theology, therefore, the two primary categories which serve as *principia* (and thus ground all other disciplines) are the existence and nature of God, and the doctrine of revelation (both general and special). And while we do not have the time to work out the relationship between these two *principia*, we should note at least the following.

First, the juxtaposition, so familiar in the confessions of the Reformation, between the doctrine of Scripture (revelation) and the doctrine of the existence and nature of God relates specifically to a particular understanding of who God is and of how he may be known. In other words, for human beings, the one *principium* entails the other. To seek to know God apart from his revelation is to begin in the wrong place. Knowledge of God is *first* given, not demonstrated. Once properly *received*, it is, at the same time, recognized that revelation is the necessary foundation of that which we know.

Second, it was in this context that Franciscus Junius (1545–1602) developed a categorization of the knowledge of God that relates directly to our theological understanding of *principia*. In attempting to articulate the relationship of God's own knowledge to our knowledge of God, Junius made a distinction between *archetypal* knowledge and *ectypal* knowledge. Archetypal knowledge is that knowledge which God alone has. It is knowledge of God that partakes of all the essential divine attributes. Hence, it is knowledge that just *is* God himself (given the simplicity of God).

Ectypal knowledge is true knowledge that has its foundation in God's archetypal knowledge. This knowledge is not identical with God's archetypal knowledge. It could not be since archetypal knowledge is—like God—infinite, eternal, and immutable. But it is nevertheless *true* knowledge, even though finite and limited, because it has its roots in, and thus is consistent with, God's own essential and exhaustive knowledge of himself and of everything else. God himself has ectypal knowledge, based on his archetypal knowledge, and that ectypal knowledge is given to his human creatures by way of revelation. Thus, as creatures made in God's image, the knowledge that we have is ectypal knowledge.

Third, this is all just another way of saying that the only way in which we can know God—or anything else, initially—is if God graciously chooses to reveal himself to us. That revelation comes in and through creation (thus knowledge of creation presupposes knowledge of God), and through his spoken (written) Word. As creatures, therefore, there is an inextricable link—an inextricable *principial* link—between God and his revelation. From the perspective of the creature, we cannot have one without the other. And that is just to say that the *principia* of theology entail each other. We know God properly by his revelation, and we know his revelation by knowing him properly.

Covenant Foundations

It is this notion of God as a revealing God that constitutes what is meant by *covenant*. Covenant, in the way I am using it, means "God's voluntary condescension in order to *relate* himself to his creation, and specifically to his human creatures." The *Westminster Confession of Faith* 7.1 puts it this way:

> The distance between God and the creature is so great, that although reasonable creatures do owe obedience unto Him as their Creator, yet they could never have any fruition of Him as their blessedness and reward, but by some voluntary condescension on God's part, which he hath been pleased to express by way of covenant.

The God whom Christianity confesses is a God who condescends. He condescends to speak creation into existence. His creation reaches its apex, climactically, as God condescends to create human beings *in his image*. An image, by definition, entails a relationship; no image can be what it is without its original. To be the image of God, therefore, human beings must be in a relationship to the God who made them. That relationship can be denominated as "covenant." It is a relationship that is unilaterally initiated by God, and it includes the privilege and responsibility of being the image of God. That is, we must first and foremost recognize our utterly *dependent* character as image. All that we do, we do as image. All that we undertake to know and to be, we undertake as image. Our responsibility in everything that we are, do, and undertake is to seek to reflect the image of the one whose we are, and who himself is the only one who is *not* dependent.

When God creates male and female as image, he speaks to them. That speech to them is in order that they might be obedient images that "reflect" his character. He tells them to be responsible rulers—*under him*—of the earth. They are to "subdue" it. In naming the animals, God was demonstrating Adam's rule over the animals, even as God's sovereignty was manifested as he brought the animals to Adam to name. Not only so, but even as Adam and Eve were commanded to rule the earth to God's glory, God demonstrated his ownership of the earth by picking out a tree over which Adam and Eve had no control or rule, and which would demonstrate God's unfettered rule as well as their responsibility toward him.

All of these events presuppose a covenant relationship, which itself presupposes the God who was "in the beginning." To be the image of God means to be related to God. That relationship entails a real responsibility toward the God who made us.[8]

Philosophy is one of those tasks. It is meant to take the good gifts that God has given in creation and to develop those gifts to the glory of God. But so many of these developments have not been good, useful, or productive. In our various tasks—including philosophy—we have taken aspects of God's creation and developed bad, harmful, and destructive means. But even these harmful and destructive products are covenantally qualified. And here a further word of explanation is in order.

The tree of the knowledge of good and evil, which God had sovereignly appointed as a demonstrable sign of Adam and Eve's relationship to him, was the test case for Adam and Eve. Their responsibility was to do as God required; they were not to eat from it.

But they did eat from it. They were tempted by Satan, and they succumbed to that temptation. When they ate from the forbidden tree, the

---

8. Space does not allow a discussion of God's "common" grace. Suffice it to say that those who do their work "in Adam" can, nevertheless, because of God's mercy over a cursed creation, continue to be somewhat productive and useful in their endeavors. But these come not *because of*, but *in spite of*, the rejection of the true foundation of God and his revelation. For more on common grace, see Cornelius Van Til, *Common Grace and the Gospel*, ed. K. Scott Oliphint (Phillipsburg, NJ: P&R, 2015).

relationship that they had enjoyed with God as a happy and fulfilling one became one of punishment and curse. Because Adam was designated by God as the covenant head or representative of all creation, the curse extended to the entirety of that creation. This means that the way things are now is not the way they were created to be. Instead of everything remaining "very good" as it was originally created, humanity—and the earth on which we live—are all "cursed." That is, all of us as we are "in Adam" have an intrinsic opposition and abhorrence to God's original, created intent.

But—and this is the key point—even amidst this opposition, the relationship that God established at the beginning of creation is in no way erased. Indeed, it *cannot* be erased. Its *character* has changed, but the relationship remains intact. That relationship began in harmony with God's desire and intent for creation. Adam and Eve were created as "very good" along with the rest of creation. But once Adam opposed that desire and intent, the goodness of creation began to carry a curse. *But that curse is itself covenantal.* In other words, to be cursed is to be in an unhappy and unfulfilling relationship to God, a relationship characterized by our opposition to and attempted destruction of all that God originally designed for his creation.

But the God who justly cursed his creation because of Adam's sin also provided a way out of that curse. He promised that the seed of the woman would crush the head of the serpent. In other words, he promised that a way would be provided so that the curse would one day be defeated and the goodness of creation would reach its consummate climax.

This "way out" that God provided finds its focus in that ultimate and preeminent covenantal condescension of God, i.e., in the person of Jesus Christ. In Christ, the second person of the Trinity, the Son of God, took to himself a human nature, even while remaining fully God, so that he could resolve the curse and clean up the mess that Adam began and that we perpetuate. Adam's sin brought death to humanity, and we have been perpetuating that sin ever since, with the result that death continues to assert itself as supreme in every person's life. But the "second Adam," Jesus Christ, obeyed perfectly, and thus conquered the death that Adam's sin brought to creation.

For all of humanity, there are two—and only two—representatives, and each person can have just one of them. Each person either *covenantally* remains in Adam, and thus continues in the disobedience that Adam began, or is *covenantally* in Christ, and thus begins by grace to thwart that disobedience and to "think God's thoughts after him," i.e., to think and work according to what God has said (in the world and in his Word).

Death is not supreme, and it is not the end. The death of Jesus Christ was the beginning of the death of death. As an enemy, death itself will one day be destroyed. In the meantime, death makes its mark on all, but it is not the final word for any. Instead, death ushers in a new mode of existence for each of us. For those who remain *covenantally* in Adam, that new mode of existence is an extension of the curse. For those who are *covenantally* in Christ, the new mode of existence culminates in the reality of what the original creation was meant to be. In either case, however, there is—as there always will be—a *covenant* relationship between God and every person. Just as a mirror image always requires a "relationship" with the original, so also all human beings, as image of God, will always be in some kind of relationship to their Creator. He is always present with us, and our responsibility to image him is, therefore, always before us.

For those who are and remain in Adam as their covenant head, opposition to God continues in earnest. That which is accomplished by any who remain in Adam is ultimately destructive and subversive of God's original design for creation. Those who are in Adam live and breathe as those who are suppressing and opposing all that God originally instilled in his creation.

For those who are in Christ, the tasks that are undertaken and carried out in him will take into account all that we have said thus far. Those tasks will be framed within the reality that he has covenantally revealed to us in his Word and his world, and will work—as much as is possible in a sin-cursed world—in conformity to what he has said.

These truths have ramifications and implications too numerous to mention. What they mean for philosophy, however, is that for philosophy to be done properly, it must be done—not in the context of those principles and practices that are indicative of the curse—but in light of and in line with those principles and practices that are part and parcel of the restoration of the curse as it is found in Christ. In other words, philosophy is either *covenant*-breaking philosophy as it in Adam opposes what God originally designed, or it is by grace *covenant*-keeping philosophy as it in Christ attempts to "demolish arguments and every pretension that sets itself up against the knowledge of God, and . . . take captive every thought to make it obedient to Christ" (2 Cor 10:5).

The metaphysical and epistemological implications of this covenant model are now before us, and they cannot be separated. We recognize that the one God—Father, Son, and Holy Spirit—is absolutely independent in and of himself; he is "I AM WHO I AM" (Exod 3:14). We also see that God freely determined to condescend in order that we might know and serve him. The focus of that condescension is in his Son, who is the Word (John 1:1). For the Christian, this focus is found in his Word—Scripture—which tells us who God is and what he has done. The *principium* of Scripture is meant to ground anything else that we affirm in theology and in any other discipline.

But the written Word of God does not come in a vacuum. God has been speaking (nonverbally) "since the creation of the world" (Ps 19:1–2; Rom 1:20). That speech of God makes clear to everyone his "invisible qualities—his eternal power and divine nature" (Rom 1:20). So clear is this revelation of God in creation that it renders us all "without excuse" before him. Though our covenant-breaking tendency is always to suppress what is clearly revealed, that revelation nevertheless gets through so that—as the image of God—we all know him truly. It is, says the apostle Paul, *the truth* that we suppress (Rom 1:18). It is truth that comes, not by way of demonstration or proof, but solely through the ever-revealing activity of the God who made us. What he reveals is "clearly seen" and "understood" because it comes from him. In Adam, however, we are intent to hold it down and never bring it up.

It is these two modes of God's revelation—the "natural" and the "special"—that must be the ground and foundation of everything else that we attempt to know in God's world as his covenant creatures. Because he has condescended to reveal himself, we can begin our endeavors with *the truth*, a truth that comes from outside of us and that is grounded in the only one whose knowledge is without error or lack. This knowledge is a gracious gift, and it is accepted for what it is only by grace, through faith. It is not an elitist commodity; it is there for any who seek it. Without it, however, the best one is able to acquire is a skewed and selfish menagerie of ideas that is impossible in the end to account for reality, or for our knowledge of it.

Faith and Reason

What I have expressed thus far is probably compatible, more or less, with other models presented in this book, with the exception of the conflict model.[9] The truths expressed above are truths that require an adequate *faith* in order to be affirmed.[10] That is, to this point I have attempted to summarize what (many) orthodox Christians have *believed*, according to God's special revelation in his Word, throughout the history of the church. Disagreements in application may come, of course, but they will come within the context of affirmations of the truths described above. Those disagreements are important, and it is a useful exercise to try to soften as many of those as possible in order to promote as much harmony as we can, as we seek to live together in the various rooms of our one "house."

With respect to a conflict model, however, there is only one room—not many—and one house. Those who require theological *principia* for the proper work of philosophy are in direct opposition to those who think theological *principia* to be foolish or irrational. Likewise, those who embrace the conflict approach cannot countenance any suggestion of the need for theological foundations. Like Seuss's Sneetches, the plain-bellied Sneetches cannot live in the same room with the star-bellied kind. The two simply cannot live together at all.

But maybe it's not as bad as all that, at least from a covenantal perspective. It might be useful, therefore, to delineate some of the ways that the covenant and conflict approaches disagree and then to express some of the ways that—given the covenantal model—harmony might be a possibility.

In the context of a discussion between a covenant and a conflict model, we can see the age-old problem of the relation of faith and reason come to the fore. That problem is, in many ways, compatible with our

---

9. I should note here that at the time of writing this essay, I had yet to read the other, initial presentations in this book, so my suppositions here may be off the mark with respect to the specific authors herein.

10. Just to be clear, faith, in its historic and biblical sense, is not divorced from knowledge. It necessarily includes knowledge, as well as assent and trust.

explanation of a covenantal (i.e., faith) approach in contrast to some aspects of a conflict (i.e., denial of faith) approach. The terminology here can be confusing rather than helpful. For example, we should recognize (though this is a discussion that cannot be entered into here) that each of these views requires both (some kind of) faith and reason. The point of contention is not in the *use* of these two but in the *kinds* used: what *kind* of faith and what *kind* of reason used in each of these views helps set the boundaries and the relationship between them.

So how should a covenant model think about its relationship to our standard rules of thought (i.e., reason)? To put it in the more common vernacular, what is faith's role with respect to reason and vice versa? How might we think about reason and its abilities? And how might that affect the way we think about philosophy? To the first question first.

If we think of reason as a necessary and necessarily useful tool with respect to all of our thinking, the natural question to ask is not *whether* we use our reason, but rather what is the proper *use* of reason with respect to our knowledge. Just as a hammer is ill equipped to tighten a screw, though it be a tool suitably fitted for its proper use, so also reason is ill equipped to perform any function for which it is not made. What, then, is the proper use of reason with respect to faith, i.e., with respect to the truths given in a covenant model?

First, we have to recognize the necessity of "enlightened" reason in a covenantal model. One of the things that a proper exercise of Christian faith does is it begins to *renew* our reasoning, which, in Adam, is damaged by sin. That has a number of implications and applications, but what it means at minimum is that a foundational commitment to God's revelation sets the boundaries and provides the proper structure within which our thinking is to operate. This is, in part, what is meant by theological *foundations*.

Continuing the analogy, without a proper foundation for a house, the house itself cannot stand. Rooms might be built; they may be elaborate and impressive. But they cannot stand as they are. They will soon need to be torn down and replaced, or perhaps deconstructed in order to be reconstructed on a proper foundation. So also with the exercise of reason apart from theological (faith) foundations.

This may be what stands behind Peter van Inwagen's honest confession with respect to the "rooms" built in the history of metaphysics.

His frustration in writing a book on metaphysics is that there is no established body of literature with which he can begin and to which he can appeal. He contrasts metaphysical theories with the body of knowledge presently available in geology, and he notes:

> In the end we must confess that we have no idea why there is no established body of metaphysical results. It cannot be denied that this is a fact, however, and the beginning student of metaphysics should keep this fact and its implications in mind. One of its implications is that the author of this book . . . is [not] in a position in relation to you that is like the position of the author of [a] text . . . in geology. . . . All of these people will be the masters of a certain body of knowledge, and, on many matters, if you disagree with them you will simply be wrong. In metaphysics, however, you are perfectly free to disagree with anything the acknowledged experts say—other than their assertions about what philosophers have said in the past or are saying at present.[11]

If van Inwagen is correct (and—like all else in philosophy—it can be debated), then it appears that the best one can have in a study of metaphysics is a *description* of elaborate and impressive "rooms." These rooms are the result of brilliant and erudite thinkers; they can be meticulous in their detail and opulent in their furnishings. There is no foundation, however, and thus nothing secure on which the various rooms have been built. Time and tide have laid waste to each and every room, and those who begin to build again, or who seek to reconstruct the rooms of the past, continue to neglect to lay a foundation on which the rooms might stand.

In advocating for a covenantal model of the relationship between theology and philosophy, therefore, I am advocating for a view of reason that should recognize and acknowledge its own foundations. It should recognize its *place*, as it is designed to be used by those who affirm their utterly dependent status. It should recognize its *boundaries*, as it confesses its inability exhaustively to understand *anything* in creation. It should also recognize its *obligation* to turn from its covenant rebellion

---

11. Peter van Inwagen, *Metaphysics*, 2nd ed., Dimensions of Philosophy Series (Boulder: Westview, 2002), 12.

against the God who created and sustains all things, and to remain in covenantal conformity to what he has revealed. This is what I mean by "enlightened" reason.

Once enlightened, it is reason's task to judge as to the consistency and coherence of biblical truth.[12] In subjection to God's revealed truth, reason is to function as an arbiter of the consistency and coherence of God's Word and world. Reason is only able to function in this capacity after it has been restored and renewed by the grace of God in Jesus Christ. Along with this renewal come covenantal obligations. We are obliged to stand on the foundations provided as we build the various rooms of the house. Or, to use another analogy, a covenantal model recognizes the fence around the yard beyond which we ought not to go, but it also relishes in the space to move that the yard provides.

Therefore, in a covenantal model, reason is never meant to be the final arbiter with regard to what is possible and what is impossible. God alone is the origin of the possible, and thus the determining factor of what is impossible. But this means that a covenantal model recognizes the limits of our rules of thought. There is a "fence" built around those rules as well. This point, it seems to me, was the primary one that Cornelius Van Til was concerned to make with respect to the law of contradiction:

> It is therefore pointless for Christians to tell non-Christians that Christianity [i.e., the covenant model] is "in accord with the law of contradiction" unless they explain what they mean by this. For the non-Christian will take this statement to mean something entirely different from what the Christian ought to mean by it. The non-Christian does not believe in creation. Therefore, for him the law of contradiction is, like all other laws, something that does not find its ultimate source in the creative activity of God. Accordingly, the non-Christian will seek to do by means of the law of contradiction what the Christian has done for him by God. For the Christian, God legislates as to what is possible and what is impossible for man. For the non-Christian, man determines this for himself. Either

---

12. Francis Turretin, *Institutes of Elenctic Theology*, ed. James T. Dennison Jr., 3 vols. (Phillipsburg, NJ: P&R, 1994), 1:32ff. In what follows I will depend on, and follow closely, the discussion of Turretin (1623–1687) on the proper use of reason in theology.

positively or negatively the non-Christian will determine the field of possibility and therewith the stream of history by means of the law of contradiction.[13]

Given this model, and entailed by it, we affirm that reason always functions as a servant—never a master—in our own respective disciplines. Reason's proper place is to provide whatever tools might be helpful for us to carry out our own tasks. It also means that the law of contradiction, and the use of that law, can never finally and solely determine whether or not a particular Christian doctrine is true. That determination is left to revelation. What reason can do is help to organize, articulate, and expand those truths in such a way as to clarify their meaning.

Although the judgment of contradiction is allowed to reason in matters of faith [i.e., in a covenantal model], it does not follow that the human intellect becomes the rule of divine power (as if God could not do more things than human reason can conceive). God's being able to do something above nature and human conception . . . is different from his being able to do something contrary to nature and the principles of natural religion (which is most false).[14]

Thirdly, and following on the points just made, our tools of reasoning are in service to our own covenantal model, especially with respect to the organization and articulation of our interpretations of the Word and of the world. In a covenantal model, we use reason to understand Scripture (theology, to understand the "Word") and then also to inform and understand philosophy (and every other discipline, to understand the "world"). As Turretin notes, given the Reformation principle of *Sola Scriptura*, interpretations of Scripture and of the created world are given to us, in the first and foundational place, by way of Scripture itself. For theology, this means that we do not need another external source in order to compare and bring together the truth as God has given it to us in his Word. (This does not mean that philosophy cannot aid theology

---

13. Van Til, *Common Grace and the Gospel*, 230. Note also Turretin: "Nor is the power of God in this manner limited by the rule of our intellect, but our mind judges from the word what (according to the nature of a thing established by God) may be called possible or impossible" (*Institutes*, 1:34).

14. Turretin, *Institutes*, 1:34.

in the latter's articulation and understanding of its truths. More on that below.)

> The judgment of contradiction belongs to reason . . . with conformity to Scripture itself which clearly interprets itself and requires no other interpreter to establish its sense. Thus reason enlightened by the Holy Spirit through the word is able to consider and to judge from the word (according to the rules of good and necessary consequence) how the parts of a doctrine cohere, and what may or may not follow from them.[15]

Given these truths—that "enlightened" reason is to judge of the consistency of doctrine, is never to take a magisterial but rather a ministerial role with respect to its activity, and is to help articulate and organize our interpretations of all of God's creation—we can now move to discuss the relationship more specifically—not of reason to theology—but of philosophy to theology.

Faith and Philosophy

As we have affirmed, the question as to the differences between philosophy and theology will revolve around the answers to the questions of philosophy's and theology's *principia*. What is philosophy's *principium cognoscendi* ("foundation of knowledge")? That, of course, depends on whom you ask. Someone may say that philosophy's *principium cognoscendi* is reason itself. Without reason's asking and answering questions, there could be no philosophy at all.

To answer this question is also to answer the question of authority. The foundation or source of a discipline, in this sense, gives it its justification as well; it points to its boundaries and its rules or laws. If reason is the *principium cognoscendi* of philosophy, then philosophy's boundaries are determined by reason, its authority lies in reason, and its rules and laws are the rules and laws of reason. Not only so, but it seems that the *principium essendi* ("foundation of existence") has been made identical to the *principium cognoscendi*. This, it seems to me, creates numerous problems.

The first problem lies in the area of authority. Those who would

---

15. Turretin, *Institutes*, 1:33.

tout the tools of reason as the *principium cognoscendi* of philosophy would simply say that philosophy's authority is only as strong as the laws of logic, or the force of a sound argument, or something similar. In that way, one accepts philosophy's conclusions as one accepts these laws and forces. But nagging questions still remain. Whence these laws, and what kind of laws are they? Are they eternal, unchangeable laws? Conventions of society? Are they so intuitive that no one can rationally disagree? How would we know such things? The point here is not to refute the tools of reason given to us by God but to recognize that those tools cannot bear the weight that a foundation requires. They can be adequate tools to build the rooms of the foundation, but they need a foundation if the rooms are to stand.

The standard view in theology is that the *principium essendi* for all things is God himself. As the one who provides the ground of all existence, he also provides what is needed for us to understand him and his revelation to us in his world and his Word. The *principium cognoscendi* is revelation itself. In a covenantal model, the *principium cognoscendi externum* ("external principle of knowledge") is God's special revelation in his Word, and the *principium cognoscendi internum* ("internal principle of knowledge") is the knowledge of God that comes in and through creation, and in God's Word, all of which can only be acknowledged by faith.

Now, the specific question is, just what should a covenantal model believe the relationship of philosophy to theology to be? A covenantal model affirms, as we have noted, that God is the *principium essendi* of all disciplines, since it is from God alone that any and every discipline derives any and every thing that it is and has. On this view, as well, the *principium cognoscendi* is the revelation of God, both natural (in the world) and special (in his Word). If that is the case, then it is also the case that every discipline is related directly to these two *principia*. The only way properly to understand God's revelation is through God's own revealed Word. Thus, it is theology that sets the boundaries and the parameters, the rules and the laws, for all other disciplines. The late South African philosopher Hendrik Stoker put it this way:

> The distinction between theology and philosophy does not, according to my opinion, coincide with that between the revelation of God

in his Word on the one hand and the cosmos (or created universe) on the other. This is the case, because on the one hand theology also deals with God's revelation in creation, the cosmos, viewed in the light of his Word-revelation, whereas the Scriptures on the other hand disclose not only who God is and what his relation to all "things" is, but also matters concerning the created universe (or the cosmos) as such. (God's Word even makes assertions on matters relating to the field of some particular science or other, for instance that the laborer [note: not labor] is worthy of his [not of its] reward.) Because to the field of theology belong the ultimate problems, it may be called the "*scientia prima inter pares* [i.e., first science among equals]."[16]

To ascribe to theology a foundational status does not mean that there is *no* relationship between it and other disciplines. As a matter of fact, alert readers will have already noted one way in which Aristotle's notion of *principia* was adapted by theology. Given a covenantal structure of the relationship between theology and philosophy, there are many—and I would say, historically speaking, *necessary*—ways in which philosophy has aided theology.

Again, Francis Turretin provides some help here. He notes four primary *uses* of philosophy in theology (once it is established that philosophy's role is as handmaid, not mistress, to theology).

There is, he says, a specifically apologetic thrust to the use of philosophy in theology. In this sense, theologians should be quick to use philosophy and its tools when and where they can to demonstrate something of Christianity's own truth. According to Turretin, one of the primary uses of philosophy for theology is that

> it serves as a means of convincing the Gentiles and preparing them
> for the Christian faith. . . . So God wishes us to apply all the truths
> of the lower sciences to theology and after rescuing them from the
> Gentiles (as holders of a bad faith) to take and appropriate them
> to Christ who is the truth, for the building of the mystic temple;
> as formerly Moses enriched and adorned the tabernacle with

---

16. Hendrik G. Stoker, "Reconnoitering the Theory of Knowledge of Professor Dr. Cornelius Van Til," in *Jerusalem and Athens: Critical Discussions on the Philosophy and Apologetics of Cornelius Van Til*, ed. E. R. Geehan (Phillipsburg, NJ: P&R, 1977), 39.

the Egyptian gold, and Solomon procured the assistance of the Sidonians and Syrians in building the temple.[17]

An example from Scripture might help to illuminate this point (see Acts 17:16–34). As Paul waited in Athens for Silas and Timothy, he was moved and provoked because of the abundance of idolatry that was present, and explicitly so, throughout this center of intellectual activity. So he set out to defend the Christian faith, both in the synagogues and in the marketplace. In the course of his defense, some Epicurean and Stoic philosophers became curious (or, perhaps agitated) because of Paul's strange teaching that one who had walked the earth had also risen from the dead.

This would have been abhorrent to many, since there were views afoot at the time that there was a cyclical pattern to human life and to the universe. For one to rise from the dead would mean, rather, that there was a continuity between death and "after death" that would give the lie to some Greek views of humanity and of history. Therefore, they wanted Paul's teaching to be evaluated by the intellectuals in Athens. The hill of Aries was designed so that just such evaluations could take place. So Paul goes before the philosophers and other Athenians in order to defend the Christian faith.

Without going into the details of Paul's encounter, there are a couple of specific passages that help us understand something of the *ministerial* use of philosophy for theology. Paul does not begin his address by attempting by way of a syllogism to "prove" to the philosophers that the Christian God exists. That is, he was unconcerned to set forth demonstrations that would conclude for the existence of the triune God. Rather, Paul begins by telling his audience just what kind of god the Christian God is. Though the philosophers at Athens had concluded that there was some god who could not be known at all, Paul begins by proclaiming to them just what kind of god this is that they think is unknown.

So, in opposition to what they have concluded their gods to be, Paul wants them to recognize that God is the one "who made the world and everything in it"; he "is the Lord of heaven and earth and does not live in

---

17. Turretin, *Institutes*, 1:45f. All four points that we will list are taken from Turretin's discussion.

temples built by human hands. And he is not served by human hands, as if he needed anything. Rather, he himself gives everyone life and breath and everything else" (Acts 17:24–25). This sovereign Creator, says Paul, "From one man ... made all the nations, that they should inhabit the whole earth; and he marked out their appointed times in history and the boundaries of their lands" (Acts 17:26).

After this description of God, Paul does something that is quite fascinating and that points us in a particular direction with respect to our topic. He quotes from two separate Greek philosopher-poets.

Why does Paul do this? Is it the case that Paul is quoting from these Greek poets in order to affirm the Greeks in what they had thus far concluded with respect to God? Is Paul attempting simply to add to their otherwise coherent (though incomplete) knowledge of the true God? It doesn't seem so, and for the following reasons.

First, notice Paul's quotations: "'For in him we live and move and have our being.' As some of your own poets have said, 'We are his offspring'" (Acts 17:28).[18] The question we might ask in the first place is, "Is it true that 'in him we live and move and have our being?'" That is, is Paul using these quotations because the poets have accurately described the true God, albeit incompletely?

The answer to the first question depends on at least a couple of factors. Without engaging the entire debate concerning propositions, let's agree for our purposes that propositions are bearers of truth value; they can be either true or false. Let's also agree that propositions are expressed in sentences, such as "in him we live and move and have our being."

In that case, what we have in Paul's quotations are propositions—expressed in sentences—whose meaning depends not simply on the linguistic meaning of the sentences themselves but on the references of the indexical elements of the sentences themselves. For example, when Paul says to those on Mars Hill, "In him we live . . . ," to whom is Paul referring? He is obviously referring to the true God, the God whom he has just described to his listeners, the triune God who "made the world and everything in it," who is "Lord of heaven and earth," who

18. The first quotation (ἐν αὐτῷ γὰρ ζῶμεν καὶ κινούμεθα καὶ ἐσμέν) is likely from Epimenides of Crete; the latter (τοῦ γὰρ καὶ γένος ἐσμέν) from Aratus's poem "Phaenomena."

"does not live in temples built by human hands," who is not "served by human hands, as if he needed anything," who "gives everyone life and breath and everything else," who "from one man … made all the nations, that they should inhabit the whole earth," and who "marked out their appointed times in history and the boundaries of their lands." In other words, there was no question to whom Paul was referring when he borrowed the quotations from Epimenides and from Aratus. Given that Paul's reference was to the true and triune God, the propositions are true; they express the truth of the matter as it really is.

Worth noting, however, is that when Epimenides and Aratus wrote these words, the propositions themselves were false. The "him" to which they both refer is not the triune God but is, rather, a false god (likely Zeus). Thus, the reference of the indexical elements of the propositions as uttered by Paul is the true God, whereas the reference of the indexical elements of the same propositions when uttered by the Greek poets is an idol.

So why does Paul use the very poets who have, in the context of Paul's listeners, promoted not Christianity or true religion but idolatry? In part, the answer is "persuasion." Paul knew the reason idolatry existed in Athens was not due to ignorance on the part of the idolaters but due rather to an attempt at complete suppression of the truth as it is found in God's general revelation. But that revelation cannot be fully and completely suppressed. For, as Paul says, the suppression is worked out in terms of an exchange of the revealed truth for a lie, an exchange which results in the worship and service of some false god or gods (Rom 1:18–25). Paul was able to take these statements and transplant them back into their proper biblical context and thus to move them from false and idolatrous expressions to expressions of the truth. In doing that, he took something with which his audience would be familiar and "recontextualized" it. He changed its truth value and its meaning, so that that which was familiar to them became also that which communicated the truth to them—truth that they all knew but were seeking to suppress (Rom 1:18). There is value, therefore, in using the language of the philosophers and poets to show them just how it is that the truth of Christianity fulfills the aspirations expressed in that language.

Philosophy might also serve theology as a "testimony of consent in things known by nature." Here Turretin has in mind the fact that, to the extent that philosophy has its focus in natural revelation (which has its ultimate foundation in special revelation), it can be used to better confirm those things which are revealed by God, things which are true and certain in themselves.[19] This is the case because natural and special revelation are meant always to be seen together. Both reveal God and the truth of God, all of which are brought together as one truth. This can perhaps be seen in the way, for example, that notions of design present in philosophical discussions today serve to "better confirm" the truth of God's creating and controlling activity.[20]

Philosophy can help theology in its ability to distinguish and to clarify the truth as it is found in Scripture as well as in God's revelation generally. "For although reason receives the principles of religion from the light of faith, yet (this light preceding) it ought to judge from these principles how the parts of the heavenly doctrine cohere and mutually establish each other; what is consistent with and what is contrary to them."[21]

We should note in this regard that, contrary to a steady stream of criticism, the categories and terms that philosophy has given to theology to aid in the latter's expression of the truth of Scripture, though not always completely perspicuous, have been immensely helpful in warding off heresy and in helping the church to confess and confirm what is given to her in Scripture. Utilizing terms such as *hypostasis* or *ousia* has benefited the church immensely in its confession of God as one essence (*ousia*) in three *persons* (*hypostases*).[22] When the need of the hour is the deepening, enriching, elucidating, and expounding of what God

---

19. The central truths of theology, according to Turretin, "are founded upon certain and indubitable principles and truths known *per se*" (*Institutes*, 1:47). With theological *principia* in place, therefore, philosophy—given its subservient status—may help clarify what is otherwise known.

20. This "confirmation" does not address the stickier problem of the use of design arguments for apologetic purposes. Those arguments can, of course, be used, just so long as one's approach neither sacrifices nor undermines the *principia* of theology, i.e., just so long as one's *principium cognoscendi* (Scripture), as grounded in the *principium essendi* (the triune God), are not compromised in the method used to set forth such arguments.

21. Turretin, *Institutes*, 1:45.

22. The terms themselves were not automatically or immediately adopted by the church. They had to be debated and discussed to ensure that they were expressing the biblical truth of God's triunity. See G. L. Prestige, *God in Patristic Thought* (London: William Heinneman Ltd., 1936).

has taught the church for the past two millennia, philosophy can be extremely useful.

Finally, notes Turretin, philosophy can benefit theology in that "the mind may be furnished and prepared by these inferior systems for the reception and management of a higher science."[23] In other words, because philosophy focuses on such "big" questions as the nature of reality, of knowledge, and of ethics, it can be a useful *preparation* for theology's discussion of those questions and its answers. Discussions about the nature of ultimate reality, for example, can acquaint one with the proposed answers, the means of establishing those answers, and the counterpoints offered to them. All of this can serve to *prepare* one to receive the biblical response, "In the beginning, God. . . ."

However, a word of warning is here in order. Until and unless one is grounded resolutely in the *principia* of theology, the danger of eclipsing those *principia* can be almost overwhelming if one continues in the study of philosophy, and perhaps especially in the study of the philosophy of religion. Any quick search for an article or essay in philosophy or philosophy of religion will show the historic truths of Christianity to be under attack. Not only so, but philosophy, because of its subject matter and its general methodology, has an allure to many that is sirenically seductive in its force. So, with respect to philosophy's aiding theology, Turretin writes: "This must however be done so carefully that a too great love of philosophy may not captivate us and that we may not regard it as a mistress, but as a handmaid."[24] If we let philosophy rule over theology, then we will in effect destroy the proper and foundational status of theology itself, including its *principia*.

Four Faults

Perhaps many of the errors in thinking about the relationship of theology to philosophy lie in a failure to grasp the boundaries of each. In that light, four errors, all of which are interrelated and discussed by Turretin, are worth a mention here.

The first error has to do with an illegitimate transfer of principle from philosophy to theology. Specifically, Turretin notes that errors

---

23. Turretin, *Institutes*, 1:45.
24. Turretin, *Institutes*, 1:45.

maintained by philosophy, such as that virgins cannot be mothers, unduly tread on the *principia* of theology and thus undermine philosophy's own foundation. Turretin puts it this way:

> What philosophy teaches must be understood of its own kingdom and of natural causes, not of the kingdom of grace and in a supernatural order. Therefore, they are at fault who use such arguments against the creation of the world, the incarnation and the resurrection of the dead because Scripture teaches us that these things were the results not of natural causes, but of the omnipotence of God.[25]

Because theological *principia* must ground and found philosophy and its tasks, we dare not allow philosophical affirmations to rule out the plain truth of God's Word.

Second, and like unto the first error, we must not let teachings of philosophy that contradict theological *principia* be introduced into theology in such a way as to deny Scripture. For example, Aristotle's belief that the world was eternal must not be imported into theology or defended as a theological truth, given that it serves to undermine the teaching of Scripture with regard to the beginning of creation.

According to Turretin, the third error occurs "when philosophy assumes to itself the office of a master in articles of faith, not content with that of a servant (as was done by the Scholastics who placed Aristotle upon the throne; and by the Socinians who would not admit the doctrines of the Trinity, of the incarnation, etc. because they did not seem to be in accordance with the principles of philosophy)."[26] It may be impossible to overstate the seriousness of this error.

The Christian faith *begins* with a confession that is utterly mysterious. It begins with a trust in and commitment to one who is fully God and fully man in one person. Philosophy has no tools at its disposal to prove or to support this truth. Certainly it has tools to help explain it, or to say it with different terms. But the tools of reason are unable to put this together satisfactorily. Without it, however, there is no Christianity. This is another reason why philosophy must serve, not

---

25. Turretin, *Institutes*, 1:45.
26. Turretin, *Institutes*, 1:46.

rule over, theological *principia*. Without that order, Christianity cannot even take a first step.

Fourth, Turretin warns against introducing more new phrases or concepts than are necessary into theology "under which . . . new and dangerous errors lie concealed."[27] This was one of the concerns in the debates over appropriate terminology for describing the Trinity. Does the notion of *persona*, for example, inappropriately convey the idea that Father, Son, and Holy Spirit are simply "masks" that God uses to reveal himself in different ways? Trinitarian theology requires that the three not simply be "ways" of the one God to appear, but that they be sub-sistences that are real. In order to avoid this error, one must be acutely aware of the concepts, principles, and presuppositions that accompany philosophical language in order to reconfigure them—or perhaps to keep from borrowing them altogether.

Hendrik Stoker explains this danger well. In his "letter" to Cornelius Van Til, as Stoker builds on theology in order to understand properly the tasks of philosophy, Stoker notes concerning Van Til's use of phil-osophical language:

> No one may deny you the right of giving new meanings to distinctive old terms as long as you clearly define them. And that you do. But there is a deeper issue at stake. The distinctive old terms concerned may have been formed in answer to (and they thus may presuppose in some way or other) false problems. For instance, the interesting and complicated history of the term universal (from Socrates up to the modern absolute idealists) presupposes the (according to my view, false) problem whether and to what extent reality can or may be grasped in terms of general concepts of thought, thereby implying (in some way or other) that reality should conform to the "nature" of general concepts of human thought; and the terms "rational," "rationality," and "rationalism" presuppose a (according to my views, wrong) special stress on reason (*Vernunft*) as distinct from understanding (*Verstand*). To what extent is it possible, by giving Christian meanings to such distinctive technical old terms used in non-Christian philosophy, based as they may be on non-Christian

---

27. Turretin, *Institutes*, 1:46.

and accordingly false problems, wholly to avoid the predilective or preferential slant which the false problems gave these terms?[28]

This is a fair question, and fair warning for any who want to commandeer philosophy's concepts and terms for the sake of clarification in theology. Sometimes such commandeering may not be possible; sometimes, though possible, not wise; sometimes, both possible and perhaps wise, but clearly in need of elaboration and explanation within the context of orthodox theology.

As we attempt to set forth a covenantal approach to philosophy, we recognize that reason's finest hour can only be realized as it is nurtured, caused to grow, and produced within the warmth of Christian faith. Philosophy can only develop, and develop deeply, when the faith of Christian theology give it its proper *raison d'être*.

Covenantal Philosophy

The end product, and application, of a covenantal view is expressed well by Alvin Plantinga. With a modification or two relative to my own concerns in this essay, Plantinga's call for more "autonomy" among Christian (covenantal) philosophers, and for more "integrality," is a perfect place to begin to apply the notions given here to the task of philosophy. I'll quote Plantinga with my own slight modifications in brackets:

> [Covenantal] philosophers . . . are the philosophers of the Christian community; and it is part of their task as [covenantal] philosophers to serve the Christian community. But the Christian community has its own questions, its own concerns, its own topics for investigation, its own agenda and its own research program. [Covenantal] philosophers ought not merely take their inspiration from what's going on at Princeton or Berkeley or Harvard, attractive and scintillating as that may be; for perhaps those questions and topics are not the ones, or not the only ones, they should be thinking about as the philosophers of the Christian community. There are other philosophical topics the Christian community must work at, and other topics the Christian community must work at philosophically.

---

28. Stoker, "Reconnoitering the Theory of Knowledge of Professor Dr. Cornelius Van Til," 53–54.

And obviously, [covenantal] philosophers are the ones who must do the philosophical work involved. If they devote their best efforts to the topics fashionable to the non-Christian philosophical world, they will neglect a crucial and central part of their task as [covenantal] philosophers. What is needed here is more independence, more autonomy with respect to the projects and concerns of the non-theistic philosophical world.[29]

One supplement to Plantinga's advice here is necessary. Plantinga addresses his advice to any and all theists. But that will not suffice in a covenantal approach to philosophy. Paul's concern at Athens was not that theism was lacking; it was, rather, that the "theisms" present in his audience were actually idols, gods made in man's images.

Only in a covenantal approach to philosophy is there real condescension. Only there do we find God in Christ coming to speak what we could not discover on our own and do for us what we were unable to do. When we acknowledge that condescension, that speech as the very *principium* on which we endeavor to live, then philosophy takes its proper place as a search for wisdom to the praise of the one who made us and who will forever continue his covenant relation with us. Covenantal philosophy is the love of wisdom come to its own.

---

29. Alvin Plantinga and James F. Sennett, *The Analytic Theist: A Collection of Alvin Plantinga's Work in Philosophy of Religion* (Grand Rapids: Eerdmans, 1998), 298.

GRAHAM OPPY

Scott Oliphint makes the following six claims:

1. Theology provides *principia*—foundations, beginning points, sources, first principles—for philosophy (72–73).
2. *Principia* "are necessarily and immutably true" and "must be known *per se* . . . as both immediate and indemonstrable" (74).
3. The two *principia* for theology are:
   i. "There must be a reason why things exist."
   ii. "The foundation of knowledge cannot be self-generated" (73).
4. Theological *principia* "rely on someone who transcends the existence and knowledge of a human being and who has existence and knowledge intrinsically" (75).
5. "In theology . . . the two primary categories which serve as *principia* . . . are the existence and nature of God and the doctrine of revelation" (76).
6. "The *principia* of theology entail each other" (77).

Claims (2), (3), and (6) require that *principia* are truth-apt entities: sentences, statements, propositions, or the like. However, claim (5) requires that *principia* are not truth-apt entities: "the existence and nature of God" is a term, and so not truth apt. Jointly, claims 1–6 are inconsistent.

The supposition that *principia* are truth apt leads naturally to the thought that *principia* are axioms. This thought is supported by many of the claims that Oliphint makes for *principia*. Consider, for example:

1. "First principles are those which anyone must have when he comes to study anything at all" (75).
2. "First principles . . . cannot be something that someone demonstrates as a result of . . . reasoning or argument" (75).

I see no reason to suppose that there is any sense in which disciplines are based on axioms. Anyone who comes to study anything at all must have certain capacities and abilities: they must be able to reason, to draw inferences, to make observations, to learn from the writings and words of others, and so forth. As Lewis Carroll's dialogue between Achilles and the tortoise suggests, there is good reason to think that possession of these capacities and abilities is prior to the acquisition of principles. While there are some disciplines in which axiomatization plays a limited role, in most disciplines axiomatization is not even of theoretical interest.

I think it is doubtful that there is any good sense in which there could be foundations for our disciplines that are "transcendental in nature" (76). Oliphint claims that *principia* "provide for the possibility of anything else; in a particular science . . . they provide for the possibility of that science" (76). Suppose we ask: What makes the discipline of chemistry possible? Plausibly, there is a multipart answer. First, there is the chemical constitution of the natural world. Second, there is our ability to recognize and understand the chemical constitution of the natural world (grounded in our ability to reason, draw inferences, make observations, learn from the writings and words of others, and so on). Third, there are the social institutions that we have developed—learned academies, universities, schools, and so forth—that promote and enable the study of chemistry. It is these things together that make the discipline of chemistry possible. But none of these things is "transcendental."

Oliphint believes: (a) the existence and nature of God is metaphysically fundamental; (b) revelation is epistemologically fundamental; and (c) God has revealed both (a) and (b) to everyone. According to Oliphint: ultimately, everything else that exists owes its existence to God's creative activities; ultimately, everything else is the way that it is because of the way that God is; ultimately, whatever we know, we know because God reveals it to us; and all of these facts about what is ultimately the case have been revealed to every single human being. Taking account of these points, we might say that Oliphant believes: God is metaphysical foundation, source, and beginning point; God's revelation is epistemological foundation, source, and beginning point; and these facts about foundation are divinely revealed common knowledge.

I disagree with Oliphint about all of this. There is no God. *A for-tiori*, there has been no revelation from God, there is no such thing as God's nature, and there has been no universal revelation of God's existence, God's nature, and God's role in our knowledge. Given that we disagree about *these* things, there is the possibility of entering into genuine dialogue about them. The obvious disciplinary location for genuine dialogue on these matters is philosophy. In order to enter into genuine dialogue, we identify the things that we agree upon and the things that we disagree upon. We then try to determine whether there is any way of reducing our disagreement drawing solely upon those things in which we agree. If we find that there is no progress to be made, then the best that we can do is agree to disagree. But, in advance, it is unduly pessimistic to suppose that there is no possibility that we could reduce our disagreement drawing solely on those things upon which we agree.

Oliphint claims that the source of existence must be something in which existence is intrinsic to its nature. This need not be a claim that divides theists and naturalists. If we suppose that there is a first cause, then there are two options: either it is contingent or it is necessary. If we are theists, the first cause is God; if we are naturalists, the first cause is the initial state of natural reality. Some theists suppose that God is necessary; other theists suppose that God is contingent. Some naturalists suppose that the initial state of natural reality is necessary; other naturalists suppose that it is contingent. If pushed to choose, I would say—albeit with no great confidence—that if there is an initial state of natural reality, then it is necessary.

Oliphint claims that the foundation of our knowledge must be necessary, external, and transcendent to us: "To rely on the contingent and relative would lead to . . . skepticism" (75). While there are many different conceptions of skepticism, perhaps the most corrosive and concerning type of skepticism in contemporary democracies is the failure to give sufficient credence to claims for which there is expert consensus. Where [genuine] experts in mathematics, or physics, or biology, or geology, or history, or economics, or sociology, or psychology, or literary theory unanimously agree, it is unwarrantable skepticism for nonexperts to invest their credence in dissenting opinions. It is not common for naturalists to be subject to this corrosive and concerning kind of skepticism. Nor, of course, is it common for naturalists to be skeptical about the existence of an external world, or the existence of other minds, or about the meaningfulness of the language that we speak, or about the correctness of moral judgments on which there is more or less uniform consensus. Perhaps Oliphint thinks that it is a form of skepticism—or relativism—to deny that (a) the existence and nature of God is metaphysically fundamental; (b) revelation is epistemologically fundamental; and (c) God has revealed both (a) and (b) to everyone. But to think that is to fail to properly distinguish between skepticism and reasonable disagreement.

It may also be that Oliphint thinks that it is a form of skepticism to hold that there is no expert consensus on philosophical questions. Where I think that philosophical questions are just those questions for which we do not know—and perhaps cannot even imagine—how to produce agreed answers using agreed methods, it may be that Oliphint thinks that there is expert consensus on claims 1–8 and the other claims that he espouses. If so, I strongly disagree. It is about as obvious as anything can be that thoughtful, intelligent, reflective, serious, well-informed, upstanding people disagree about the claims that Oliphint makes. Moreover, the distribution of dissent is very widespread. It is not just that such people belong to other religions—Hinduism, Buddhism, Judaism, Islam, Sikhism, Shintoism, Daoism, and so on—or embrace nonreligious worldviews—naturalism, humanism, rationalism, and so forth; the vast majority of such people who are *Christians* also disagree with Oliphint about claims 1–8 and the other claims he endorses.

These points about depth and breadth of disagreement are not intended to establish that Oliphint's view is "foolish or irrational" (82). When we come to philosophical discussion, we cannot but start from a position in which we think that the particular beliefs of those who disagree with us are false: I cannot believe that p unless I think that those who believe that not p have a false belief. But, when we come to philosophical discussion, we cannot but start from a position in which we think that some of our own beliefs are false. It would be both foolish and arrogant for any one of us to claim infallibility with respect to questions for which we do not know—and perhaps cannot even imagine—how to produce agreed answers using agreed methods. I can reasonably believe that *some* of my philosophical beliefs are false, even though I cannot reasonably believe, for any particular philosophical belief that I hold, that *it* is false. Given what philosophy is, we all stand to gain by entering into genuine discussion with thoughtful, intelligent, reflective, serious, well-informed, upstanding people whose beliefs differ from our own.

Oliphint takes philosophy to be exhausted by metaphysics, epistemology, and ethics (71). Moreover, he supposes that those who think that philosophy is not subservient to theology will maintain that reason is the *principium cognoscendi* of philosophy, that philosophy's boundaries are determined by reason, that philosophy's authority lies in reason, that the rules and laws of philosophy are the rules and laws of reason, and that philosophy's authority is only as strong as the laws of logic and the force of sound argument (84f.). I don't accept any of this.

If *principia* are truth apt, then reason is not even of the right category to be a *principium* for philosophy. Moreover, however considerations about *principia* for philosophy play out, it is not true that the boundaries of philosophy are determined by reason, and not true that philosophy's authority lies in reason, and not true that the rules and laws of philosophy are the rules and laws of reason, and not true that philosophy's authority is only as strong as the laws of logic and the force of sound argument.

The boundaries of philosophy are not determined by reason; rather, those boundaries are determined by the questions for which we know how to produce agreed answers using agreed methods. On the boundary of every discipline, there are philosophical questions that belong to the philosophy of that discipline—philosophy of mathematics, philosophy of physics, philosophy of psychology, and so on—for which we do not yet know how to produce agreed answers using the agreed methods of that discipline. Moreover, the core of philosophy—areas where there are large constellations of questions for which we do not know how to produce agreed answers using agreed methods—includes much more than metaphysics, epistemology, and ethics: for example, aesthetics, formal logic, metaphilosophy, and history of philosophy.

There is no good sense in which philosophers have authority. No one has expertise—let alone authority—with respect to the *answering* of philosophical questions. There just is no expert agreement on the liar paradox, or the two-envelope problem, or Pascal's wager, or the implications of peer disagreement, or the permissibility of eating meat, or the existence of objective chance, and so on. The lack of authority of philosophers is mirrored by the lack of authority of philosophy: philosophy can hardly have authoritative deliverances if philosophers are unable to make authoritative deliverances.

There is a very important distinction between (a) laws of argumentation and logic and (b) laws of reasoning and inference. The rules and laws that govern rational updating of belief are very different from the rules and laws that govern the construction of valid arguments. To take one obvious example: *ex falso quodlibet* is a fine rule of logic but a disastrous rule of inference. Once we have observed this distinction, we should, I think, quickly come to the conclusion that while philosophers, like participants in every other discipline, employ both rules and laws of logic and rules and laws of inference, there are no distinctively philosophical rules and laws.

TIMOTHY MCGREW

Scott Oliphint's essay offers a position on the relation of Christian faith and philosophy that is deeply influenced by the Reformed scholastics and by the Dutch wing of the modern Reformed movement. Since Oliphint and I are both theologically conservative Protestants with a high regard for the value of Scripture, it might seem that we would have much in common when it comes to broader questions of faith and reason.

Alas! Matters are not so simple. Where Oliphint draws inspiration from Franciscus Junius, Francis Turretin, Abraham Kuyper, and Cornelius Van Til, my list of intellectual heroes includes instead names like Joseph Butler, George Campbell, Thomas Chalmers, and B. B. Warfield. In some ways, we represent the wide divergence between contemporary Westminster and Old Princeton, a divergence illustrated in our very different answers to the fundamental question posed in this volume.

At the outset, Oliphint defines *Christianity* as the theology that came out of the Reformation era. He has, of course, every right to choose his own ground. But there is something a bit odd about *defining* Christianity as something that emerged in the 16th century, however deep its roots may be. In the closing paragraph, he comes back to his preferred position and makes the further claim that "only in a covenantal approach to philosophy . . . do we find God in Christ coming to speak what we could not discover on our own and do for us what we were unable to do" (98). This assertion suggests that his initial definition was not a mere verbal infelicity. Does Oliphint really think that every dissenter from his covenantal approach—a good Lutheran, for example—believes that we could have discovered the doctrine of the atonement without revelation or that Christ merely did for us something we could just as well have done for ourselves? I am reluctant to attribute such a position to him. But I am not sure how else to read that claim.

Oliphint emphasizes the necessity for foundations or fundamental principles in various disciplines, including philosophy and theology, and there is one sense in which I would agree. A true explanation for the existence of the universe will involve not only the existence of God the creator but also further information about his attributes, character, and ends.

That agreement will not, of course, be shared by those who think that theology is akin to phrenology, a discipline devoted to the investigation of something that is not there. For this reason, the question of how one might reasonably believe that there is a God and that Christianity is true is of fundamental importance.

But when we turn to the "principle of knowledge," our agreement dissolves. Oliphint says that this principle "affirms that the foundation of knowledge cannot be self-generated," and he also says that this principle and the principle of existence are "mutually dependent (with respect to human beings)" (73) and "entail each other" (77). I cannot think of an interpretation of either of these claims that would make them both true and interesting. A quarter century's work in epistemology and philosophy of science have persuaded me that the skeptics are wrong and the representative realists are, broadly speaking, right. Objectivity is not an unattainable goal. We can and do reasonably believe many things about an external world on the basis of experiences that are externally *caused* (and therefore not self-generated) but intrinsically subjective.[1] True theological principles need not be *presupposed*, any more than one needs to start with Newton's laws in order to arrive at a knowledge of Newtonian physics. The public evidence, to which our subjective experiences give us access, suffices to show the truth of the central metaphysical claims of theology, as Paul points out in Romans 1, so that they may justly be drawn as conclusions even though they were not assumed *ab initio*.

Oliphint supports his position by appealing to Aristotle's view of first principles. But that view seems to me to be wrong, and its errors are amply illustrated by the history of the gradual breakdown of Aristotle's

---

1. My own contributions to this discussion may be found in *The Foundations of Knowledge* (Lanham, MD: Littlefield Adams, 1995), "A Defense of Strong Foundationalism," in *The Theory of Knowledge: Classic and Contemporary Readings*, ed. Louis Pojman, 2nd ed. (Belmont, CA: Wadsworth, 1998), and Timothy McGrew and Lydia McGrew, *Internalism and Epistemology: The Architecture of Reason* (New York: Routledge, 2007).

physics. The *principia essendi* of most disciplines, from astronomy to theology, are not indemonstrable, immediately evident, and so forth—they are almost invariably the conclusions of chains of reasoning, some of it rather recondite, like Kepler's discovery of the orbit of Mars. And the *principia cognoscendi* need not entail the *principia essendi*. All that is required is that we have data and means of inference sufficient to permit reasonable determination of the relevant metaphysical truths. Not everyone will follow the evidence where it leads, particularly when the conclusions are theological. Nevertheless, the evidence *does* point to these conclusions.

I am not denying the need for special revelation; I insist upon it. There are things we need to know that we could never have known unless they were disclosed. But neither the content of that revelation nor its status *as* revelation form, in my view, an appropriate starting point for theological investigation. Rather, as Thomas Chalmers points out, we can and must test the credentials of various purported revelations—the Judeo-Christian Scriptures, the Quran, the Book of Mormon—in order to determine where, if anywhere, there is a revelation from God.

> Reason can judge of the external evidences for Christianity, because it can discern the merits of human testimony: and it can perceive the truth or the falsehood of such obvious credentials as the performance of a miracle, or the fulfilment of a prophecy.... [But a]fter we have established Christianity to be an authentic message from God upon those historical grounds, on which the reason and experience of man entitle him to form his conclusions, nothing remains for us but an unconditional surrender of the mind to the subject of the message. We have a right to sit in judgment over the credentials of heaven's ambassador, but we have no right to sit in judgment over the information he gives us.[2]

In quoting Chalmers to this purpose, I am directly and self-consciously contrasting my own position with the presuppositional methodology of Oliphint's mentor Cornelius Van Til. In his *Christian-Theistic Evidences*, Van Til spends several chapters critiquing a broadly

---

2. Thomas Chalmers, *The Evidence and Authority of the Christian Revelation*, 4th ed. (Edinburgh: William Blackwood, 1817), 275–77.

evidentialist methodology of the kind I endorse, using Butler's *Analogy of Religion* as a foil. He concludes that David Hume, having articulated a *consistent* empiricism, undermined the force of Butler's reasoning.

> Hume's empiricism was far more critical and consistent than that of Butler. We proceed to see what happens to the conception of probability on the basis of Hume's empiricism. If all knowledge is based upon experience, and experience is interpreted without the presupposition of the "Author of nature" as Hume claims it is, we cannot expect that one thing rather than another will happen in the future. From the point of view of logic, one thing as well as another might take place in the future. But why is it then that we expect the course and constitution of nature to remain the same? *"Wherein consists the difference betwixt incredulity and belief?"* asks Hume. The answer is once more that it is in nothing but custom and feeling.[3]

As for reported miracles, Van Til claims that Hume undermined the credibility of miracle reports chiefly by showing that, on empiricist grounds, *"There is no reason to think that a God who could work miracles can be proved to exist."*[4] In particular, according to Van Til, Hume demolished the empirical arguments—cosmological and teleological—for the existence of God in his *Dialogues concerning Natural Religion*.

> The upshot of the whole dialogue is, . . . that the representative of Butler's type of thought virtually admits defeat. He will not give up his mode of appeal to fact. Yet he realizes that with this mode of appeal to fact he cannot prove anything more than a finite god. In fact, though he does not admit it, he really cannot prove anything.[5]

For anyone who, like Van Til, has fallen under the spell of the great Scottish skeptic and acquiesced in these melancholy conclusions, I have good news. *Hume was wrong.* He was wrong about inductive inference, and his critique of induction, influential as it was, displays the poverty

---

3. Cornelius Van Til, *In Defense of the Faith, Volume IV: Christian-Theistic Evidences* (Phillipsburg, NJ: Presbyterian & Reformed, 1978), 22.

4. Ibid., 26.

5. Ibid., 32.

of his own understanding of probable inference.[6] He was wrong in the objections he raised against the credibility of reported miracles and was resoundingly refuted on this subject by his own contemporaries, as even some modern agnostics have realized.[7] His criticisms of the traditional arguments for the existence of God are riddled with conceptual errors, as even atheists have pointed out.[8] In any event, there is no need to prove the existence of God, or even to render it more likely than not, before the testimony to miracles can be taken seriously.[9] And apart from those errors, Hume never engages with the explanatory versions of those arguments. He is mired in a deductivist framework for explicating such arguments and never considers—in fact, never reveals any awareness of—nonmonotonic forms of reasoning.

When someone starts out on the wrong foot, as I believe Van Til has done by his concessions to Hume, it is not surprising that problems tend to resurface throughout his philosophical system. To pick just one illustration, Oliphint quotes with apparent approval Van Til's criticism of the non-Christian for whom

> the law of contradiction is, like all other laws, something that does not find its ultimate source in the creative activity of God. Accordingly, the non-Christian will seek to do by means of the law of contradiction what the Christian has done for him by God. For the Christian, God legislates as to what is possible and what is impossible for man. For the non-Christian, man determines this for himself. Either positively or negatively the non-Christian will

---

6. See, for example, Henry Kyburg, "The Justification of Induction," *The Journal of Philosophy* 53 (1956): 394–400, Donald Williams, *The Ground of Induction* (New York: Russell & Russell, 1963), and David C. Stove, *The Rationality of Induction* (Oxford: Oxford University Press, 1986). I consider and refute a wide range of objections to this approach to the justification of induction in my paper, "Direct Inference and the Problem of Induction," *The Monist* 84 (2001): 153–78.

7. See William Adams, *An Essay in Answer to Mr. Hume's Essay on Miracles*, 3rd ed. (London: B. White, 1767), George Campbell, *A Dissertation on Miracles* (Edinburgh: A. Kincaid & J. Bell, 1762), John Douglas, *The Criterion* (London: A. Millar, 1757), John Earman, *Hume's Abject Failure* (Oxford: Oxford University Press, 2000), and Timothy McGrew and Lydia McGrew, "The Argument from Miracles," in *The Blackwell Companion to Natural Theology*, ed. William Lane Craig and J. P. Moreland (New York: Blackwell, 2009), 593–662.

8. See the devastating critique by D. C. Stove, "Part IX of Hume's Dialogues," *The Philosophical Quarterly* 28 (1978): 300–309.

9. This is a point on which thinkers as diverse as Van Til, R. C. Sproul, and J. L. Mackie have been confused. See McGrew and McGrew, "The Argument from Miracles," 639–41.

determine the field of possibility and therewith the stream of history by means of the law of contradiction.[10]

I find this sort of radical logical voluntarism unintelligible. I have no idea what it would even mean for what is logically possible and impossible to be the result of a creative act of God; the very notion of action seems to presuppose distinctions between actor and act that are intelligible only in terms of fundamental principles of logic.[11] And the alternative is misdrawn. Relatively few non-Christians would maintain man determines for himself what is logically possible or impossible.

It is painful to have to point out things like this, since Van Til has inspired so many ardent and loyal disciples. But in my view, deep problems pervade almost every aspect of Van Til's thought—his epistemology, his history of philosophy, his description of the position of non-Christians, and his exegesis of Scripture. It is my considered opinion that there is no point trying to correct his system piece by piece. One must simply start over on very different principles.

This is, I am reasonably confident, the very judgment that Oliphint would make of my own position, and I certainly do not grudge him the right to say so. I have been blunt here partly because there is a long history of abortive interaction and unproductive dialogue between presuppositionalists and Christians of a more evidential persuasion. I think the only hope of progress in that discussion is to make it clear at the outset how very deep our disagreements really are.

There is one point where I agree with Oliphint: the God whom Christianity confesses is a God who condescends (77). Both in the helping of man when he was fallen and become miserable and in the making of man when man was nothing, God has shown his mercy and condescension to his creation. And that same mercy will be extended to those who come to him through a faulty epistemology, whichever way the fault may lie. It is all those who come to him, not just those who come with their evidential or presuppositional epistemology straightened out, who will never be rejected (John 6:37). Such is the divine humility.

---

10. Cornelius Van Til, *An Introduction to Systematic Theology* (Syllabus, 1961), 256. Quoted by Oliphint (pp. 85–86) from Van Til's work *Common Grace and the Gospel*, 230.

11. I may recover a bit of philosophical piety here by acknowledging that this point was first worked out by Aristotle in his *Metaphysics*, Book Γ.

PAUL K. MOSER

K. Scott Oliphint offers a "covenantal" perspective on philosophy entailing that "Christianity trumps philosophy" (71). It allegedly trumps philosophy on the basis of two considerations. First, "it must be the case that the theological foundations that were reasserted during the time of the Reformation must be the starting point for philosophy (and for any other science)" (72). Second, a covenantal perspective "seek[s] to affirm the *theological* necessity of any philosophical activity that aims at truth" (72). Oliphint uses the term *principia* to identify standards that include "a foundation, a beginning point, a source, or a first principle" for thinking, knowing, and existing. In particular, he holds that "the *principia* of theology provide those truths that are requisite for any other discipline, in that they provide the foundation for *all being* and for *all knowing*" (76).

Oliphint extends his foundation beyond theology to include the Bible, or Scripture. He states: "For the Christian, this focus [of God's condescending revelation] is found in his Word—Scripture—which tells us who God is and what he has done. The *principium* of Scripture is meant to ground anything else that we affirm in theology and in any other discipline" (81). The Bible, then, becomes a "starting point" or "foundation" for "anything else that we affirm." He applies this position as follows: "We must not let teachings of philosophy that contradict theological *principia* be introduced into theology in such a way as to deny Scripture. For example, Aristotle's belief that the world was eternal must not be imported into theology or defended as a theological truth, given that it serves to undermine the teaching of Scripture with regard to the beginning of creation" (95). Oliphint likewise would exclude any teachings from other disciplines that contradict the Bible, whether they come from science, ordinary experience, or extraordinary experience. The Bible as the "starting point" thus faces no outside threat according to the covenantal perspective.

A noteworthy implication of the covenantal perspective is this: "Without [knowing in God's world as his covenant creature], . . . the best one is able to acquire is a skewed and selfish menagerie of ideas that is impossible in the end to account for reality, or for our knowledge of it" (81–82). Part of the alleged problem is that human reason has been corrupted by human sin. Oliphint states: "One of the things that a proper exercise of Christian faith does is it begins to *renew* our reasoning, which, in Adam, is damaged by sin" (83). This renewal of reason demands agreement with "biblical truth": "In subjection to God's revealed truth, reason is to function as an arbiter of the consistency and coherence of God's Word and world" (85). Even the principle of noncontradiction (roughly, "two contradictory statements cannot both be true at the same time") is deficient as a test for truth apart from the Bible: "The law of contradiction, and the use of that law, can never finally and solely determine whether or not a particular Christian doctrine is true. That determination is left to revelation" (86). So the Bible as the starting point does not face an outside threat even from the principle of noncontradiction.

Oliphint has offered the Bible and the theology of the Reformation (including the theology of John Calvin and the *Westminster Confession of Faith*) as "the starting point for philosophy (and for any other science)" (72). Philosophy, logic, and other disciplines suffer the grave defects of human sin when they are not subjected to the proposed "starting point": the Bible and the theology of the Reformation. This is a relatively simple story about the nature of human thinking, knowing, and existing, but it must face at least two serious problems.

First, the various Jewish-Christian Bibles we have are human compilations over time, even if they include God's revelation and hence are not merely human. For better or worse, humans need to decide what to include in the canon of God's revelation and what to exclude, and their decision needs to meet standards of reasonableness (if their decision is to be taken seriously by a wide range of people). The focus of such deliberation is what the Bible itself includes, and some standard plays a role here. Clearly, one cannot appeal to the Bible itself when the contents of the Bible are under question. It would be viciously circular, or question begging, to invoke the Bible itself to settle what belongs to the Bible. Many inquirers want to know why these books, and not other books, belong in the Bible, and for this a standard other than the Bible is needed. Otherwise, we make no explanatory progress and risk epistemic dogmatism and hence arbitrariness about a normative status for the Bible in inquiry. The Bible, then, will not serve as a "starting point" in the way suggested by the covenantal perspective. It does not justify itself and needs a prior starting point if we are to avoid a dogmatic circle. Otherwise one might as well use a covenantal perspective to promote the Quran, for instance, rather than the Bible. The following point clarifies the main problem by generalizing it.

Second, the covenantal perspective runs afoul of a crucial distinction for human inquiry: the distinction between a *merely ontic* starting point and an *apologetic* starting point. This problem is typical of various Reformed and presuppositional approaches to Christian theology, and it accounts for their seeming to be authoritarian and dogmatic in an evidentially arbitrary manner. We can approach the crucial distinction with a simple question: What is the alleged starting point a starting point *for*? A typical answer is that it is a starting point for all ontic matters, matters concerning reality, including the reality of thinking, knowing, and existing. The starting point becomes the place to (begin to) answer questions about such matters. *If* the covenantal perspective is true, the Bible and Reformed theology serve as an ontic starting point in that manner. Why, however, should one affirm that the previous antecedent ("the covenantal perspective is true") is actually true? The question makes good sense if we understand "should" in an epistemic sense, that is, to concern what is supported by one's overall *evidence*. We can ignore the question only at the risk of evidential dogmatism and arbitrariness. In that case, we may end up preaching only to the choir and ignoring the needs of an important audience of inquirers. The covenantal perspective seems to leave us there, with inadequate apologetic resources.

We need to attend to a starting point that is conceptually irreducible to a merely ontic starting point: an apologetic starting point. Such a starting point aims to relate to doxastic outsiders (people with beliefs different from ours) in a way that is free of circularity or question begging. It aims to represent pertinent evidence that is not just an affirmation of the ontic claims in question. Evidence need not itself be an argument (consider perceptual evidence of household objects), and therefore an apologetic starting point need not be an argument. Some parts of the

Bible invoked by the covenantal perspective suggest an apologetic starting point that is irreducible to a merely ontic Christian starting point. This means that the covenantal perspective fails by its own standard for a starting point. We should clarify this point.

We can make good sense of the Bible only if we distinguish between (a) its endorsed *truths about God*, that is, its theology, and (b) its reported unique *actions of God in human experience*. If we make its endorsed truths the starting point, as the covenantal perspective does, we will preclude epistemically prior factors that can supply foundational evidence for at least some of the endorsed truths. We then will be left with an epistemically arbitrary starting point, devoid of a needed apologetic basis attentive to outsiders. This is where Oliphint's covenantal perspective fails us. So we need an alternative, and we find one in the New Testament itself.

Various New Testament writers suggest an apologetic starting point that is irreducible to the merely ontic starting point of the covenantal perspective. Some of these writers attribute to Jesus himself a position on the needed apologetic starting point. For instance, John's Gospel represents Jesus as saying that God (and Jesus) "will come" (ἐλευσόμεθα) to people who are suitably receptive to them (John 14:23). This coming would be a unique divine action in human experience, but what kind of action would it be? According to John's Gospel, Jesus reports that he "will manifest" (ἐμφανίσω) himself to the people in question (14:21). How?

We find key aspects of the answer in the New Testament reports about the coming of God's "Spirit" (πνεῦμα) to human experience. This pneumatic evidence in action is omitted by the covenantal starting point, and it is irreducible to the Bible or Reformed theology as a starting point. God's Spirit, as portrayed in the New Testament, is an *intentional, personal agent* and is identified with the Spirit of the risen Christ (Rom 8:9); neither the Bible nor Christian theology is such an agent. So we should not identify or conflate these different categories or realities. They do not constitute the same starting point because they are ontically different.

The author of 1 John suggests that people can know the abiding presence of God, courtesy of the Spirit God "gave" to people (1 John 3:24). This giving of God's Spirit gains clarity in the following statement by the apostle Paul: "Hope [in God] does not disappoint us, because God's love (ἀγάπη) has been poured into (ἐκκέχυται) our hearts through the Holy Spirit who has been given (δοθέντος) to us" (Rom 5:5). Paul has in mind not only psychological disappointment but also cognitive, or epistemic, disappointment. That is, he has supporting *evidence* in mind, and this evidence includes something being *given* by God in intentional action toward human experience. So this evidence does not reduce to the Bible or Christian theology. We find closely related statements of Paul's epistemic position in his talk of God's Spirit as "bearing witness" (συμμαρτυρεῖ) to God for humans (Rom 8:16) and as being God's "guarantee" (ἀρραβών) to humans (2 Cor 1:22, 5:5; cf. Eph 1:14). The relevant notions of "witness" and "guarantee" have epistemic, or evidential, significance in Paul's account.

God's evidential self-manifestation, according to Paul, is one of divine redemptive love (ἀγάπη) in human experience, and humans do not need to embrace it to experience it; they can ignore or reject it. This is the kind of love that Jesus manifested on behalf of God for humans in his Gethsemane decision to undergo the suffering and death of Calvary. As Paul would put it, "God proves his love for us in that while we still were sinners Christ died for us" (Rom 5:8 NRSV). God then seeks to "pour out" this love in our human experience as an evidential guarantee in the present (Rom 5:5). This pouring out, however, is not coercive toward human wills as if their receptivity were irrelevant. As a result, John's Gospel portrays Jesus as saying: "Anyone who resolves to do the will of God will know whether the teaching is from God or whether I am speaking on my own" (John 7:17 NRSV). This suggests a role for human receptivity in receiving the key evidence from God. In addition, this role can figure in divine hiding relative to some unprepared humans at some times, for their redemptive good (see, e.g., Matt 11:25; Luke 10:21; John 16:12).[12]

We now see that the New Testament itself offers an alternative to the starting point endorsed by the covenantal perspective. We can clarify its apologetic value by casting it as *apparent* divine action in human experience and then asking what best explains the experience in question:

---

12. For development of this perspective, see Paul K. Moser, *The Severity of God* (Cambridge: Cambridge University Press, 2013).

An intervention of God or something else? In this mode, we can face all relevant evidence and avoid quick dismissal of doxastic outsiders. We also can acknowledge that divine perfect love would extend to doxastic outsiders, including in their experience. We then can inquire whether some human experiences include unique actions that are divine, and not human, in origin.[13] Philosophy does well to attend to such inquiry.

13. For relevant discussion, see Herbert H. Farmer, *Towards Belief in God* (London: Macmillan, 1943).

A REJOINDER

K. SCOTT OLIPHINT

Let me first say what an enjoyable process this has been. I have learned from my three interlocutors and am glad to have been involved in this discussion. This response will be necessarily and unsatisfactorily brief. In the limited space remaining, I'll simply pick out a thing or two that require some clarification. There is much more to say, of course, but all good and enjoyable things must come to an end.

In his response to me, McGrew writes, "There is something a bit odd about *defining* Christianity as something that emerged in the 16th century, however deep its roots may be" (105). It would have been good for McGrew to employ his substantial philosophical acumen here and, instead of impugning something to me that I did not say, reiterate what I *did* say and recognize it for what it was—an initial point of clarification in my essay. What I did not say is that Christianity is *defined* in the way I explained. Instead, when asked to write on the notion of "Christianity trumps philosophy," I was clarifying the way in which *I* was going to use the terms "Christianity," "philosophy," and "trumps." What I said was, "By 'Christianity' *I mean* the theology that came out of the Reformation (including the post-Reformation) era, as expressed in the creeds and confessions of that era" (72, emphasis added). Since this clarification comes at the beginning of my essay where I am attempting to explain *what I mean* by "Christianity," by "philosophy," and by "trumps," my statement involved not a *defini-tion* of Christianity but—in order to be clear about my position—it described, as I said in the essay, what "I mean" when I use those terms in my discussion. This is almost too obvious to be pointed out, but unfortunately it needs to be said in response to McGrew's caricature of what I said. His further elaboration and question with respect to

117

my "definition" illustrate and elaborate his initial misconstrual to the point of erecting a straw man.

With respect to my assertion that the *principium cognoscendi* and the *principium essendi* are mutually dependent and that they mutually entail each other, McGrew notes, "I cannot think of an interpretation of either of these claims that would make them both true and interesting" (106). He then refers to the past twenty-five years of philosophy as the foundation of his own view. However, a look at virtually any Reformed treatise on theology would provide a rich and full interpretation and articulation of these *principia* and the reasons for their necessity. I, on the other hand, cannot think of anything in the past twenty-five years of philosophy that would recognize, much less understand, the importance of *principia* for philosophy.

More substantively, McGrew and Moser offer similar responses to my appeal to God's revelation as our *principium cognoscendi*. According to McGrew, "Neither the content of that revelation nor its status *as* revelation form, in my view, an appropriate starting point for theological investigation" (107). Moser fills the same objection out a bit more:

> Clearly, one cannot appeal to the Bible itself when the contents of the Bible are under question. It would be viciously circular, or question begging, to invoke the Bible itself to settle what belongs to the Bible. Many inquirers want to know why these books, and not other books, belong in the Bible, and for this a standard other than the Bible is needed. Otherwise, we make no explanatory progress and risk epistemic dogmatism and hence arbitrariness about a normative status for the Bible in inquiry. The Bible, then, will not serve as a "starting point" in the way suggested by the covenantal perspective. It does not justify itself and needs a prior starting point if we are to avoid a dogmatic circle. Otherwise one might as well use a covenantal perspective to promote the Quran, for instance, rather than the Bible. (112–13)

The substance of this objection, perhaps more than any other, displays the deep theological differences that remain between the three of us.

In the *Westminster Confession of Faith*, the first chapter affirms the status of God's written revelation, especially as that revelation relates to the authority of the church (or of any person). As these scholars and pastors gathered to write this Protestant confession, they wrote (WCF 1.4):

> The authority of the Holy Scripture, for which it ought to be believed and obeyed, depends not upon the testimony of any man or Church; but wholly upon God (who is truth itself) the author thereof: and therefore it is to be received, because it is the Word of God.

The confession of Protestantism, then, was that Holy Scripture must be self-attesting in its authority. It cannot derive its authority from someone or something other than God (who is truth itself). This portion of the Confession came on the heels of much discussion and debate among theologians about the nature and status of a final authority, a *principium*. The conclusion was that God and his revelation must be the foundation on which anything else could rest.[1]

The question of circularity has been discussed for centuries and continues to be discussed today, especially when matters of *principia* are debated. The question, however, is not whether there is some form of circularity—all positions must have that—but which *principia* are able to sustain the substantial load that they must bear if they are to account for existence and knowledge. John Owen, the prince of Puritans, argued convincingly (in my estimation) that the circular reasoning of Roman Catholicism with respect to its own assumed authority was wholly inadequate to bear such a heavy load.[2] The same would be true for any person or any data.

To say that Holy Scripture is foundational, however, does not mean that it stands alone with no support or witness to its intrinsic authority. The *Westminster Confession* in the next section affirms this (1.5):

> We may be moved and induced by the testimony of the Church to an high and reverend esteem of the Holy Scripture. And the heavenliness of the matter, the efficacy of the doctrine, the majesty

---

1. This is one of the reasons that virtually every Reformed confession has these two *principia*—God and his revelation—as the first two chapters.

2. See John Owen, *The Works of John Owen*, ed. William H. Goold (Edinburgh: T&T Clark, n.d.), 8.524ff.

of the style, the consent of all the parts, the scope of the whole (which is, to give all glory to God), the full discovery it makes of the only way of man's salvation, the many other incomparable excellencies, and the entire perfection thereof, *are arguments* whereby it doth abundantly evidence itself to be the Word of God: yet notwithstanding, our full persuasion and assurance of the infallible truth and divine authority thereof, is from the inward work of the Holy Spirit bearing witness by and with the Word in our hearts (emphasis mine).

In other words, the assertion of the *principial* authority of Scripture does not give license to a bare and naked affirmation with no argument to testify to its authority. The testimony of the church (throughout history) plays a key role, as do the content, style, coherence, etc. of what Scripture says. Because of this, for example, Scripture can be compared with profit to other purported revelations from God (e.g., the Quran). The Bible does not exhibit and attest to its authority in a vacuum.

There can be no objection, therefore, in the use and testimony of other data, other factors, the church, etc. that show the *principial* status of Scripture. The point of *principia* is that any other data and factors cannot bear the weight or take the place of Scripture's foundational authority. It is that authority that provides for the legitimate use and content of philosophy as well as for all other science. Whether one believes this or not is not the immediate issue; the point is that God and Scripture as *principia* provide the rationale for such enterprises. No other supposed rationale can carry such a heavy load.

Finally, whatever the differences Moser, McGrew, and I have, we are all agreed that there is *some kind* of important relationship between Christianity and philosophy. Oppy, on the other hand, would not agree (since he denies God's existence), and I heartily commend him for joining with us in our discussion. I am grateful for his measured and thoughtful response to my essay. In that light, I want to try to provide a bit more clarity.

The first thing to note is that there is no inconsistency in my claims 1–6 as Oppy claims and as he delineates them (99). He is troubled by the lack of truth aptness to claim (5). He writes that "'the existence and nature of God' is a term, and so not truth apt" (99). There are a number of ways to dissolve this purported inconsistency. The most obvious way is to remember that "truth aptness" must itself be grounded in something. Or to put the matter differently, God—who "is truth itself" as noted above—is the *principium essendi* who both grounds and founds any truth aptness that might obtain. So while it might make some sense to promote my claim (5), as Oppy numbers it, to claim (1), so that the other five claims all flow from and are thus dependent on the first, there can be no inconsistency in the six claims with respect to their truth. God's existence includes the existence of truth itself (which is a person before it is a property). Any truth aptness follows from that. The assertion that my claim (5) renders the six claims jointly inconsistent rules out the Christian position from the outset.

As far as the rest of Oppy's discussion concerning the *principia*, he disagrees with me about all of it (101). In spite of that disagreement, Oppy rightly notes that there is "the possibility of entering into genuine dialogue" about our disagreements (101). I hope our discussions here have shown that to be the case. I also agree that philosophy is *one way* to engage that dialogue. But it is not the only way and not the best way. To defer our disagreements about God and his revelation to the domain of philosophy is to assign a role to philosophy that it cannot adequately play. When it does try to play such a role, strange ideas ensue. For example, with respect to my admission that God's existence is intrinsic to him, Oppy supposes that naturalists can account for existence this way:

> If we suppose that there is a first cause, then there are two options: either it is contingent or it is necessary. If we are theists, the first cause is God; if we are naturalists, the first cause is the initial state of natural reality. . . . Some naturalists suppose that the initial state of natural reality is necessary; other naturalists suppose that it is contingent. If pushed to choose, I would say—albeit with no great confidence—that if there is an initial state of natural reality, then it is necessary. (101)

But this discussion points out the urgent need for *principia*. How could it be, we could ask, that someone could seriously assert that the natural is able to account for itself? There is no evidence for such a claim, and it is far from intuitive to think so. It's as if Oppy finds himself at the shore of a wide and deep lake and assumes to himself the burden of asserting that there is no such thing as rain. The lake *must* be able to account for itself; whether it is necessary or contingent, it must be self-contained. With nose to the grindstone and eyes never looking up, he commits himself to a lifetime of studying this self-contained and self-explanatory lake. The problem is that whenever it rains, he has to find a way, against all evidence and rationality, to refer the rainwater's origin to the lake itself.

Christianity is not a philosophy. It cannot be adequately named and gamed using philosophical tools. Instead, it is that which breathes life into true philosophy, birthing it and providing for its flourishing. God's good gifts, of course, including Oppy's considerable brilliance, can be enjoyed by all, even by those who deny him. Like the Prodigal Son, he can attempt to run from God, but it is impossible to escape him. A true and proper philosophy requires a personal foundation of the triune God who has spoken. Such *principia* are not accessed and agreed upon ultimately by way of philosophical discussion and argument but, for all four of us, can only be accessed by way of true repentance and trust in Christ. Once accessed in that way, philosophy finds its only real home. In that home, it can properly and meaningfully grow into a mature, healthy adult rather than remaining a thin, anemic orphan, perpetually meandering about with nowhere to lay its head.

CONVERGENCE MODEL

TIMOTHY MCGREW

Apologia pro vita sua

One of my most vivid memories from my student days is of a conversation with Fr. Edward Gannon, a quirky, brilliant, chain-smoking Jesuit who had designed the honors program at the University of Scranton. Gannon had a habit of adopting undergraduates and making sure they were headed in the proper direction—with a helpful shove from behind, if need be. I had transferred into the University to study philosophy, and Gannon soon hauled me into his office for conversation and counsel.

It came out (I no longer remember how) that I was reading my way through a stack of books by the great Catholic scholar Etienne Gilson. Gannon, who was not a sentimental man, grew pensive at the mention of Gilson's name, his eyes fixed on the middle distance. "I saw him once, at a conference," he said, his normally gravelly voice softened almost to wistfulness by a vision of something I could not see. And then, with a mixture of emphasis and bafflement: "He was a *philosopher*, and he was a *Christian*, and *he saw no contradiction!*"

As a philosopher by training and vocation and a Christian by conviction and commitment, I have grown accustomed to hearing that there must be, if not an outright contradiction, at least some tension between Athens and Jerusalem. Being a professional philosopher means (or ought to mean) devoting one's life to reasoned inquiry into fundamental questions of metaphysics and epistemology and value. Being a Christian means, among other things, holding certain beliefs that are presently unpopular in philosophical circles—beliefs about God and man and nature and sin and revelation and redemption—and entering sincerely into the spiritual life of the Christian community in prayer and worship and repentance and forgiveness and discipleship. To some who stand outside of that community, perhaps outside of any religion at all, these beliefs and actions and commitments may seem baffling. Why would a philosopher voluntarily subscribe to a cluster of outmoded concepts and antiquated beliefs? Why clutter one's life with spiritual disciplines and activities that must interfere with unfettered inquiry and the search for truth? To some within that community, the idea of opening inquiry into questions touched on by the Christian faith may seem nearly as sacrilegious as it would be to come to the wrong conclusion about them. ("You're going to study philosophy?" someone I barely knew said to me with a shake of his head. "You could get really messed up.")

I think these criticisms are equally mistaken. Rather, I think there is a convergence: philosophy confirms Christianity, and Christianity completes philosophy. But to explain what this means, I must first give at least a sketch of how I conceive of philosophy and a brief outline of what Christianity actually involves.

Philosophy

Philosophy today is not a set of substantive beliefs; it is a discipline. Professional philosophers (when they are worthy of the name) share a set of techniques and formal tools, and they work with an inherited set of problems developed and preserved in a literature that spans two and a half millennia. Over the course of that much time, some things have changed. Disciplines like psychology and physics have broken off from philosophy and assumed an autonomous identity when their subject matter proved relatively tractable to experimental inquiry, though there remain deep and interesting problems in those disciplines that experimentation cannot resolve. But plenty of questions remain that are not within the province of any of the special sciences and that can be resolved, if at all, only by means of the characteristic tools and techniques of philosophy.

To say that philosophy is a discipline is not to say that philosophers are disciplined in the sense in which soldiers might be disciplined. Philosophers are a fractious bunch. They love to argue—so much so, that in the previous paragraph I have probably managed to antagonize a sizeable majority of the credentialed philosophers now living. Some who are deeply involved in the project of "naturalizing" philosophy would maintain that all of the questions philosophy used to try to answer must be handed off to the sciences. On this view, philosophy departments can be shut down right now without any loss; the only interesting and answerable questions can and must be left to specialized empirical disciplines. Others, slightly more generous, would maintain that philosophy and the special sciences are ultimately trying to answer the same questions by different means. So philosophers may be allowed to keep their jobs and might even make genuine contributions to human knowledge without changing careers, though in the end their labors will be redundant. In some quarters, the idea that philosophy is not a set of substantive beliefs would be roundly condemned; in others, the notion that there are such things as *beliefs* at all is openly derided. And for every technique and tool that one could mention—conceptual analysis, linguistic analysis, formal logic, probability theory, introspection, appeal to intuition—there are whole schools of thought devoted to denouncing their usefulness.

I have said that philosophy is not a set of *substantive* beliefs. But to do philosophy well, one must start somewhere, have some beliefs or commitments. And among these, the laws of logic have a special standing; they are topic-neutral conditions for rational thought, and they are not negotiable. True, in formal logic we study so-called "deviant" logics, where the truth conditions or implication sets for the same inscriptions differ. But the changes in meaning introduced when we try to give an interpretation to the symbols undermine the suggestion that they are instances of an alternative rationality. One does occasionally encounter a sincere, fuddled attempt to deny the laws of logic outright. In graduate school, a fellow student much enamored of Heidegger and Derrida tried to explain continental philosophy to me: "What you need to understand is that, in continental philosophy, those three laws of logic, noncontradiction, excluded middle, and . . . and . . . I can't remember the third one, but I have it written down somewhere, *they don't hold*." So much the worse for continental philosophy.

Are there other beliefs that are nonnegotiable? As a neoclassical foundationalist, I think there are some beliefs about oneself and one's present experience that one cannot form in the normal way without being justified, indeed *completely* justified, in holding them. The literature on epistemic justification, even from within a broadly internalist standpoint, is vast, and strong foundationalism is decidedly out of fashion at present. But what of it? Foundationalism is neither the only nor the most unfashionable philosophical position I hold. The changing winds of fashion have never seemed to me to be a good reason for abandoning anything. Popularity is a rotten test of truth.

Not everyone agrees. There is at present a flourishing literature on the epistemology of disagreement. A key question in this literature is what one should do upon discovering that an epistemic peer—sometimes this is fleshed out as a person one recognizes as having comparable education, abilities, and attainments to one's own—disagrees with one's judgment regarding some proposition P about an issue that lies within one's field of professional competence. Suppose I hold that P is true, and I discover that my respected colleague Dr. X disagrees. Should this discovery shake my confidence in P?

In the usual sort of case, I think the answer is that it should not, or at any rate not much. For in the usual case I have my reasons for believing that P, and I have done my best to judge how the total evidence bears on it. If Dr. X disagrees, that fact itself gives me some reason to doubt that Dr. X is fully informed or fully rational with respect to this particular point. My judgment is defeasible, of course. Perhaps Dr. X will sway me with his complex, multilayered argument, or with his subtle critique of my line of reasoning, or with the introduction of some new and relevant information of which I was previously unaware. And of course, if I have given the matter no previous consideration and am merely offering my casual opinion, then the case may be quite different. But when I am in possession of arguments and reasons, the mere fact that we have a disagreement generally casts more doubt on the suggestion that Dr. X is my peer than it does on P.

Putting the case like that assumes that there are such things as reasons of which we are sometimes aware, that we can actually base our beliefs, at least some of the time consciously, on those reasons, and that when we do, the reasons can justify the beliefs. This sort of internalism is the standpoint of untutored common sense, and after decades of work in the field of epistemology I see no reason to abandon it. At the present time, various forms of externalism are popular among both secular and Christian philosophers. Take, for example, the reliabilism of Alvin Plantinga, who redefines the term *knowledge* as (approximately) true belief arrived at by the proper functioning of a cognitive module that is operating in the environment for which it was designed. I am persuaded that all versions of externalism, including Plantinga's version, collapse into a very deep and troubling form of skepticism. Since I have written reasonably extensively on this issue, I will say nothing more about the matter here.[1] Nor will I take any notice of the fatal turn to relativism exhibited in the work of writers like Thomas Kuhn.[2] Readers who disagree may complain that my framing of subsequent issues in terms of reasons and justification is tendentious. They are welcome to try to reformulate what I have to say in their preferred idiom so long as they do not saddle me with the reformulations.

Whatever their official positions in epistemology, philosophers, like everyone else, reason from data, and they are usually not overly fussy about whether that reasoning takes them across disciplinary lines. Epistemologists—many of them—read the literature of cognitive psychology; philosophers of science poke their noses into biology and physics and sociology and other fields; metaphysicians work along (and sometimes cross over) the borders that philosophy shares with modern physics and set theory; ethicists ponder the implications of empirical studies like the Zimbardo prison experiment and write books about the uses of casuistry. I say this by way of a preface, for in what follows I will be drawing not only on some of the sciences but, particularly heavily, on historical data that might properly be said to belong to ancient history or New Testament studies. Such appropriation may be audacious, but it is no very great divergence from normal philosophical practice. The question is not so much whether a philosopher will draw upon material claimed by other disciplines as which ones, and how much, and how well.

---

1. See Timothy and Lydia McGrew, *Internalism and Epistemology* (New York: Routledge, 2007).
2. See Timothy McGrew, "Scientific Progress, Relativism, and Self-Refutation," *Electronic Journal of Analytic Philosophy* 2 (1994).

Natural Theology

Arguments for and against the existence of God, and arguments for and against the truth of Christianity, form a vast field of inquiry, and the books written on these subjects would fill a sizeable library. It is not my intention here to add another volume to that library. I will give only an outline of a handful of arguments, making no attempt at anything like a full treatment of even a single issue, and I will leave unmentioned most of the intricate dialectical swordplay that philosophers find so absorbing. Instead, I want to touch on some of the more general methodological issues in order to explain how I would, in some cases, handle these subjects differently from others, including those who share some or all of my conclusions. But for the record I will say that these are all lines of argument that I find interesting and, cumulatively, compelling. I would not lay a hand on any one of them if I were not persuaded that it has real substance and force.

The great German philosopher Immanuel Kant repeatedly stressed the importance of three topics in philosophy: God, freedom, and immortality. Three things make these issues fundamental. First, they raise very deep conceptual problems. Second, the answers to the associated questions—Is there a God? If so, what is God like? Are we free? If so, in what sense? Will we survive our physical death? If so, what will that mode of existence be like?—have profound implications for how we should now live. Third, common human experience does not seem at first blush to shed too much light on these questions. In his *Ecclesiastical History of the English People*, the Venerable Bede recounts a story of a local king who asked one of his counselors what he ought to think about Paulinus's preaching of Christianity. The counselor's response expresses what is, I suspect, a very common state in the minds of many people when they first begin to contemplate the big questions:

> The present life of man upon earth, O king, seems to me, in comparison with that time which is unknown to us, like to the swift flight of a sparrow through the house wherein you sit at supper in winter, with your ealdormen and thegns, while the fire blazes in the midst, and the hall is warmed, but the wintry storms of rain or snow are raging abroad. The sparrow, flying in at one door and

immediately out at another, whilst he is within, is safe from the wintry tempest; but after a short space of fair weather, he immediately vanishes out of your sight, passing from winter into winter again. So this life of man appears for a little while, but of what is to follow or what went before we know nothing at all.

This is the sentiment at the starting point of their reflections, though it need not and I think should not be the end. But to find our way forward, we need to look into natural theology, a subdiscipline of the philosophy of religion devoted to the study of arguments for (and, in its broader forms, against) the existence of a deity. The history of this discipline is long and complex. In its Western form, it stretches back at least to the days of the earliest Greek philosophers, where a form of the cosmological argument can be found in Plato. But in Judaism the idea can be found earlier. Psalm 19, for example, opens with the assertion that

> the heavens declare the glory of God;
> the skies proclaim the work of his hands.

The tradition of natural theology in Judaism remained strong through the beginning of the Christian era, where Paul's famous appeal in Romans 1 strongly echoes the more detailed presentation of cosmological and teleological reasoning in such intertestamental works as *Wisdom of Solomon*.

From time to time, some ardent Christians—usually adherents of a certain branch of the Reformed tradition or followers of Karl Barth—have tried to deny that there is any actual natural theology in Scripture and to explain away the plain meaning of the texts mentioned here. Calvin famously reads Romans 1 as referring not to natural theology but to the *sensus divinitatis*, an inborn faculty by which, in his view, all men are given immediate and infallible knowledge of the existence and nature of God. I can see no rational ground for taking this point of view, which seems to me to torture both the biblical text and the principles of sound historical investigation. That some people may have direct experiences of God is something I should not wish to deny. But the further claim that everyone possesses a faculty of this sort seems to me not only groundless but flatly contrary to the experience of many believers.

130 FOUR VIEWS ON CHRISTIANITY AND PHILOSOPHY

The project of developing a positive natural theology can take various forms. It will be convenient here to make a rough classification of approaches in terms of the data from which the arguments begin, the patterns of inference used, the conclusions drawn, and the level of confidence ascribed to those conclusions. Different schools of thought tend to gravitate to different local sectors of the space thus described; different practitioners even within the same school of thought may also differ to a smaller extent from one another.

My own approach takes for data some very broad features of reality which, I am persuaded, ought to be available to nearly any rational person regardless of his religious commitments. In particular, I think there are legitimate arguments to be made from, *inter alia*, the origin of the universe, the origin of life, the fact of consciousness, and the existence of objective good and evil. But I would develop some of these arguments in a manner somewhat different from that in which they are often put forward, and for that reason I need to explain what I would and would not claim for them.

First, I should say a word about what counts as a *good* argument. It is tempting to say that a good argument is one that persuades other inquirers—all of them, or most of them, or all of them who are rational—of the truth of its conclusion.[3] There is something right about connecting goodness in an argument with rationality and persuasiveness. But I think this definition is at once too broad, too narrow, and out of focus. It is too broad, since bad arguments can and often do persuade even the majority of inquirers. The history of philosophy, like the history of science, is littered with examples; if I am not mistaken, contemporary philosophy affords us with many examples of this as well. It is too narrow, since (as I will try to illustrate) there may be arguments that are in a recognizable and important sense good and yet do not, and even should not, persuade most rational inquirers of the truth of their conclusions. And it is out of focus, since it does not provide the conceptual resources to represent the fact that the goodness of arguments, like the goodness of many other things, can come in degrees.

What, then, should we understand to be meant by referring to an

---

3. Graham Oppy offers something like this as a definition of a *successful* argument, with some additional qualifications, in *Arguing about Gods* (Cambridge: Cambridge University Press, 2006), xv, 1, 6–15.

argument as *good*? There are several irreducible notions of goodness, and which one is appropriate will depend in part on the dialectical context. Two, in particular, seem relevant to many discussions in the philosophy of religion. First, an argument may be good in the sense that it shows, from premises widely available to rational inquirers, that its conclusion has a nonnegligible probability. That probability need not exceed 50%. If an argument were to show that (say) 10% is a lower bound on the probability that there is a god of some sort, then philosophers should (and some would) sit up and take notice.

Second, an argument may be good in the sense that and to the extent that it shifts the ratio of probabilities in favor of its conclusion. This is a sense that is easier to show mathematically than to put into plain English, but the basic idea is to compare the probability of the conclusion C to the probability of its negation, $\sim$C. If taking evidence E into account shifts that ratio in a direction favorable to C, then E is evidence for C. For example, an argument that lifts the probability of C from 1% to 25% changes that ratio from $P(C)/P(\sim C) = 1/99$ to $P(C|E)/P(C|\sim E) = 1/3 = .25/.75$. Even though 25% is not a probability that would underwrite belief in C, the evidence E provides significant *confirmation* for C. A number of such arguments taken together may provide a cumulative case of great power for C.[4]

Using these two definitions of goodness, we can briefly explore a few arguments. To start with, the core of the Kalam cosmological argument can be cast as a simple deductive argument from two premises:

1. Whatever begins to exist is caused to exist by something else
2. The physical universe began to exist

Therefore,

3. The physical universe was caused to exist by something else

From the standpoint of logical structure, the argument is impeccable; if the premises are true, the conclusion must also be true. But four features of the argument call for further comment.

First—and this is an issue that applies to many arguments in

---

4. These issues are treated at greater length in Timothy McGrew and John DePoe, "Natural Theology and the Uses of Argument," *Philosophia Christi* 15 (2013): 299–309.

philosophy and in everyday life—the premises may not be certain. Uncertainty in the premises introduces the possibility of uncertainty in the conclusion. How much uncertainty, and why only the possibility of it? It turns out that if we work within the framework of epistemic probability, this question admits of a mathematically precise answer: the maximum uncertainty of the conclusion is the sum of the uncertainties of the premises, where the uncertainty of P, written $U(P)$, is equal to 1 minus the probability of P.[5] A consequence of this formal fact, put a little less formally, is that if each of the two premises of the Kalam is somewhat more likely than not, then the conclusion is at least on the table for discussion. If the probability of premise 1 is 80%, and the probability of premise 2 is 60%, then the *minimum* probability of the conclusion is 40%—and it may well be greater, with no upper bound on it lower than 100%.

As it happens, I think both premises are more likely than not, and most of the people with whom I have discussed the argument are inclined to agree, even if they are shy of putting specific numerical probabilities into the mix. The numbers help to illustrate the point, but it is the point that matters, not the numbers.

Second, premise 1 of the Kalam argument is logically stronger than it needs to be. A weaker claim—entailed by premise 1 but not entailing it, and therefore (omitting here some technicalities that would be of interest mainly to those who already know about them) more probable than premise 1 is—would suffice for the validity of the argument, namely:

1*. If the physical universe began to exist, then the physical universe was caused to exist by something else

I have used premise 1 instead of 1* both because it is a customary way of presenting the argument and because it has a certain intuitive appeal when stated generally. But in all strictness, a lower bound for the conclusion estimated from the uncertainties in premises 1 and 2 may well be too pessimistic.

One does occasionally encounter the rejoinder that premise 1, in

---

5. If the sum of the uncertainties of the premises equals or exceeds 1, then the maximum uncertainty of the conclusion is 1, and hence its minimum probability is 0—which is not terribly helpful, since we knew that already.

its full generality, is undermined by examples from quantum theory, such as radioactive decay. But this objection is misconceived. The alpha particles that are emitted in the decay of uranium-238 into thorium-234 are simply two protons and two neutrons from the nucleus of the original uranium atom; they do not come into being *ex nihilo* at the time of decay. There are puzzles about causation in quantum mechanics, but they do not touch premise 1. And even if they did, it is a further question whether they would have any bearing on 1*.

Third, there are multiple lines of argument that have been marshaled to defend premise 2. Two *a priori* philosophical arguments regarding actual infinities and the traversal of an infinite series have provoked very lively debate. For my part, I have always found the empirical arguments for premise 2 more persuasive. Our best cosmology does seem to be telling us that the physical universe does not have an infinite past. The Borde-Guth-Vilenkin theorem tells us that this characteristic holds generally for universes that are on average expanding and that comply with the constraints of general relativity. Thermodynamics strongly suggests that if our universe had an infinite past, then barring divine intervention, it would have reached a state of maximum entropy already. It is of course possible that all of these scientific clues are misleading us. But possibility is cheap, and we do not need our premises to be certain in order for the argument to do significant work—in this case, the work of putting a nonphysical cause of the existence of the physical universe on the table for serious discussion.

Fourth, the conclusion of the Kalam argument falls short of claiming that God exists, particularly the God of the Judeo-Christian tradition. Someone may reasonably object that for all the Kalam argument proves, the cause of the universe's existence might be Thor, or Quetzalcoatl, or a committee of nonphysical beings who have since outlived their usefulness. It does not force even those who embrace its premises as certainties to the conclusion that the triune God of Christianity exists.

True enough. But the Kalam significantly reduces the available ways to avoid that conclusion, because it directly undermines the assumption that reference to physical reality supplies the answers to every legitimate question about our world. This is obviously relevant to the subject of God's existence. Naturalism—the view that the physical world studied by the natural sciences is the whole of reality, or at least the whole of causally efficacious reality—is today the metaphysical view of choice for atheists. If naturalism can be shown to be hopeless, or seriously defective, or even open to significant doubt, then the number of ways to be a consistent and reasonable atheist has been sharply narrowed. There are various ways to build upon the conclusion at line 3 to argue for more, but for present purposes we need not take the discussion in that direction. It is enough if the argument calls naturalism into question.

Something similar goes for the very simple version of the moral argument that I have in mind:

1. If naturalism is true, then there are no objective moral values
2. There are objective moral values

Therefore,

3. Naturalism is false

Again, the premises need not be certain for the argument to do significant work, though in this case, few people seem inclined to ascribe intermediate probabilities to either of them. For my part, I should say that premise 1 is as reasonable as nearly any claim in the whole of metaethics, and premise 2 is so obvious that we should use it as a touchstone for evaluating ethical systems. In introductory courses, I sometimes propose for the class's consideration the proposition that it is morally wrong, always, everywhere, for everyone, to burn babies in gasoline as a spectator sport. Usually only one or two students are hardy enough in their relativism to deny it. But such examples, though they may help to make its truth more vivid, are not *arguments* for it. Here, I believe, we have hit ethical bedrock.

The more common version of the moral argument substitutes, for premise 1, a somewhat stronger claim:

1* If God does not exist, then there are no objective moral values

We are then invited to derive, from 1* and 2, the stronger conclusion:

3* God exists

This version of the argument invites the old objection that Plato raises in his *Euthyphro*, and the advocates of this bolder version of the moral argument typically respond by articulating sophisticated versions of a divine command theory. Whether such a theory is wholly satisfactory is a question that does not concern me here, though in my judgment it can be developed in a way that blocks the Euthyphro dilemma. Obviously, 3* is a more exciting conclusion than 3. Conversely, 1* is a more burdensome premise to defend than 1. I am content to let the simpler version of the argument do the work of undermining naturalism and move on.

A third argument that does significant work in the cause of theism is the argument from the existence of consciousness. One need not follow Descartes through his entire audacious program of establishing medicine, mechanics, and morals on indubitable foundations to acknowledge that he selected a starting point that cannot be coherently denied. Incoherent denials are another matter. Many years ago, at a conference in Quine's honor in San Marino, I spent a few fascinating hours talking with a graduate student from Princeton who insisted that he had no conscious experiences whatsoever. We made, I am sorry to say, little progress.

Here, I should prefer to put the argument in a probabilistic form, or at any rate an explanatory form, rather than a deductive one. Theism and naturalism, though they do not exhaust the logical space, certainly span a large portion of it for many people in the Western world. In our comparison of their relative merits, we may ask (among other things) what we should be led to expect on each hypothesis. In my judgment as an interested spectator and occasional participant in discussions regarding the naturalist project in the philosophy of mind, the earnest endeavor to make the world safe for naturalism is hopeless. In a universe without consciousness, we have not the slightest reason to expect that consciousness will arise. Even some major philosophers of mind who are card-carrying naturalists—famously, Colin McGinn—have come to the conclusion that we are not capable of answering the question of how consciousness emerges from a nonconscious world. But if theism is true, then consciousness is built into the universe on the ground floor.

Mere theism does not, of course, entail that the deity will create other conscious beings, and someone might object on this ground that the comparison of probabilities does not clearly favor theism over naturalism. But I do not think this objection is as serious as it may first seem. A universe where there is already a conscious being is one where there is at least a plausible chance that more conscious beings will be generated; a universe where there is not cannot be on the same footing. I may speculate on the probability that a cup of tea is brewing in the house that I am passing, and this is a point on which, *a priori*, it would be rash to be certain. But be that probability great or small, it is surely much greater if the house is occupied than if it is standing vacant.

Consciousness is not the only point of leverage we find in the philosophy of mind. Two others seem worth pursuing, namely, the intentionality of our thoughts and the trustworthiness of our reason. The argument from intentionality takes rise from the fact that we can think about other things, including things not present to our senses: I can think about the satellites of Jupiter, though I am writing indoors and thus (lamentably) cannot at the present moment see the starry sky above. It is notoriously difficult, within a purely naturalistic framework, to give an account of how intentionality is supposed to work. And for the trustworthiness of our reason, the case is comparably bleak. Long before C. S. Lewis made the argument from reason part of his Broadcast Talks, Arthur James Balfour had articulated a version of it in *The Foundations of Belief*. Balfour's formulation of the challenge is not the most careful or rigorous available, but like Lewis he had a knack for making the central idea vivid. Balfour applies the principle this way:

> [F]or a creed to be truly consistent, there must exist a correspon-
> dence between the account it gives of the origin of its beliefs and the
> estimate it entertains of their value; in other words, there must be
> a harmony between the accepted value of results and the accepted
> theory of causes. . . . If, underlying the rational apparatus by which
> scientific beliefs are formally justified, there is a wholly non-rational
> machinery by which they are in fact produced, if we are of opinion
> that in the last resort our stock of convictions is determined by the
> blind interaction of natural forces and, so far as we know, by these
> alone, then there is a discord between one portion of our scheme of
> thought and another, between our estimate of values and our theory
> of origins, which may properly be described as inconsistency.[6]

---

6. Arthur James Balfour, *The Foundations of Belief*, 8th ed. (New York: Longmans, Green and Co., 1918), xviii–xix. Victor Reppert updates this argument in his book *C. S. Lewis's Dangerous Idea* (Downers Grove: InterVarsity Press, 2003).

Balfour pursues this suggestive line of argument through other areas, including aesthetics and ethics. The force any given individual finds in the argument will, of course, be inversely proportional to his willingness to bite the bullet. Someone who is unmoved by beauty, or who regards the moral sense as a genetic or sociological accident, will escape the charge of a grave mismatch between his estimate of value and his theory of origin for aesthetic and moral value. That is not to say that all is well with him. He has far graver problems. And if he bites the bullet on the value of reason, then inconsistency with his professed belief is, paradoxically, his only hope.

The Problem of Evil

The principal philosophical argument against the existence of God is the venerable problem of evil—of physical suffering and pain, in particular. The objection is not always filled out fully, but when it is, it runs something like this:

1. If God exists, he is all-powerful, all-knowing, and perfectly good
2. If God is all-powerful, he is able to prevent evil
3. If God is all-knowing, he is aware of any possibility of evil
4. If God is perfectly good, he always wishes to prevent any evil
5. If God is able to prevent evil and aware of any possibility of evil, and he always wishes to prevent any evil, then there is no evil
6. There is evil

Therefore,

7. God does not exist

This argument, or one much like it cast in a similar deductive form, is sometimes called *the logical problem of evil*.

This argument is *valid*: if the premises of the argument were all true, the conclusion would also be true. But are the premises true? Premise 1 is a consequence of the traditional definition of God. Premise 2 is undoubtedly true in one sense, though we will need to return to this point in a moment. Premise 3 also seems true, assuming that knowledge can be extended to what is possible and not yet actual; let us grant this assumption. Premise 5 seems obvious, and premise 6 is undeniably true.

When we take a closer look at premise 4, however, the argument begins to unravel. The problem is that premise 4 is not qualified in any way. And there seem to be at least two important qualifications that need to be included.

First, some evils must be allowed as a consequence of allowing certain goods. It seems quite reasonable to suppose that the existence of free creatures who can choose to love and worship God and use their freedom for one another's benefit is a very good thing. Yet genuine freedom carries with it the possibility of abuse; a creature who can freely do good to another is also a being who can withhold good or do harm. The existence of the good carries with it the possibility of some kinds of evil.

Second, some evils are necessary for good consequences to come. If my enduring suffering of a certain kind, for a certain time, is required for the formation of a virtuous and compassionate character, would it be good of God not to allow my character to be formed (and improved) in this way? A good parent may allow a child to suffer a temporary pain or loss for a time—a pain or loss that the parent could have prevented—for the sake of developing the child's character.

This line of thought can be extended to the parent's direct intervention. All punishment is painful in some respect. But a parent who never punished an erring child would not be a good parent. So it seems that God may well have perfectly good reasons for allowing evil to exist. Premise 4, stated in this bald, unqualified way, is false. This consideration alone is enough to undermine the logical problem of evil.

But if God does have those reasons, then we need to rethink the way that premise 2 is stated. God is able to prevent any evil *that he has not already determined must be permitted for the sake of a greater good*. But it would be inconsistent to demand that God both permit and prevent the same evil.

Someone might accept this analysis but try to shift to a different strategy. Even if it is possible that God has adequate moral reasons for allowing some evil, perhaps the quantity and variety of evil we see in this world counts as evidence (maybe overwhelming evidence) against the existence of God. This challenge is known as *the evidential problem of evil*.

But would it really count as evidence against the existence of God—a loving God who permits evil only for good reasons? In order for this argument to have any serious force, it must be the case that we would not expect what we find if there were such a God. We should admit that we do not know God's reasons for permitting many *particular* evils. But the reasons for particular evils are precisely what we would not expect to know, if there were a God. After all, if he exists, presumably *God knows something we don't.* We are in a somewhat better position for understanding why a good God would permit certain *types* of evils; here, the same kinds of reasons come into play that draw the sting of the logical problem of evil.

As for the quantity of evil, two considerations mitigate the evidential force of the argument. First, there is the matter of diminishing returns. If there may be good reasons for God's permitting some evil and suffering, then those same reasons may *prima facie* apply to other instances of evil and suffering as well. Once admit that God may have reasons for allowing one person to die of cancer, and there is no obvious barrier to the application of those same reasons to thousands of other cases. So each subsequent example has less force than the first one.

Second, we are not in a strong position to say that there may not be other reasons for both the type and quantity of evils we see. The existence of even some reasons we can understand suggests (to say no more) that there may also be some reasons that at present we cannot. I do not wish to take this line of reasoning in the direction of any very strong form of skeptical theism. But once again, the consideration that if God exists, he knows something we don't should induce in us at least some humility about the extent of our ability to justify the ways of God to man.

There are two further points that are not always given the serious consideration that they deserve. First, in the Judeo-Christian view, things are not the way they were supposed to be. Both human nature and the physical world have been twisted off in a direction that gives rise to moral and natural evils. And in the Christian view, God has himself entered human history, not to make our suffering stop but to participate in it in the most appalling way. Such a view leads us to expect more in the way of sorrow and suffering than a generic benevolent theism would, and consequently that sorrow and that suffering, though no less painful, do not have the same force against Christianity as they do against a sort of Precious Moments theism where the deity's principal role seems to be to ensure that we are all happy in our own way.

Second, it is not necessary for a sincere and rational believer to deny that evil—whether particular evils or the distressing fact of the wide scope of some sorts of evil—counts as evidence against the existence of God. In many areas of life, from scientific reasoning to historical investigation to auto mechanics, we make up our minds in favor of a position despite the existence of some counterevidence. What is necessary for rational belief in God's existence is not the elimination of all evidence to the contrary or the satisfactory solution of all objections but rather a balance of evidence that substantially favors acceptance. If there are serious reasons to believe in God, we must take seriously the possibility that they overcome any evidential force that arises from the problem of evil.

Giving a dispassionate analysis of the problem of evil is one thing; living with suffering (particularly the suffering of those we love) is another. The argument may not be the devastating *intellectual* challenge it is sometimes believed to be, but it is certainly a profound *existential* challenge. Our vivid sense of right and wrong should motivate us to act differently, to be wise and humane and generous to those who are suffering.

And perhaps it should do more than that. In his book *Mere Christianity*, C. S. Lewis points out that our very ideas of right and wrong offer us a clue to the nature of reality. In a purely material universe of the sort that philosophical naturalism offers us, there is no room for objective right and wrong. There is nothing tragic about the suffering of the innocent, nothing noble about Mother Teresa or Lillian Doerksen or Raoul Wallenberg. The very existence of *real* evils and *real* goods is an important piece of evidence that naturalistic atheism is wrong. The more vividly we are aware of the reality of objective value, the more certain we will be that the naturalist's picture of the world is missing something vital at its heart.

In his final book, written in 1952 just a few years before his death, the British philosopher and lifelong atheist C. E. M. Joad gives a remarkable testimony to what he calls "The Significance of Evil":

> [T]o believe, as I have grown to believe, in the fundamental and in this life ineradicable nature of human sinfulness is intolerable, unless there is some source of guidance and assistance outside ourselves to which we can turn for comfort and assurance. Presently

the facts of sin and evil came to present themselves with such over-whelming strength that unless one were able to seek assistance, if not for the overcoming of them, at least for the not succumbing to them, one would give way to despair. The more I knew of it, the more Christianity seemed to offer just that strengthening and assistance. And with that the rationalist-optimist philosophy, by the light of which I had hitherto done my best to live, came to seem intolerably trivial and superficial—a shallow-rooted plant which, growing to maturity amid the lush and leisured optimism of the nineteenth century, was quite unfitted to withstand the bleaker winds that blow through ours. I abandoned it, and in abandoning it found myself a Christian.[7]

Christianity

The factual bases for the arguments that I have briefly discussed above play the role of clues. They point toward a conclusion richer than they can establish by themselves. Because they typically involve either uncertain or nonobvious premises or nondeductive forms of reasoning (or both), it is always possible for someone to deny the conclusions to which they point without obvious self-contradiction. For those who hold to a more ambitious program of natural theology, this may seem like minimal progress indeed. A cluster of clues suggesting that natu-ralism is false and that the universe was created by something conscious and nonphysical is a far cry from a demonstration of the existence of an eternal (or perhaps timeless) being who, by definition, possesses every perfection.

Obviously, we can go much further with the resources provided in the Christian Scriptures.[8] Here we learn not only that there is a God but something of his character and actions. We learn not only that we are free but also why. We learn not only that we are destined for immortal life but also how we must live with a view to that life. Above all, we come to see Jesus Christ as the culmination of centuries of prophetic promise, and to recognize the cross and the empty tomb as the great turning point of history. Natural theology may suggest that there is a

---

7. C. E. M. Joad, *The Recovery of Belief* (London: Faber and Faber, 1952), 82.

8. Whether we will go in precisely the same direction, to the God of classical theism, is another question.

deity, but it cannot tell me whether there is redemption for sin, nor can it answer the vital question of the Philippian jailer: "What must I do to be saved?"

But the appeal to Scripture kicks the evidential can just one step down the road. To many people it seems obvious that the appeal to any particular religious tradition, while it may be motivated by social solidarity or filial piety, cannot possibly be backed up by cogent evidence. In fact, in the main stream of Western academia, it is apparently thought safe to neglect even passing acquaintance with the Christian Scriptures. One day in the department mailroom a young philosopher of my acquaintance, a truly brilliant fellow with a doctorate from a fine school and a promising future ahead of him, asked me what I was reading. "It's a book on the four Gospels," I replied. His brows quirked in confusion. "The four Gospels?" He had never heard of them.

In those four Gospels, in brief compass, we have four narratives of a remarkable life. Jesus, as he emerges in each of these portraits, gives answers to those great questions with which philosophers continue to wrestle. He does not offer them, like Socrates does, as conjectures, apologizing for the uncertainty of his reasoning; he teaches with authority. He speaks in images drawn from the life of his listeners. He has compassion on the poor but is pitiless and scathing with the self-satisfied intelligentsia and religious leadership of his day. He speaks with women and touches lepers, but he drives the money changers out of the temple with a whip. He heals the lame and the desperate, and he appeals openly and repeatedly to his mighty works as authentication of his divine commission and prerogatives. But when crowds pursue him out of idle curiosity, he contemptuously refuses to gratify them with a miracle. He tears through the dialectical traps his enemies lay for him with such savage intelligence that when he is done, no one dares to ask him any further questions. But he teaches that a childlike trust in God is a prerequisite to entry into the kingdom of heaven. He tells his disciples that he is going to die, and he throws the words of Daniel 7 in the teeth of the Sanhedrin who are meeting to condemn him to that death. But when his disciples are bickering about which of them will be greatest in the kingdom to come, he girds himself like a servant and washes their feet. The Jesus portrayed in the Gospels is unlike any character we would have invented; one needs only to read the gnostic so-called "gospels" to see how wide the contrast is between a portrait drawn from life and one fashioned by mere imagination.[9] There is something vivid and profoundly compelling about this brilliant, compassionate, angry young man.

It is a pity that the scope and strength of the evidence for the basic historicity of the Gospels is not more widely appreciated. Even in conservative Christian circles, the most common approach to the defense of the faith is a "minimal facts" argument that bypasses the question of the general reliability of the Gospels altogether. But there is much to be said on the affirmative side of that question. The external evidence for their traditional authorship is unanimous and, by comparison with what we have for the works of other ancient writers like Thucydides, very early and extensive.[10] The internal interconnections of the Gospels—not simply their telling some of the same stories in approximately the same way, but the way that one Gospel will supply details that explain puzzling features of another—are extensive and crisscross the texts in all directions. The Synoptics—Matthew, Mark, and Luke—explain John. John explains the Synoptics. The Synoptics explain one another.[11] A thoughtful cross comparison of the character of Jesus displays the unity of the portrait, particularly when we compare things like Jesus's characteristic methods of teaching in the Synoptics with his method of teaching displayed in separate scenes narrated only in John.[12] Each of the Gospels makes contact at multiple points with data from archaeology and from non-Christian historical sources.[13]

The book of Acts, a continuation of the Gospel of Luke that

9. Of the many good books on the wide difference between the four Evangelists and the second century "gospels," one of the best and most accessible is David Marshall, *The Truth about Jesus and the "Lost Gospels"* (Eugene, OR: Harvest House, 2007).

10. It is remarkable that Bart Ehrman in his textbook, *The New Testament: A Historical Introduction to the Early Christian Writings*, 2nd ed. (New York: Oxford University Press, 2000), omits all mention of the patristic testimony to the authorship of the Gospels. It is difficult to imagine someone's omitting the principal external evidence for authorship in an introduction to any other set of ancient writings.

11. Some of this evidence can be found in older works, such as John James Blunt, *Undesigned Coincidences* (New York: Robert Carter & Brothers, 1855). While a few of Blunt's specific arguments have been superseded by subsequent textual discoveries, and a few others are not as cogent as he thinks, the majority of them are still worth careful examination.

12. This is just one of the numerous subsidiary lines of evidence traced by William Paley in *A View of the Evidences of Christianity* (London: John W. Parker and Son, 1859). See Part 2, chapter 4.

13. I have touched on some of this external evidence in various public lectures; interested readers can easily find them online.

describes the growth of Christianity as it spreads out from Judea and across the Roman Empire, covers a wider geographical surface area than the Gospels and, correspondingly, is confirmed even in its details by a dazzling array of external evidence.[14] The book of Acts displays the life of the Christian community, a life interwoven with institutions that would be inexplicable unless the climactic events of the Gospels had taken place more or less as they are described.[15] That narrative is itself cross confirmed by the major letters of Paul, an active participant in the events narrated—most strikingly in the seven letters acknowledged almost universally to be genuine.[16] In any matter not religious, such an array of historical evidence would leave no reasonable doubt that the main outlines of the facts and even many of the details were correctly reported.

The common counterargument is that the Gospels contradict one another, not just here or there (for that might be said of nearly any independent source in ancient or even more modern history), but so extensively that they cannot be taken as reliable records.[17] A good illustration of the popular view of the matter can be found in the second chapter of Bart Ehrman's book *Jesus, Interrupted*, which proposes to introduce Ehrman's readers to "a world of contradictions." His cataract of examples, viewed at a distance, looks impressive. But most of them will not survive even a moderately close investigation. I am not speaking here of desperate attempts to harmonize every small detail by far-fetched conjectures. I am talking about the basic charity in reading that we would accord to the documents of secular history, the sort of honesty in quotation that would prevent us, were the subject matter not the Christian Scriptures, from omitting inconvenient

14. In his monumental work *The Book of Acts in the Setting of Hellenistic History*, WUNT 49 (Tübingen: Mohr Siebeck, 1989), Colin Hemer lists eighty-four such points of confirmation for the latter half of the book of Acts.

15. This line of argument is worked out with subtlety and care in Stanley Leathes, *The Religion of the Christ*, 2nd ed. (New York: Pott, Young, and Co., 1876).

16. This argument is developed in great detail in William Paley, *Horae Paulinae* (London: SPCK, 1877), an edition made more valuable by the annotations provided by the editor, John Saul Howson. Like Blunt's work, Paley's requires occasional updating but is substantially sound.

17. For an amusing account of the striking manner in which the reports of immediate eyewitnesses diverge, see Archibald Forbes, "Napoleon the Third at Sedan," in *The Nineteenth Century* 31 (1892): 419–32. Yet note what Forbes says at the outset: as to the salient facts, the historian's task will be easy enough.

words when giving quotations in order to manufacture an appearance of contradiction—an appearance that would be destroyed by a quotation of the immediate context.

This is a harsh criticism, and though there is no space here to give a detailed account of dozens of examples, I should offer at least one or two clear instances of this sort of chicanery. Here is one of Ehrman's examples, in his own words:

> [I]n John's Gospel, Jesus performs his first miracle in chapter 2, when he turns the water into wine (a favorite miracle story on college campuses), and we're told that "this was the first sign that Jesus did" (John 2:11). Later in that chapter we're told that Jesus did "many signs" in Jerusalem (John 2:23). And then, in chapter 4, he heals the son of a centurion, and the author says, "This was the second sign that Jesus did" (John 4:54). Huh? One sign, many signs, and then the second sign?[18]

What happens if we look up these verses for ourselves? Continuing John 2:11 a few words beyond the point where Ehrman adroitly cuts it off, we read:

> What Jesus did here *in Cana of Galilee* was the first of the signs....

And when we continue John 4:54 in the same way, we read:

> This was the second sign that Jesus performed *after coming from Judea to Galilee.*

The "many signs" mentioned in John 2:23 were, as Ehrman himself admits, worked in Jerusalem, which is not in Galilee. It is perfectly obvious that John is applying the ordinal numbers to the miracles in Galilee, a consideration that makes the "contradiction" evaporate. It is equally obvious that Ehrman has deliberately crafted his presentation of the alleged problem to avoid giving his readers this information.[19]

---

18. Bart Ehrman, *Jesus, Interrupted* (New York: HarperOne, 2010), 8–9.

19. In a note buried at the back of the book, Ehrman argues that the Greek of John 4:54 probably should not be *translated* as saying that this was the second miracle Jesus worked in Galilee. But this claim, right or wrong, is irrelevant. The meaning does not need to be secured by an explicit construction in the Greek of that verse. It is already obvious from the double reference to Galilee in John 2:11 and John 4:54.

Or consider this case where uncharitable reading has foisted an absurdity upon the evangelist:

> In Matthew, Jesus' disciples procure two animals for him, a donkey and a colt; they spread their garments over the two of them, and Jesus rode into town straddling them both (Matthew 21:7). It's an odd image, but Matthew made Jesus fulfill the prophecy of Scripture quite literally.[20]

No great expertise in Greek is required to see that "garments" is an admissible antecedent for "them." As the renowned Greek scholar A. T. Robertson drily remarks,

> The garments, of course. The words in Gk. might refer to the two animals, but such reference is by no means necessary. Matthew is not careful to distinguish, but common sense can do it.[21]

When "discrepancies" generated by incomplete quotations, tendentious (even ridiculous) readings and translations, arguments from silence, and completely trivial variations are set aside, Ehrman's list of errors shrinks from fifty or sixty to perhaps five or six. Those cases deserve (and have received) thoughtful scholarly treatment. But even if we were without further investigation to brand every one of them as a genuine mistake, such a small handful of errors would not, collectively, suffice to impugn the basic historical integrity of the narratives. Weighed in the balance against the positive evidence, they are insignificant.

The lines of evidence for the basic historicity of the Gospels converge and provide an incredibly strong case: multiple and early attestation in documents that boast both external and internal signs of authenticity and genuineness, the cross comparison afforded by numerous letters on the one hand and a history evidently written independently of the letters on the other, multiple points of contact between the historical narratives and archaeology and nonbiblical documents from Roman and Jewish writers, and a vivid picture of the life of the Christian community that presupposes the central facts of the Gospels. Such evidence would be

---

20. Ehrman, *Jesus, Interrupted*, 59.
21. A. T. Robertson, *A Commentary on the Gospel according to Matthew* (New York: Macmillan, 1911), 220 n. 7.

more than adequate to secure assent were it not for one fact that is, for many philosophers, of overriding significance.

The documents contain reports of miracles.

Of Miracles

The late Christopher Hitchens, in his debates with Christians, liked to put his opponents on the spot with a straight question or two, gravely asked. "Do you *really* believe that Jesus was born of a virgin? Do you *really* believe that he rose from the dead?" If the Christian answered in the affirmative, Hitchens would turn to the audience with a theatrical flourish—"Thank you. Ladies and gentlemen, my opponent has just demonstrated that science has done nothing for his worldview."

It is always a shrewd move to paint one's adversary as an enemy of science, and Hitchens rarely let slip an opportunity for good theater. But good theater is not always good reasoning. Did Hitchens *really* believe that first-century Jews didn't know where babies come from or that Roman soldiers didn't know how to kill an unarmed man? Did he doubt that peasants in an agrarian society had seen enough death to know that in the natural course of things, men who are dead—completely dead, not just mostly dead—stay that way? Christians from Pentecost onward have been shouting from the rooftops the astounding message that Jesus, who was crucified and buried, had risen bodily from the dead. Did Hitchens *really* think he could show them up by suggesting that there is something out of the ordinary about the claim?

David Hume presented the world with a false dilemma when he tried to pit reported miracles against the laws of nature. Science tells us what nature does when left to itself; miracles, if they occur at all, occur precisely because nature is *not* left to itself. Believers and skeptics agree that there is a stable causal order, a normal course of events in which virgins are not pregnant and dead men stay dead. And precisely because they are agreed on this point, it cannot be a significant piece of evidence against the occurrence of miracles. A river must flow, as one of Hume's contemporaries pointed out, before its stream can be diverted. Some conception of the ordinary course of nature is required for us even to make sense of the notion of a miracle, which otherwise could not be recognized for what it is.

Of course, many people disbelieve in the existence of God, either in the Judeo-Christian sense or in any other. A nonexistent deity raises no one from the dead. On their view, the creator is not locked out; there was never a creator to begin with. If atheism is true, miracle claims (insofar as these involve reference to a deity) must be false. So why should an atheist even bother looking into a miracle claim?

The short answer is that atheism might be wrong. Even those who strongly suspect that there is no God should not close themselves off from contrary evidence. It might take a lot to shift them from comfortable nonbelief to the uneasy suspicion that there may be something to the God idea after all. But if nothing could even in principle count against their atheism, then something like Hitchens's complaint comes back around with a vengeance: evidence does not appear to make any difference to their worldview.

Some people are comfortable in that position. They define miracles as inordinately improbable, placing them, if not out of the realm of possibility, then at least out of the reach of evidence. But I find the arguments for doing this completely unpersuasive. Any initial prejudice against miracles—any ground for assignment of a low initial probability to the claim that a miracle has occurred—cannot be any greater than the rational prejudice (great or small) against the conjunction of two claims: that there is a God who has destined his human creations for a future state of existence, and that he wants to tell them about it in such a way that they can know the message comes from him. If there is a God who wants to make such a revelation, and he wants to make it in such a way that we cannot mistake it for the mere word of man, then there is really no other way to seal it than by a miracle. A miracle would be the guarantee to us that this is a genuine word from God and not just someone's fine-sounding philosophy or a well-crafted tale. And the conjunction of those two claims should, I think, not seem to any well-informed person to be so absurdly low as to lie beyond the reach of evidence.

Still, life is short and miracle claims abound. It is all very well to speak of being open to evidence, but no sensible person goes haring off after every supernatural claim to inquire into it in detail. Even thoughtful religious believers rarely bother to look into miracle claims in any tradition other than their own. Why should the irreligious be expected to do more? And if they were, then why, it may be asked, should they begin with one religion rather than another?

The question is reasonable, and it may be as reasonably answered in terms that make no appeal to any particular religious tradition. In some circumstances, we have *prima facie* reason to doubt a miracle claim. For example, we have reason to doubt when it is reported only long after the alleged event happened, or at a great distance from the place where it happened. We have reason to doubt when the report would have been permitted to pass without examination, either because such examination would have been impossible in the nature of the case (say, with regard to an event that would leave no public traces) or because the local population would have had no motive to inquire into its truth or falsehood (because, for instance, it fell in with their own religious prejudices).[22] And it is also reasonable to doubt a miracle claim when no remotely worthy end could have been served if it had really happened—no deep questions about our origin and destiny answered, no striking teachings confirmed, no divine commission endorsed. "Let not a god intervene," as Horace wrote, "unless there be a knot worthy of a god's untying."[23]

These criteria cut a wide swath through claims of the miraculous, not because they show them definitely to be false (for a claim might fail on one or more of these points and yet be true) but because they offer a plain reason for suspicion of fraud or muddle or the growth of legend. If honest skeptics would ask the proponent of any particular miracle claim to provide some evidence that it meets the criteria, there would seldom be any serious takers. On the other hand, claims still left standing after we have applied these criteria may fairly be said to deserve a closer look. And if those skeptics would follow up with equal honesty and with the seriousness that the issues seem to merit on any that really do appear to meet the criteria, then let the epistemic chips fall where they may.

"I am not asking anyone to accept Christianity," C. S. Lewis once wrote, "if his best reasoning tells him that the weight of the evidence is against it."[24] Nor am I. Nor should anyone. But I think that the seriousness of the issues involved and the *prima facie* evidence from natural theology ought to put it on the table for thoughtful consideration even by those who have never bothered to look into the public evidence in a

---

22. I have borrowed these criteria from John Douglas, *The Criterion*, 4th ed. (Oxford: Oxford University Press, 1832).

23. *Nec Deus intersit nisi dignus vindice nodus*—Horace, *Ars Poetica* 191.

24. C. S. Lewis, *Mere Christianity* (New York: HarperOne, 2007), 116.

serious way, a group that includes—alas!—most Christians. For a serious apprehension that it *may* be true, as Joseph Butler observes in *The Analogy of Religion*, places obligations on the inquirer.[25] It can no longer be brushed aside as just one more baseless fantasy among a myriad of others.

Convergence

Philosophy, rightly and thoughtfully pursued, offers us multiple clues that point to the existence of a deity. Christianity offers us a view of God and man that goes far beyond what philosophy can attain. Yet there is, as I see it, no contradiction. Our philosophical investigations take their rise from broad features of our world or of our experience; Christianity tells us a story of God's intervention in space and time that can be tested, at multiple points, by the sort of reasoning about factual details that we rightly apply in other historical investigations. Both lead us toward the conclusion that there is a God. One simply takes us further than the other.

Neither philosophical nor historical investigation can, in strict logic, *force* us to its conclusion. But that is what we should expect. In almost every area of life, we draw conclusions and determine our actions on the basis of inconclusive data. There is no reason why the same standards ought not be applied here. And if, as I believe, the philosophical picture and the Christian one dovetail, their convergence is yet another reason to believe that both pictures are true.[26]

---

25. Joseph Butler, *The Analogy of Religion* (New York: E. P. Dutton & Co., 1906), Part 2, chapter 7 and conclusion.

26. Some of the material in this essay was commissioned for, and first appeared in, an online article for *Slate* magazine (http://www.slate.com/bigideas/are-miracles-possible/essays-and-opinions/timothy-mcgrew-opinion).

GRAHAM OPPY

Tim McGrew claims that the following argument "calls naturalism into question" (134):

1. Whatever begins to exist is caused by something else.
2. The physical universe began to exist.
3. (Therefore) The physical universe was caused to exist by something else.

Let's suppose that there is a causal network of things that cause other things to exist. Let's suppose, further, that there are first things: things that cause other things to exist but that are not themselves caused to exist. (Perhaps there is just one first thing; for the purposes of this analysis, I stipulate that it is true that there are first things if there is just one first thing.) Now, let's ask ourselves: Do first things begin to exist?

If we suppose that first things do begin to exist, then the first premise in our argument is false. So, if the argument is to have any chance of success, we need to say that first things do not begin to exist.

If we say that first things do not begin to exist, is it true that the physical universe began to exist? Well, only if the physical universe itself is not a first thing. If the initial state of the physical universe is the first state of causal reality, then—given our decision about how we are using the expression "began to exist"—it is not true that the physical universe began to exist.

McGrew thinks that there is empirical evidence in favour of premise (2). But, at best, that empirical evidence tells us that the universe does not have an infinite past. Even if that's so, we have not settled the question whether the initial state of the physical universe is the first state of causal reality.

Theism says: the physical universe was caused to exist by God. If theism is true, then the second premise of the argument is true.

Naturalism says: if there is an initial state of the physical universe, then the initial state of the physical universe is the first state of causal reality. If naturalism is true, then the second premise of the argument is false.

Obviously enough, McGrew's argument provides no reason at all to prefer theism to naturalism. Equally obviously—contrary to McGrew's explicit claim—this argument does not in any way "call naturalism into question."

What should we make of McGrew's claim that "most of the people with whom I have discussed the argument are inclined to agree [that both premises are more likely than not]" (132)? It seems plausible to me to suppose that most people would accept: (a) that all nonfirst things are caused to exist by other things; and (b) that the physical universe does not causally regress infinitely into the past. But, while premises (1) and (2) are naturally understood as expressions of (a) and (b), in the argument from premises (1) and (2) to (3), (1) and (2) cannot be interpreted in that way, on pain of rendering the argument invalid.

McGrew thinks that the following argument "undermin[es]" naturalism (135):

1. If naturalism is true, then there are no objective moral values
2. There are objective moral values
3. (Therefore) Naturalism is false

McGrew claims "premise 1 is as reasonable as nearly any claim in the whole of metaethics, and premise 2 is so obvious that we should use it as a touchstone for evaluating ethical systems" (134).

In order to assess this argument, we need to understand how we are using the expression "objective moral value." While McGrew does not give explicit guidance about this, it seems that he thinks that if it is true that it is morally wrong, always, everywhere, for everyone, to burn babies in gasoline as a spectator sport, then there are objective moral values.

I am a naturalist. There are three central tenets of my naturalism. First, causal reality just is natural reality. Second, all minds are late and local. Third, there is nothing that is divine, or sacred, or worthy of worship. I agree with McGrew that it is morally wrong, always, every-where, for everyone, to burn babies in gasoline as a spectator sport. So, by McGrew's lights, I accept premise 2: I agree that there are objective moral values. Obviously enough, though, I reject premise 1: I think that naturalism is true and that there are objective moral values; so, of course I do not think that if naturalism is true, then there are no objective moral values.

Perhaps McGrew thinks that there is some inconsistency between the tenets of my naturalism and premise 2; perhaps he thinks they can't all be true. Well, I'm a philosopher, and a naturalist, and I see no contradiction! At the very least, it is obvious that there is no *formal* contradiction between the tenets of my naturalism and premise 2. If there is a formal contradiction in my view, it must be that I am committed to some further bridging principles that connect together the subject matters of the tenets of my naturalism and premise 2. I do not believe that I am committed to any such bridging principles. Clearly, then, the argument that McGrew gave above provides no reason at all to suppose that my naturalistic view is inconsistent. This argument, too, does nothing to "undermine" naturalism or to "call it into question."

McGrew claims that there are arguments from consciousness, intentionality, reason, aesthetics, and ethics that do similarly "significant work in the cause of theism" (135). Since he does not provide these arguments for inspection, it is impossible to put them to the test. However, given that the arguments he did give do nothing to undermine naturalism or to call it in question, there ought not to be any presumption that the arguments we have not seen can do what the arguments we have seen could not. Note that I do not say that there *should* be a presumption that the arguments we have not seen cannot do what the arguments we have seen could not. In this area of philosophy, as in any other area of philosophy, every argument should be treated on its merits. Of course, I don't expect to be presented with an argument that undermines naturalism or calls it into question; but my expectations are hardly infallible. (I discuss some arguments from consciousness, intentionality, reason, aesthetics, and ethics in *The Best Argument against God*; I discuss more such arguments in *Arguing about Gods*. None of the arguments that I discuss in those works undermine naturalism or call it into question.)

McGrew's discussion of evil seems fine to me, as far as it goes. The particular logical argument from evil that he examines is unsuccessful for the reasons that he gives, and the evidential bearing on theism of facts about evil is much as he says. Of course, I reject the claims that he makes about the evidential bearing of facts about evil on naturalism. In my view, the suffering of the innocent is tragic, and the conduct of some human beings in the face of that suffering is noble (though of course there is room for argument about examples).

While the particular logical argument from evil that McGrew examines is unsuccessful, it would be hasty to conclude that there are no successful logical arguments from evil. (Similarly, even if you agree with me that the particular cosmological and moral arguments that McGrew presents in his chapter are unsuccessful, it would be hasty to conclude that there are no successful cosmological arguments and no successful moral arguments.) Logical arguments from evil have three kinds of premises: (a) premises that attribute properties to God (e.g., being omnipotent, omniscient, perfectly good, and the sole creator of all else); (b) premises that make claims about evil (e.g., that there are these particularly horrendous evils that have occurred in the course of history); and (c) premises that make claims that connect together divine attributes and evil (e.g., that a perfectly good being would eliminate evil if it could do so at no cost). Since we can be sure that we haven't yet examined all logical arguments from evil, any generalizations that we make about the failure of logical arguments from evil should involve some measure of caution.

Although the evidential bearing on theism of facts about evil is much as McGrew says, it is worth noting that theists often incur theoretical costs in order to accommodate facts about evil. Suppose, for example, that you think natural evil is the work of fallen angels. The postulation of fallen angels is an additional theoretical cost for theism relative to naturalism. Given that naturalists don't need to make new postulations in order to account for natural evil, this marks a theoretical advantage for naturalism over theism. If all else were equal, naturalism would trump any version of theism that postulated fallen angels in order to account for natural evil.

McGrew says that "the lines of evidence for the basic historicity of the Gospels converge and provide an incredibly strong case" (146). He writes further, "In any matter not religious, such an array of historical evidence would leave no reasonable doubt that the main outlines of the facts and even many of the details were correctly reported" (144). Whether there is anything to argue about here depends upon what you mean by "basic historicity" and "main outline of the facts." While some scholars want to argue that none of the naturalistically acceptable parts of the New Testament are true, I see no reason in principle why naturalists cannot allow that most of the naturalistically acceptable parts of the New Testament are true. It is no affront to naturalism that there was in the first century an inspirational teacher who was put to death by the Romans, and whose followers launched what eventually became a global religion.

The *interesting* question about historicity concerns all of those parts of the New Testament that are not naturalistically acceptable: the resurrection, the ascension, the performance of miracles, the fulfilment of prophecy, the existence and actions of God, and so on. Are there good reasons to think that the New Testament is reliable with respect to all of *these* kinds of details?

Here, it seems to me that the answer is negative. There is no independent confirmation for any of the naturalistically unacceptable details found in the New Testament texts. Where naturalistically unacceptable details are recorded in non-Christian texts, what is provided is evidently derivative from the Christian texts. Moreover, there is no other kind of evidence—e.g., archaeological remains—that supports any of the naturalistically unacceptable claims. And there are naturalistically unacceptable claims in the New Testament that one would expect to have been noted in non-Christian texts if they actually occurred. (For example, a failure of the sun for three hours in the middle of the day— with the attendant failure of the planets for three hours in the middle of the night on the other side of the globe—would have made it into astronomical records the world over.)

When we read Suetonius's account of Augustus's conception, we have no trouble identifying the fact that it is not an accurate historical record of events. The naturalistic unacceptability of the narrative is alone sufficient to tell us that the report involves some gilding of the lily. The point generalizes. We all rely upon judgments about naturalistic acceptability in making decisions about the reliability of texts and authors, both ancient and modern. In order to make exceptions to this universal critical practice, we need to have very substantial reasons. McGrew thinks that it is enough that a report does not fall into a narrow range of categories: (a) written after the fact; (b) written in a distant location; (c) almost certain to have been allowed to pass without comment; and/or (d) recording an event that would have served no remotely worthy end. The fact that it appears that Suetonius's account of Augustus's conception passes this test suggests a rather different principle: *wherever* there is naturalistic unacceptability, there is plain reason for suspicion of "fraud, or muddle, or growth of legend."

K. SCOTT OLIPHINT

I enjoyed reading Timothy McGrew's "convergence model" of Christianity and philosophy. Not surprisingly, there are a number of things his model has in common with my covenant model. McGrew's discussion of the cogency and consistency of the four Gospels is very helpful. Especially in light of Bart Ehrman's deceptions, McGrew helps us see that those who refuse to recognize the authority of Scripture will inevitably begin to invent problems with Scripture that don't exist. The source of such inventions is not the *text* of Scripture itself but the *antipathy* one holds to it.

And it is just at this point of revelational antipathy where McGrew's model differs from a covenantal approach. The differences will not be, strictly speaking, *philosophical* but will be at root *theological*. The best way to begin to address these differences is to begin with McGrew's assessment of Romans 1:

> Calvin famously reads Romans 1 as referring not to natural theology but to the *sensus divinitatis*, an inborn faculty by which, in his view, all men are given immediate and infallible knowledge of the existence and nature of God. I can see no rational ground for taking this point of view, which seems to me to *torture both the biblical text and the principles of sound historical investigation*. That some people may have direct experiences of God is something I should not wish to deny. But the further claim that everyone possesses a faculty of this sort seems to me not only groundless but flatly contrary to the experience of many believers. (129, my emphasis)

In light of this assessment, it is important, crucially so, to call McGrew's brief analysis of Romans 1:18ff. seriously into question. McGrew acknowledges the possibility of some experiential knowledge of God, but he "can see no rational ground" for understanding this section of Romans as teaching that there is such a faculty as the *sensus divinitatis*.[1] The problem is, that is exactly and explicitly what the apostle Paul *says*.

The overall logic of Paul's argument in Romans 1:18ff. is to show that *all people* are sinners and thus deserving of God's righteous justice and judgment. "What shall we conclude then? Do we have any advantage? Not at all! *For we have already made the charge that Jews and Gentiles alike are all under the power of sin*" (Rom 3:9; emphasis mine). That is, Paul's concern in Romans 1:18–3:20 is to argue the universal sinfulness of humanity.

Thus, Paul's initial concern with respect to the revelation of the wrath of God against all unrighteousness is to articulate the *reasons* for God's wrath (1:18). The first reason that he gives is that all of us, if and when we remain in our sins (and do not put our trust in Christ), "suppress the truth" (1:18). The fact of a suppression of the truth entails that it is *truth* that is suppressed. So, minimally, Scripture is confirming that all people who remain in their sins and who abide under God's wrath are subjects of that wrath, in part because (1) they all *have* the truth, and (2) they sinfully attempt to hold it down (*katechontōn*; v. 18). The next two verses describe what that truth *is*, and *how* someone comes to possess it. The truth that all have is "what may be known about God," (1:19) which includes God's "eternal power and divine nature" (1:20). The *how* of this truth includes the fact that what can be known about God is what God himself makes plain (v. 19), and that God makes himself plain in the things that have been made (v. 20).

So clear and unavoidable is this truth about God, which God himself makes plain through all that he has made, that it renders all of us "without excuse" before God (v. 20). The clear fact of Paul's teaching in this text is that, supposing there exists someone who does not know God, that person would have an excuse for his unbelief. He would stand before God and say to him, "I didn't know you." But Scripture will not allow such an excuse. It is in "*knowing God*" (*gnontes ton theon*; v. 21) that

---

1. For Calvin (following Paul), the *sensus divinitatis* is not simply knowledge of God but, as inextricably wedded to the image of God that all people are, it is *true knowledge* that all people everywhere at all times and in all places have of the true God. See, for example, John Calvin, *Institutes of the Christian Religion*, ed. John T. McNeill, trans. Ford Lewis Battles, vol. 1, The Library of Christian Classics (Louisville: Westminster John Knox, 2011), chapters 3–5.

we stand accused before him. This universal knowledge of God is what Calvin means when he argues for a *sensus divinitatis*.

Paul goes on to affirm that due to this suppression of the knowledge of God, God gives people over (1:24, 26, 28). He gives them over as an expression of his wrath to homosexuality (1:26–27), to use Paul's initial example, and to all manner of sinfulness (1:28–31).

In 1:32, the apostle summarizes his previous discussion and sets up the discussion to follow in chapter 2:

> Although they know God's righteous decree that those who do such things deserve death, they not only continue to do these very things but also approve of those who practice them.

In other words, included in the *sensus divinitatis* is a universal knowledge of God's "righteous decree" or his righteous requirements (*dikaiōma*). Included in every person's knowledge of those requirements is the knowledge that our transgressions of them are worthy of death. With the knowledge of God's character comes the knowledge of those things that violate that character. In this sense, embedded in the human condition is the knowledge of the problem of evil, as that evil is understood in light of God's character, and the knowledge that *we* are a significant part of that problem.

Paul goes on in chapter 2 of Romans to discuss that revelation of God as it is written on human hearts, to which our consciences dynamically respond (v. 15). That, too, is an aspect of the *sensus*.

Much more could be said in light of the above passages of holy Scripture, but we should be able at least to conclude that any exegesis that does not take the position above would, of necessity, itself be torturous. Whether or not this universal and persistent knowledge of God—the *sensus divinitatis*—is best denominated a "faculty" may be up for debate. But the fact that every person did, does, and will have it is unmistakable in the text of Scripture. It seems, therefore, to be an overstatement *in excelsis* to say as McGrew does that this discussion "tortures the biblical text." Rather, it takes the plain meaning of Paul's words, together with the clear logic of his argument, and recognizes Scripture's teaching on what must be the plight of every sinner apart from Christ.

The other part of McGrew's objection to Scripture's notion of a *sensus divinitatis* is that it tortures the "principles of sound historical investigation." Given what we have seen above concerning God's revelation in and through creation, this is the point where McGrew's helpful analysis of Ehrman extends more deeply and broadly. Ehrman's problems with Scripture stem not from the text of Scripture—the *data* of Scripture—but from his *initial* rejection of it as the Word of God. In an analogous way, according to Paul's argument in Romans, anyone who begins with the rejection of God or with any supposition that assumes God is *not* known through the things he has made will inevitably skew and distort the *data* of creation, in that they will hold down and suppress the clear knowledge of God given in all creation.

Given this, there can be no *mere* rational principle or *mere* historical investigation. Principles and investigations, in that they are attached to *persons*, will begin either with an assumption that God is *not* clearly revealed in all that he has made or that he is. There can be no such thing, therefore, as "sound historical investigation" that begins its activity from a religiously neutral standpoint.

McGrew avers that the notion of universal knowledge of God is opposed to sound historical investigation and is "flatly contrary to the experience of many believers" (129). But what are the criteria by which this "sound" historical investigation takes place or by which we might measure such "experience"? Suppose, for example, that the vast majority of people on the earth were committed to some kind of religion. Such a commitment might be interpreted, via "sound" historical investigation, as people innocently seeking for something higher and bigger than themselves. Or, if Romans 1–2 is correct, it could be interpreted as a suppression of the truth in unrighteousness. So also for "experience."

This is the way, for example, that Paul understood the religions of the Athenians in Acts 17. He was moved by the rampant idolatry there. But he did not interpret that idolatry as an innocent quest for something higher and bigger. Instead he told them that their "unknown God" was actually the God who needs nothing, who made everything, and in whom they live, move, and exist. In other words, Paul appealed to the truth of God that the Athenians already knew by way of natural revelation, and in that appeal he called them to repent of their idolatry.

As with Ehrman, so also with interpretations of data and history, it is the bias at the beginning that will go a long way toward determining the conclusions. If we see such interpretations of data, history, rationality, evidence, etc. through the spectacles of Scripture rather than through some supposedly "neutral" notion of fact gathering, then we will begin to see the world the way God has interpreted it rather than interpreting God on the basis of our own preferred way of seeing. We will then see all people who remain in their sins as working diligently to hold down, suppress, hide, deny, subvert, and pervert the clear knowledge of God that is continually given by God through and in the things he has made.

What determines the direction of historical investigation, of the gathering of evidence, and of rationality itself are the *principia* on the basis of which such things are carried out. It is for this reason that probability arguments of natural theology give away too much in their attempt to demonstrate a god. Not only do they assume that "evidence" (including background knowledge) will be understood in the same way by theist and atheist alike but they also, and more importantly, operate on the assumption that God has *not* made himself clearly known to all who are made in his image. They assume, contrary to Scripture's plain meaning, that those who do not believe in God *have an excuse*. They will be able to stand before God and declare that they never knew him.

But sin, in Scripture, is what it is—always and everywhere—in the context of the character of God. Sin is what it is *only* because God is who he is. Without the knowledge of God, strictly speaking, there can be no sin. This, again, is the reason that Paul's sizable list of sins in Romans 1:26–31 is what it is against the backdrop of what God is doing as he clearly reveals himself in creation, and as that revelation gets through to all made in his image. Sin is defined against the backdrop of the universal knowledge of God.

One final point in this regard needs development but will have to remain here simply as stated. Romans 1:24, 26, and 28, in speaking of God's wrathful activity in giving people over to their sins, presupposes that people are not as sinful and wicked as they could be. They are not so, *not* because a little bit of "goodness" remains in them or because they have a "spark of divinity" in them, but because God in his goodness restrains our devoted penchant to oppose him. Because of God's restraint of sin, there is much that those who are apart from Christ can accomplish. But we should recognize that such accomplishments are (1) *in spite of*, and not because of, the presumed neutrality or autonomy of unbelievers, and (2) they are what they are only because Christianity is what it is. That is, accomplishments by those outside of Christ are evidence that God is good to all people and that such accomplishments only have their proper home in the context of the Christian position.[2] Since all facts are, first of all, *God* interpreted, any interpretation by those outside of Christ that approximates God's interpretation does so because God is actively restraining the depravity that reigns in every unbelieving heart.

The "remedy" for the wrath of God—which is to say, the remedy for any and all unbelieving activity, be it in philosophy, or historical investigation, or evidence gathering, or . . . —is the grace of God in Jesus Christ. Once one begins one's task according to that grace, through faith, then philosophy and all other disciplines take their proper place.

---

2. In the words of Geerhardus Vos, "There is something in sinful man that is not compatible with sin, that protests against sin. But that is not something good in him. It is the voice of God in him who bears witness to what is right" (*Reformed Dogmatics*, ed. Richard B. Gaffin, trans. Annemie Godbehere et al., vol. 1 [Bellingham, WA: Lexham, 2012–2014], 87).

PAUL K. MOSER

Timothy McGrew offers a "convergence" perspective: "Philosophy confirms Christianity, and Christianity completes philosophy" (124). This is a hopeful perspective in its main claim, but grounded hope will need clear notions of "confirms" and "completes." McGrew looks to natural theology to advance his perspective. He states: "To find our way forward [toward convergence], we need to look into natural theology, a subdiscipline of the philosophy of religion devoted to the study of arguments for (and, in its broader forms, against) the existence of a deity" (129). Citing Psalm 19, McGrew claims that "the tradition of natural theology in Judaism remained strong through the beginning of the Christian era, where Paul's famous appeal in Romans 1 strongly echoes the more detailed presentation of cosmological and teleological reasoning in such intertestamental works as *Wisdom of Solomon*" (129). Evaluation of the convergence perspective requires an assessment of the natural theology in question and the claim about Romans 1.

McGrew's first argument of natural theology is a Kalam argument, the conclusion of which is that "the physical universe was caused to exist by something else" (131). Clearly, this conclusion does not take us to the Christian God or to any God. McGrew states: "The conclusion of the Kalam argument falls short of claiming that God exists, particularly the God of the Judeo-Christian tradition" (133). Even so, he claims the following: "There are various ways to build upon the conclusion . . . to argue for more, but for present purposes we need not take the discussion in that direction. It is enough if the argument calls naturalism into question" (134). Many (if not most) contemporary philosophers doubt, on the basis of reasons, that the Kalam argument calls naturalism into question, but we need not digress to that matter. (I mention this because McGrew reports that "most of the people with whom I have discussed the argument are inclined to agree" that the argument's premises are more likely than not.) Instead, we should note that a case for Christian faith would require more than calling naturalism into question. It would need to identify adequate evidence for the reality of the Christian God. A serious question is whether the arguments of natural theology can supply such evidence.

McGrew's second argument of natural theology concludes that "naturalism is false" (134). Here also many philosophers will have doubts, on the basis of reasons, about this conclusion, but the relevant shortcoming is that it does not yield adequate evidence for the Christian God. A neo-Platonist, for instance, could be content with the conclusion offered. Likewise, theorists from a wide range of other, non-Christian perspectives could be content with it.

The third argument of natural theology offered is an argument from the existence of consciousness. McGrew writes: "In a universe without consciousness, we have not the slightest reason to expect that consciousness will arise. . . . But if theism is true, then consciousness is built into the universe on the ground floor" (135). We can grant these claims, for the sake of argument, but then ask what exactly they contribute to a Christian perspective or even to "mere theism." Many philosophers will grant that "in a universe without consciousness, we have not the slightest reason to expect that consciousness will arise." Even so, they will not take this to indicate that the consciousness in our universe is evidence for Christian theism or even mere theism. McGrew adds that "it is notoriously difficult, within a purely naturalistic framework, to give an account of how intentionality is supposed to work" (136). This is notoriously difficult, but if truth be told, it is notoriously difficult too in a theistic—including a Christian theistic—framework. The main point, however, is that the argument from consciousness, like the previous two arguments, fails to supply adequate evidence for Christian theism.

McGrew offers a fittingly modest assessment of the value of his arguments: "The factual bases for the arguments that I have briefly discussed above play the role of clues. They point toward a conclusion richer than they can establish by themselves. Because they typically involve either uncertain or nonobvious premises or nondeductive forms of reasoning (or both), it is always possible for someone to deny the conclusions to which they point without obvious self-contradiction" (141). What the factual bases of the arguments are "clues" *for* or "point toward" will depend on what constitutes ultimate reality, and the arguments do not settle that matter. In addition, the talk of a "clue" and "point[ing] toward" is sufficiently vague to leave us puzzled. The pressing question is how the kind of "clue" or "pointing toward" in question relates to adequate evidence for Christian theism.

McGrew finds clues for theism in philosophy itself. He writes:

> Philosophy, rightly and thoughtfully pursued, offers us multiple clues that point to the existence of a deity. Christianity offers us a view of God and man that goes far beyond what philosophy can attain. . . . Our philosophical investigations take their rise from broad features of our world or of our experience; Christianity tells us a story of God's intervention in space and time that can be tested, at multiple points, by the sort of reasoning about factual details that we rightly apply in other historical investigations. Both lead us toward the conclusion that there is a God (150).

Here again the vagueness in the talk of "clues" and "point to" hinder assessment, including confirmation, of the claim at hand. In addition, if philosophy does "point to" a deity, we need a robust case to answer a simple question: *Which* deity? The quasi deity of Plato's *Timaeus*? Or the quasi deity of Aristotle's *Metaphysics*? Or some other deity? In any case, we lack a case for the pointing of philosophy to the Christian God, the God of Abraham, Isaac, Jacob, and Jesus. I also doubt that we should leave the testing of Christian theism at the level of testing in "other historical investigations." Christian theism does rest on historical claims, but it also exceeds them in its position on God's work in the present.

Given the gist of the convergence perspective, particularly its claim that "philosophy confirms Christianity," we might have expected a case for the position that the arguments of natural theology *confirm* Christian theism. McGrew, however, offers a more modest claim: "I think that the seriousness of the issues involved and the *prima facie* evidence from natural theology ought to put [Christianity] on the table for thoughtful consideration even by those who have never bothered to look into the public evidence in a serious way, a group that includes—alas!—most Christians" (149–50). Putting Christianity on the table for thoughtful consideration does seem advisable, but it does not bring adequate evidence for (endorsing) Christian theism. In addition, it seems that

Christianity, owing to its potential explanatory value at least, should be on the table for thoughtful consideration even if all of the arguments of natural theology fail. It is unclear, at any rate, why McGrew thinks that the case for Christian theism depends on arguments of natural theology. The writers of the New Testament did not hold this view, and therefore the New Testament itself is free of arguments of natural theology.

McGrew tries to locate natural theology in Paul's Epistle to the Romans. He claims: "The tradition of natural theology in Judaism remained strong through the beginning of the Christian era, where Paul's famous appeal in Romans 1 strongly echoes the more detailed presentation of cosmological and teleological reasoning in such inter-testamental works as *Wisdom of Solomon*" (129). It is noteworthy that McGrew understands "natural theology" in terms of "arguments for (and, in its broader forms, against) the existence of a deity" (129). Many Christian apologists have made this kind of claim about Paul's position in Romans 1, but the claim to find natural theology there does not withstand scrutiny.

Paul does not use an argument of natural theology in his early speech at Athens (Acts 17:16–31) or in the first chapter of his later Epistle to the Romans. He nowhere infers that God exists on the basis of premises suitable to natural theology. In particular, Romans 1 does not include a natural-theology argument from nature to God or from anything in nature to God. Paul comments as follows in Romans 1:19–20: "What can be known about God is plain to them, because God has shown it to them. Ever since the creation of the world his eternal power and divine nature, invisible though they are, have been understood and seen through the things he has made" (NRSV). Paul claims that "*God* has shown" things about God to humans, but he does not suggest that there is a natural-theology argument from nature (or from some features of nature) for God's existence. As a result, there is no suggestion in Romans of a design argument or a first-cause argument for God's existence. The arguments of natural theology find no foothold in Paul.

The numerous Christian apologists who attribute natural theology to Paul postulate something foreign to Paul in connection with his actual statements. Their position rests on misleading exegesis, and we have no need or good reason to undertake such exegesis. The God acknowledged by Paul can self-manifest God's reality *through* nature to humans without supplying any kind of argument of natural theology. Paul assumed as much and hence avoided any argument from natural theology for God's existence. A rough analogy is that I can reveal myself to you through my cell phone, but there is no good argument from the existence of the cell phone to my existence. An agent's using something as a means to self-manifestation does not entail that the thing used supplies an argument for that agent's existence. Many Christian apologists miss this important point in their zeal for the arguments of natural theology. They are looking in the wrong place for the needed evidence, which Paul finds in the interpersonal work of God's intervening personal Spirit (see, e.g., Rom 5:5, 8:15–16; 2 Cor 1:22; cf. Eph 1:13–14).[3]

The New Testament writers could have used arguments of natural theology, but they chose not to do so. This is significant, and it raises the question of why they avoided such arguments. Obviously, they were not fideists who opposed the use of evidence or arguments regarding God. Instead, I propose, they valued evidence that was not speculative in a way that is subject to quick doubt and easy rejection. In short, they sought a kind of resilient evidence that was not supplied by arguments of natural theology. The core of this evidence was God's self-manifestation in human experience, in keeping with God's being *sui generis* and worthy of worship. It would be a mistake, then, to assume that Christian apologists can improve on the New Testament writers by offering arguments of natural theology. I suggest, in particular, that it would show poor philosophical judgment to suppose that one could improve significantly on the religious epistemology of the apostle Paul.

I conclude with a dilemma for advocates of the arguments of natural theology. Those arguments, including those offered by McGrew, do not lead us to a God worthy of worship and hence do not take us to the Christian God. This raises a pressing question: What kind of evidence could take one from the lesser gods of natural theology (if we can get even to such gods) to the Christian God? Either we have such evidence or we do not. If we do have such evidence, say from divine self-manifestation to humans, why should we suppose that the tenuous contribution of natural theology is needed after all? It seems in that

---

3. For illumination of this interpersonal work, see Herbert H. Farmer, *The World and God* (London: Nisbet, 1935). See also Paul K. Moser, *The Severity of God* (Cambridge: Cambridge University Press, 2013).

case that the contribution of natural theology is epistemically dispensable. If, however, we do not have the evidence in question, we should refrain from claiming that natural theology "leads to" Christian theism. I recommend, finally, that we thus refrain.

TIMOTHY MCGREW

Ad Moser

Paul Moser does not like natural theology. If he were content to say merely that some of the arguments for the existence of God do not seem cogent to him or that those arguments do not take us all the way to the Christian God, we would have some common ground. I said quite explicitly in my opening essay that the factual bases of these arguments are clues that point toward a conclusion richer than they can establish by themselves.

But Moser goes further: he finds the very idea of clues that point toward the existence of God to be vague and puzzling. I am puzzled by his puzzlement. Does Moser really not know what a clue is? We use them everywhere—in law, medicine, automotive repair, history, cosmology, forensic detection—and in all of these areas we get along well enough without the benefit of a technical explication. Still, to satisfy his curiosity, I am happy to explain more formally what I mean by the term. A piece of evidence E *confirms* a hypothesis H just in case $P(E|H) > P(E|{\sim}H)$.[1] It is not necessary for confirmation that $P(H|E) > 0.5$. When there are multiple pieces of evidence $E_1, ..., E_n$,

$$\frac{P(H|E_1 \& ... \& E_n)}{P({\sim}H|E_1 \& ... \& E_n)} = \frac{P(H)}{P({\sim}H)} \times \frac{P(E_1|H)}{P(E_1|{\sim}H)} \times ... \times \frac{P(E_n|H \& E_1 \& ... \& E_{n-1})}{P(E_n|{\sim}H \& E_1 \& ... \& E_{n-1})}$$

---

1. This is the most widely used definition of *confirmation* in the philosophical literature today.

When those pieces of evidence work together to confirm H, each contributing something to that confirmation, I refer to them as *clues*. Readers interested in seeing how many clues may in aggregate amount to a powerful argument for H should consult Richard Swinburne's work.[2]

Moser wonders to which deity these clues point. The answer is that they point to the fact that *a deity exists*; further evidence is required to say more about that deity's identity and actions. But it is quite misleading to say, as Moser does, that they point only to the existence of a "lesser" deity, as if these arguments put some upper bound on divine power or goodness. Perhaps he is stumbling over the fact that such arguments may simultaneously raise the probability of the existence of the Christian God and non-Christian deities. But when we have a partition with more than two members, a body of evidence may simultaneously raise the probability of several incompatible hypotheses. This is not a piece of special pleading on behalf of natural theology; it is an elementary fact about confirmation and evidence.

Romans 1 presents a special problem for Moser's view, and he therefore tries to avoid its obvious implications. God might, he says, make his eternal power and divine nature known through creation in something like the way that Moser might reveal himself through a cell phone—the *existence* of the cell phone need not be evidence for the existence of Moser. I do not wish to press too hard on a point that Moser himself calls merely "a rough analogy," but I cannot see how it is supposed to help his case. Why, if that were all he means, does Paul bother referring to the physical creation at all?

Paul's language is very much of a piece not only with Psalm 19 but also with other strands of Second-Temple Jewish thought. The pseudepigraphal Wisdom of Solomon, which in the first century was one of the most popular and widely read pieces of Jewish wisdom literature, contains an explicit piece of natural theology that fairly begs to be laid side by side with Romans 1:

> For all people who were ignorant of God were foolish by nature;
> and they were unable from the good things that are seen to know

---

2. For example, Richard Swinburne, *The Existence of God*, 2nd ed. (Oxford: Oxford University Press, 2004), chapter 1.

the one who exists, nor did they recognize the artisan while paying heed to his works; but they supposed that either fire or wind or swift air, or the circle of the stars, or turbulent water, or the luminaries of heaven were the gods that rule the world. If through delight in the beauty of these things people assumed them to be gods, let them know how much better than these is their Lord, for the author of beauty created them. And if people were amazed at their power and working, let them perceive from them how much more powerful is the one who formed them. For from the greatness and beauty of created things comes a corresponding perception of their Creator. Yet these people are little to be blamed, for perhaps they go astray while seeking God and desiring to find him. For while they live among his works, they keep searching, and they trust in what they see, because the things that are seen are beautiful. Yet again, not even they are to be excused; for if they had the power to know so much that they could investigate the world, how did they fail to find sooner the Lord of these things? (Wis 13:1–9 NRSV)

Paul was no fool; he must have known that his language would bring this passage to the minds of at least many of his readers. I leave it to those who value the historical and sociological context of first-century Palestinian Judaism to determine whether it is Moser or the "apologists" he deprecates whose position rests on misleading exegesis, positing something foreign to Paul's thought.

"McGrew," Moser says, "thinks that the case for Christian theism depends on arguments of natural theology" (166). He is mistaken. I do not think that one must understand and accept *any* of the arguments of natural theology in order to have a rational belief in Christianity. Still, those arguments are not only interesting in their own right but also useful, since they add to the confirmation of Christianity, weaving a tough safety net beneath our beliefs. And some people cannot be induced to attend to the historical evidence at all unless they are first brought to the point of considering theism as a serious possibility. These considerations dissolve Moser's concluding "dilemma."

Ad Oppy

Reading Graham Oppy's response gave me the feeling that we had wandered into the Monty Python Argument Clinic: this isn't so much argument as simple contradiction. His critique of the Kalam argument amounts, for all I can see, to saying that whatever begins to exist is caused to exist by something else, unless that is naturalistically inconvenient. In that case, we will call it "the first state of causal reality," by which verbal maneuver we will declare it to be exempt from the causal principle. This evasion looks like a textbook example of the taxicab fallacy. Oppy is willing to take the principle as far as he wants to go, but he is quick to dismiss it before it takes him any further.

Oppy protests that he too thinks burning babies in gasoline as a spectator sport is always wrong. I should be worried if he did not! But he is left with the puzzling problem of how to account for the existence or emergence of objective moral values in a naturalistic world. The mere absence of a formal contradiction in his view would not mean that the problem of moral value "does nothing" to undermine naturalism. There are more ways to be unreasonable than by formal self-contradiction. Giving an account of the origin of a thing (say, of moral value) that makes it deeply unclear why we ought to value it as we do is one of those ways.

When we turn to the historical evidence, Oppy is willing to grant *arguendo* "that most of the naturalistically acceptable parts of the New Testament are true," but he persists in complaining that there is no "independent confirmation" for any of the "naturalistically unacceptable details" (155). As I have already argued, the objection is unreasonable. Those who were persuaded of these things almost inevitably became Christians. The one case where he spells out what he wants is the three hours of darkness during Jesus's crucifixion. Oppy interprets the Synoptic authors as saying that the sun itself ceased to shine for this period of time, and he objects that we should expect some record of this event from the astronomers. But this seems to me a serious overreading of a passage that refers at most to an auspiciously timed darkness across the land.[3]

---

3. Edward Gibbon, in his *History of the Decline and Fall of the Roman Empire*, vol. 1 (London: W. Strahan, 1776), 518, remarks with a thinly veiled sneer that although "a distinct chapter of Pliny" is "devoted to eclipses of an extraordinary nature and unusual duration," the

The real problem, I fear, is that when it comes to miracles, Oppy wants to do history *a priori*. How else to account for the fact that he thinks "the naturalistic unacceptability of the narrative is *alone* sufficient" (155; emphasis mine) for us to reject the reliability of the text? I offered some reasons to take reports of miracles seriously enough to investigate them further, such as their not being distant in time from the events they report and their not being allowed to pass unchallenged. The central Christian miracle claim, the resurrection of a crucified peasant, was proclaimed openly and in the teeth of the Jewish opposition in Jerusalem less than two months after it was supposed to have occurred. Oppy refers confidently to Suetonius's account of the conception of Augustus as if it were a parallel in these respects. But Suetonius was writing nearly two centuries after the birth of Augustus, and he was attributing a supernatural conception to a universally revered emperor who had already been worshiped as a deity for three generations. It is a very useful thing to compare the evidence of the Gospels to that of the records of secular history. But to receive the full benefit of this procedure, one must make a serious attempt to get the basic facts straight about both.

Ad Oliphint

Scott Oliphint has gone to some length to lay out his reading of the central part of Romans 1. Unfortunately, at the key point (Romans 1:20), he fails to engage with Paul's reference to "what has been made." The obvious interpretation, and one consonant with the parallels to Wisdom of Solomon, is that Paul is alluding to the visible physical evidence treated in classic arguments from natural theology and saying that anyone who fails to see the obvious implications of that evidence is without excuse. To say that Paul is referring instead to an internal awareness of God's power and majesty is to leave his reference to creation a complete mystery. That is most certainly *not* "exactly and explicitly what the apostle Paul says" (158).[4]

---

darkness at Jesus's crucifixion goes unmentioned there. But Gibbon is not being candid with his readers; the "distinct chapter" of Pliny (*Natural History* 2.30) is a mere eighteen words long. *Male verum examinat omnis corruptus judex* (Horace, *Satires* 2.2.8)—a corrupt judge does not search carefully for the truth.

4. Readers who wish to pursue this question should consult James Barr, *Biblical Faith and Natural Theology* (Oxford: Clarendon Press, 1993), chapter 3.

Oliphint and I agree in our negative appraisal of Bart Ehrman's handling of the New Testament. But Oliphint goes further, insisting that no one can come to historical investigation without either assuming *ab initio* that God is *not* clearly revealed in all creation or assuming *ab initio* that he *is*. There are undoubtedly people who come to the subject with one or the other of these assumptions, but neither experience, nor logic, nor proper exegesis suggests that such prejudication is inevitable. And it is both injurious and counterproductive to assume, without very strong reasons, that someone who is apparently seeking the truth is in fact implacably opposed to finding it.

This point is at the heart of our disagreement. Oliphint emphatically denies that there is any neutral ground between Christians and non-Christians, any possibility of examining the data without assuming one's conclusion.[5] That is why he dismisses all talk of rational principles and historical investigation that presupposes the possibility of a neutral standpoint. I am persuaded that he is wrong. Some people, by God's grace, approach the question of the truth of Christianity with a genuine desire to know whether it is true, a willingness to believe it if it is, and an expectation that the evidence, properly sifted and weighed, will tell them where the truth lies. Those who seek the truth with their whole heart will find it; for God is not only just but good.

---

5. See for example K. Scott Oliphint, *Covenantal Apologetics: Principles and Practice in Defense of our Faith* (Wheaton: Crossway, 2013), 17, 110–14, 208, 239, etc.

CONFORMATION MODEL

PAUL K. MOSER

> I [God] revealed myself to those who did not ask for me.
>
> Romans 10:20

> In the wisdom of God the world through its wisdom did not know him.
>
> 1 Corinthians 1:21

My approach to Christian philosophy offers philosophy under, or *conformed* to, God in Christ, which involves a distinctive kind of wisdom, namely, God's wisdom in Christ. If philosophy is the love and pursuit of wisdom, Christian philosophy is the love and pursuit of God's wisdom under divine authority in Christ, which calls for an ongoing volitional union with Christ, including one's belonging to God in Christ. The latter wisdom contrasts with what Paul calls "human wisdom." If someone finds this approach to Christian philosophy too demanding, a simple question arises: too demanding *for what?* The fact that this approach challenges business as usual among professional philosophers is no reason against this approach. On the contrary, we should expect such a challenge given the transformative and redemptive kind of divine wisdom found in God in Christ. The remaining question is whether we are *willing* to be conformed to this wisdom and to God in Christ. Our philosophy will be thus conformed when its motive and content are subjected fully to the good news of God in Christ. The details must be discerned by God's spiritual wisdom on offer.

How, if at all, does Christian faith benefit from philosophy of the general sort immortalized by Plato and Aristotle? We know that Christian faith benefits from the Hebrew wisdom traditions, but this does not answer the previous question. The Hebrew wisdom traditions are different in kind from the philosophy found in Plato and Aristotle. This is no surprise once we see the sharp difference between the God of the Hebrews and the gods of Plato and Aristotle. As one's God goes, so also goes one's wisdom.

This essay contends that the unique character of the Hebrew-Christian God sets Hebrew-Christian wisdom and philosophy apart, not only from the gods of the ancient philosophers (and many subsequent philosophers) but also from the wisdom and philosophy of the latter philosophers. Many Christian writers have neglected this lesson, but this essay will offer a corrective. We shall see that, in a Christian perspective, human wisdom and philosophy need to be conformed to Christ, "in whom are hidden all the treasures of wisdom and knowledge" (Col 2:3). In other words, Christ is Lord not only of our behavior but of our wisdom and philosophy as well. A denial of this would entail a denial of the lordship of Christ. I contend that wisdom and philosophy benefit Christian faith only when they are conformed to the lordship of God in Christ. The apostle Paul has the correct account of this matter (even though his account is widely ignored by Christians), and therefore we will attend to his insights and apply them to our topic.

Wisdom and Philosophy

What is Wisdom?

We may think of wisdom in general as the special knowledge that enables us to prioritize our values and valued things and to guide our plans and actions in ways that are good. In this perspective, we can distinguish between evaluative wisdom (concerning values and valued things) and practical wisdom (concerning plans and actions). Both kinds of wisdom are important in Christian faith and life, because Christians are responsible for good evaluation and good conduct. The neglect of either kind of wisdom undermines a good Christian life as well as a good human life.

Socrates seems underwhelmed by human wisdom apart from God's wisdom, because he holds that "real wisdom is the property of God," and that wisdom apart from God is "really worthless" (Plato, *Apology* 23a–b [Tredennick]). This bold perspective makes theology directly relevant—even indispensable—to an account of real wisdom. Very few philosophers, however, have followed suit. Many have tried to secure and explain wisdom without dependence on God as its source or owner, and even without acknowledging the existence of God. The results have not been encouraging.

Plato holds that wisdom leads to happiness (*Meno* 88c) but requires a kind of human "purification" (*Phaedo* 69c) because it gives humans an escape from evil (*Phaedo* 107c–d). I suspect that Plato and Socrates agreed on the latter point about wisdom. In the *Laws*, however, Plato has the Athenian say: "Righteousness, temperance, and wisdom [are] our salvation, and these have their home in the living might of the gods, though some faint trace of them is also plainly to be seen dwelling here within ourselves" (10.906b [Taylor]). Socrates may be more pessimistic here than Plato or at least than the Athenian, given his aforementioned claim in the *Apology* that wisdom in humans, apart from God, is "really worthless."

Plato's "salvation" through wisdom includes the deliverance of the human mind or soul from the world of change into acquaintance with the immutable constituents of reality (see *Phaedo* 79). Following Parmenides, Plato and Aristotle portray reality and God as immutable and impassible, and they evidently hold that perfection requires such features of God. So God is unmoved and unmovable, without passions or emotions. This view influenced Philo and Clement of Alexandria, among other thinkers in the Jewish and Christian traditions around the time of Jesus, and it still has many proponents today. The biblical story of the active, self-manifesting Hebrew-Christian God, however, does not fit with their static portrait of God.

If God is affective (having emotions), then significant lessons follow for knowing God, for faith in God, and for divine wisdom, as well as for the role of philosophy in knowing God, in faith in God, and in divine wisdom. We shall see what these lessons are in connection with the divine gift of Christ crucified, but we first need to introduce some considerations about philosophy.

What is Philosophy?

I favor an approach to "philosophy" that has normative value (and so not just *anything* can qualify as philosophy) and fits with the etymology of the term. As a *practice*, it is the love and pursuit of *wisdom*, where wisdom is an objective reality, the special kind of knowledge noted previously and not just what some person or group says it is. As *content*, philosophy is what qualifies as a suitable product of such a practice. People can model the love and pursuit of wisdom without paying dues to a professional society of philosophers or without teaching in an academic department of philosophers. In many Western societies, professional academic philosophy seems to have a monopoly on the discipline of philosophy, but that is more of an appearance than a reality. The discipline still allows for philosophers like Socrates, who had no professional or academic affiliation.

What of "Christian philosophy"? Perhaps there are as many views of what it is as there are Christian philosophers. In any case, we need at least a rough idea of Christian philosophy in order to understand how the philosophy espoused by some Christians bears on Christian faith and life. Etienne Gilson has offered what seems to be a straightforward approach at first glance: "We call Christian philosophy the use made of philosophical notions by the Christian writers. . . ."[1] The big question, of course, concerns when a notion is "philosophical" and when not. The issue is highly controversial among philosophers and resists any simple answer.

We get an idea of Gilson's position in his following remark: "Christianity, itself centered upon the living person of Christ, is less a speculative view of reality than a way of life. It is not a philosophy; it is a religion."[2] This suggests that, in Gilson's opinion, a philosophy is a "speculative view of reality" and a philosophical notion is a notion that

---

1. Etienne Gilson, *History of Christian Philosophy in the Middle Ages* (New York: Random House, 1955), v.

2. Gilson, *History of Christian Philosophy*, 5.

figures importantly (substantively, and not just formally) in a speculative view of reality. Gilson denies that Christianity, as a way of life focused upon "the living person of Christ," is a philosophy. He apparently finds its focus upon the person of Christ to be inadequately speculative as a view of reality to qualify as a philosophy. This seems plausible in contrast with traditional philosophy, and we shall return to a contrast between distinctively Christian knowing and speculative philosophy.

Gilson finds the wisdom involved in Christianity to be different from the wisdom of the philosophers. He writes: "When Saint Paul wrote that Christ was 'wisdom' [1 Cor. 1:30], ... he was saying that what the philosophers had vainly expected from their so-called wisdom, the Christians had just received from Christ, and this was not a philosophical statement; it was a religious one."[3] In Gilson's perspective, philosophers have "so-called wisdom," and they "vainly expect" something important from it. In contrast, the Christians receive wisdom from Christ that actually delivers what the philosophers had expected from their wisdom. I suspect that Gilson has the salvation of humans in mind, perhaps in light of the Platonic view—mentioned previously—that wisdom yields salvation for humans. We may assume that this salvation includes human knowledge of God, but it is controversial whether the "so-called wisdom" of the philosophers includes knowledge of God. We shall return to the latter issue.

According to Abraham Heschel, "The disturbing fact is that philosophy remains the perpetual rival to religion. It is a power that would create religion if it could. Again and again, it has tried its talent at offering answers to ultimate questions and has failed."[4] Heschel includes questions about God's reality and presence among "ultimate questions," and he holds that philosophy does not offer adequate answers to such questions. In particular, he doubts that philosophy can show that God exists: "There are no proofs for the existence of the God of Abraham. There are only witnesses."[5] One problem, according to Heschel, is that the God of Abraham is a personal, passionate agent who hides from people at times in order to instruct and challenge them. So this God

---

3. Gilson, *History of Christian Philosophy*, 6.
4. Abraham Heschel, *God in Search of Man: A Philosophy of Judaism* (New York: Jewish Publication Society of America, 1955), 11.
5. Abraham Heschel, *The Prophets* (New York: Harper & Row, 1962), 27.

is not constantly available to people for their convenient speculation or proof. This is not the God of the traditional philosophers.

Heschel finds a special task for philosophy of religion in relation to religion and philosophy. He explains: "[Philosophy of religion's] task is not only to examine the claim of religion in the face of philosophy, but also to refute the claim of philosophy when it presumes to become a substitute for religion, to prove the inadequacy of philosophy as a religion."[6] Heschel would add that philosophy of religion also has the task to challenge the claim of philosophy when it presumes to offer a way to knowledge of God. He doubts that philosophy has that capacity. I share his doubt and will explain the basis for my doubt, while contending that Christian philosophy must be conformed to Christ.

God's Wisdom and Revelation

God's Wisdom

Whatever bearing philosophy has on Christian faith, a distinctive kind of wisdom figures in the early Christian movement, starting with Jesus himself. According to Luke's Gospel, "Jesus increased in wisdom and in years, and in divine and human favor" (Luke 2:52 NRSV). In addition, Luke portrays Jesus as linking wisdom to his ministry and remarking that "wisdom is vindicated by all her children" (Luke 7:35 NRSV; cf. Matt 11:19). Even so, Jesus suggests that he himself is superior to Solomon, the famous dispenser of wisdom in the Hebrew Bible (see Luke 11:29–32; cf. Matt 12:42). In addition, he offers the following promise to his disciples: "I will give you words and a wisdom that none of your opponents will be able to withstand or contradict" (Luke 21:15 NRSV). In Mark's Gospel, some in the synagogue ask the following about Jesus: "What is this wisdom that has been given to him?" (Mark 6:2 NRSV; cf. Matt 13:54). The Synoptic Gospels, then, portray Jesus as having a reputation for wisdom, although a wisdom of a distinctive kind. We need to identify this kind of wisdom.

The apostle Paul offers a profound approach to wisdom in his letters—primarily in 1 Corinthians—but his approach is widely neglected by Christian philosophers and by Christians in general. He acknowledges God as the source of human wisdom via a divine gift in

---

6. Heschel, *God in Search of Man*, 11–12.

Christ, and his approach is more developed than that of Socrates in Plato's writings. Paul agrees with the book of Isaiah that God aims to "destroy the wisdom of the wise" (1 Cor 1:19, quoting Isa 29:14; cf. 1 Cor 3:18–20). The people called "the wise" here try to make do without God's true wisdom, understood by Paul for his time as God's wisdom in Christ. As Joseph Fitzmyer notes, "'Human wisdom' . . . denotes the mindset of some Corinthian Christians who were denying the soteriological significance of Christ's cross or crucifixion."[7] We shall see, however, that the controversy concerned more than the saving significance of the cross; it included the matter of *knowing God* via human wisdom. In Corinth, some sought wisdom that had no need for God in Christ crucified, and therefore Paul countered with the central role of Christ crucified in God's wisdom and power. This led to Paul's striking remark: "I decided to know nothing among you except Jesus Christ, and him crucified" (1 Cor 2:2 NRSV). Paul had in mind the risen Christ and not just the earthly Jesus.

Paul announces to the Corinthian Christians, "My speech and my proclamation were not with plausible words of wisdom, but with a demonstration of the Spirit and of power, *so that* your faith might not rest on human wisdom but on the power of God" (1 Cor 2:4–5, emphasis added). Paul desires that faith in God "not rest on human wisdom but on the power of God," because "in the wisdom of God, the world did not know God through [its] wisdom" (1 Cor 1:21). This concern is important in understanding the basis—including the evidential basis—of Christian faith in God; therefore, we will attend to its meaning. Paul's approach to wisdom bears on knowing God and not just on how God saves people. In other words, it has epistemological import.[8]

Paul contrasts "God's wisdom, secret and hidden, which God decreed before the ages for our glory," with this human wisdom (1 Cor 2:7 NRSV). He also contrasts "God's wisdom" with "the wisdom of the world" (1 Cor 1:20–23). I take the two contrasts to be substantially the same. One key difference between the categories contrasted is that

7. Joseph A. Fitzmyer, *First Corinthians*, AB 32 (New Haven: Yale University Press, 2008), 157.

8. As emphasized by Alexandra R. Brown in *The Cross and Human Transformation* (Minneapolis: Fortress, 1995) and in "Apocalyptic Transformation in Paul's Discourse on the Cross," *Word & World* 16 (1996): 427–36.

God's wisdom has the divine power (*dynamis*), including the power of self-giving *agapē*, to give a lasting good life with God to receptive humans as an alternative to despair, whereas human wisdom lacks such power. Only God's wisdom, then, can empower human salvation as a lasting good life anchored in good and unselfish personal relationships under God. Such life is impervious to final death just as God is.

God's wisdom includes the message of Christ crucified (1 Cor 2:7–8), and Paul speaks of "Christ [crucified] the power of God and the wisdom of God" (1 Cor 1:24). He reports that he did not proclaim the gospel "with eloquent wisdom, so that the cross of Christ might not be emptied of its power" (1 Cor 1:17 NRSV). Obscuring, diminishing, or ignoring the significance of the cross of Christ would put one at odds with the wisdom that God uses to undermine the wisdom of the world. Here we have a stark contrast between God's wisdom in the cross of Christ and the wisdom of the world, which is the kind of wisdom God seeks to destroy. Christian philosophers should attend to this important contrast.

God chose the wisdom in the cross of Christ "so that no one might boast in the presence of God" (1 Cor 1:29 NRSV). In Paul's account, God is the source of our wisdom, and the crucified Christ "has become for us wisdom from God" in order to replace our boasting in humans and our own achievements with boasting in the Lord (1 Cor 1:29–31; cf. 1 Cor 3:21). Fitzmyer explains:

> For Paul, boasting denotes the fundamental mindset of human beings in their relation to God, manifested especially in the pursuit of their own ability and wisdom. It's an attitude with which God in the Old Testament already found fault. . . . Paul insists: humans cannot bring about their salvation by wisdom in any ordinary or natural sense through allegiance to human beings or by their accomplishments. In [1 Cor] 4:7 he will insist further that one's standing before God is itself a gift: "What do you have that you did not receive?"[9]

Boasting in humans detracts from the credit due to God alone—including in the area of human knowledge of God and not only in the area of salvation. It robs God of honor appropriate to God alone in his self-revelation to humans, particularly in Christ. In doing so, it obscures

---

9. Fitzmyer, *First Corinthians*, 163–64.

human indebtedness to God and exaggerates the importance of humans in relation to God's wisdom and power. Such human pride, devoid of proper honor and gratitude toward God (Rom 1:21), leads humans to trust in a false security, such as in their own thinking about God. In contrast, God in Christ intervenes to call for trust in what is trustworthy: God and his promise of the power of new life in the crucified Christ.

What is the life-giving power in the cross of Christ? Paul writes: "God proves his love for us in that while we still were sinners Christ died for us" (Rom 5:8 NRSV). Leander Keck rightly has called this theme "the heart of Paul's christology," adding: "It is the congruence between Jesus's demeanor and God's character that makes it possible for the Jesus event to be a revelation of God's righteousness, and not of God's arbitrariness or of Jesus's victimization at the hands of God."[10] Paul would add that the congruence depends on Jesus's being the obedient "Son of God" (see Gal 2:20; Phil 2:5–8) rather than an ordinary human who—contrary to Gethsemane—opts for selfish ways over God's ways. The divine righteousness is God's perfect goodness that, in Christ crucified, offers to *ungodly* people the power to be in a right relationship with God by grace, without their earning or merit (see Rom 3:26; 4:1–5).[11]

How does "eloquent wisdom," or the wisdom of the world, threaten or obscure the power of God's righteous love in Christ? God's self-manifestation of his love for us in the death and resurrection of Christ is, of course, *God's* doing, and uniquely so. Indeed, if God's character is uniquely one of righteous love, then divine self-manifestation will be the ideal way to manifest that character, and other means will fall short. So we humans should not take credit for it or diminish its importance in our pride or our quest for achievement and credit—intellectual or otherwise. Whether in Jewish, Hellenistic, or other human wisdom that does not credit God in Christ, eloquent wisdom from humans calls attention to human speakers in their eloquence. It points to a human achievement in a way that ignores or diminishes the importance of what God has done

10. Leander Keck, "Biblical Preaching as Divine Wisdom," in *A New Look at Preaching*, ed. John Burke (Wilmington, DE: Michael Glazier, 1993), 36.

11. Cf. Ernst Käsemann, "'The Righteousness of God' in Paul," in *New Testament Questions of Today*, trans. W. J. Montague (London: SCM, 1969); idem, *Commentary on Romans*, trans. G. W. Bromiley (Grand Rapids: Eerdmans, 1980), 105–13; Leander Keck, *Paul and His Letters*, 2nd ed. (Philadelphia: Fortress, 1988), 110–22; idem, *Romans* (Nashville: Abingdon, 2005), 101–33; and Robin Scroggs, *Christology in Paul and John* (Philadelphia: Fortress, 1988), 33–41.

in Christ, the true wisdom of God. It thus runs afoul of God's unique wisdom and power.

We should mention an important lesson overlooked by many philosophers. Speculative human arguments in natural theology, including such arguments for God's existence, ignore or neglect the importance of God's unique self-manifestation of redemptive power in Christ, that is, the divine power of righteous love (see Rom 3:21–26). This is part of what makes them speculative rather than experiential toward God. Such arguments call attention to human reasoners in their speculative reasoning skills, as if God's self-manifestation is somehow deficient, unreal, dubious, shameful, or embarrassing. The apostle Paul, in contrast, invoked a divine claim to self-manifestation suggested in Isaiah 65:1: "I [God] have *shown myself* to those who did not ask for me" (Rom 10:20, emphasis added; cf. Rom 1:19).[12] The idea of God "showing himself" to humans is central to the biblical story of God's dealings with humans.[13] It also figures in Paul's blunt remark: "I am not ashamed of the gospel; it is the power of God for salvation to everyone who has faith, to the Jew first and also to the Greek" (Rom 1:16 NRSV). Paul thus did not try, or need to try, to mitigate any cognitive shame with speculative arguments from philosophy. (We shall return to this point in connection with Romans 5:5.)

The God of the crucified Christ aims to destroy speculative philosophical alternatives to the true wisdom of God in Christ. They obscure and interfere with the true, unique article from God alone, who self-manifests his righteous love without speculative philosophy. Therefore, to redeem humans with the power and wisdom of the crucified Christ, God does not need or desire human eloquence, the speculative arguments of philosophers, or anything else that puffs up humans. God has the power to self-manifest his righteous and gracious character in Christ's death and resurrection without relying on human achievement and pride. As a result, Paul states: "May I never boast of anything except the cross of our Lord Jesus Christ, by which the world has been crucified to me, and I to the world. For neither circumcision nor uncircumcision

---

12. See also Joseph A. Fitzmyer, *Romans*, AB 33 (New York: Doubleday, 1993), 600.

13. See Samuel Terrien, *The Elusive Presence* (San Francisco: Harper & Row, 1978); Paul K. Moser, "God without Argument," in *Is Faith in God Reasonable?*, ed. Corey Miller and Paul Gould (New York: Routledge, 2014).

is anything; but a new creation is everything!" (Gal 6:14–15 NRSV). In other words, God's work of making people new in Christ is the boast-worthy work. Just as God's power of original creation did not rely on humans, neither do God's power of re-creation in Christ nor human knowledge thereof await help from humans in their worldly wisdom or speculative arguments.

Revelation

Paul holds that God is self-revealed in the cross and resurrection of Christ, and this view bears on how we are to understand the relevance of philosophy to Christian faith. Leander Keck has offered the following reflection on this divine self-revelation:

> A revelatory event . . . is one which does more than trigger an insight; it becomes part of the insight permanently because it becomes the prism through which alone the insight can be seen. A revelatory event is one to which one returns again and again because it has the capacity not only to repeat the original disclosure but to keep on unfolding its meaning into one situation after another. In this case, the relation between event and revelation is intrinsic and permanent. . . . For Paul, the gospel does not merely have its origin in the event which the cross epitomizes but has its permanent criterion and center in the cross, so that the word of the cross is the means by which that event reaches hearers as a revelation which redeems.[14]

The revelation in question is event centered toward the self-manifestation of divine power. It is a God-empowered episode as a series of divine events in the domain of human life, even if some humans fail to perceive the reality of the divine episode in Christ. The "message of the cross" (1 Cor 1:18) is the message of what God has done to self-manifest his love in Christ crucified. It is no ordinary message, however, because it comes with "the power of God" for putting humans right with God (1 Cor 1:18; cf. Rom 1:16). (We shall return to this theme in connection with the power of the Spirit of God.) The message reveals God's righteousness in Christ that aims to bring all humans into a right

---

14. Keck, "Biblical Preaching," 146–47.

relationship with God, even though they are ungodly and unworthy of this relationship.

Keck has elaborated on the connection between the cross of Christ, knowledge of God, and the world's wisdom:

> It is because the story of Jesus and his cross is simultaneously the story of God's love that Paul can conclude that whoever believes this story is rightly related to the truth about God, and so redeemed from trusting a misconstrued God. Because cross/resurrection as God's act could not be integrated into what passed for knowledge of God, Paul came to see that one was forced to choose between the wisdom of the world and the foolishness of the gospel, and that if the gospel was right, the world's wisdom has been unmasked as folly in the guise of wisdom. . . . Whoever has experienced [the corrective power of God] by entrusting oneself to God as proclaimed in the gospel knows that the foolishness of God is wiser than human wisdom, and that the cross . . . is indeed stronger than human power, because, when grasped as God's deed, it has the capacity to set us right with God.[15]

The power of God in the cross of Christ and in the message of the cross is no mere affirmation or belief. It is divine power that can bring an ungodly person into a right relationship with God, freeing that person from bondage to things that prevent such a relationship. In addition, one's receiving the power is no mere belief that something is true; instead, it includes entrusting oneself to this personal power in submission to God. This is the heart of faith in God, beyond mere belief that something is true about God.

Even if God intervenes and self-manifests in the episode of Christ crucified and resurrected, we still could have a disconnect from human experience. That is, the relevant evidence of God's self-manifestation needs a basis in human experience if it is to be evidence of God *for a human person*. God can self-manifest in an objective event, but this will have interpersonal evidential significance for a human person only if the person apprehends the event somehow in his or her experience. We might propose, with Keck, that "those who believe this word of the

---

15. Ibid., 148, 154.

cross know it as both the power of God and the wisdom of God," but we cannot avoid this question from Keck: "How will they know this?"[16]

Keck offers the following answer to his question about knowing: "In a word, they have experienced the rectitude of God as rectification, the holiness of God as sanctification and the power of God as redemption because in believing the word of the cross they know that God made Christ 'our wisdom, our righteousness and sanctification and redemption,' as 1 Cor. 1:30 puts it."[17] He adds:

> Moreover, by adding the appositional phrase [in 1 Corinthians 1:30], Paul clarifies the "for us" aspect of the wisdom from God that Christ became/was made: neither a sage whose wisdom improves our thinking, nor a principle by which *we* interpret reality, but an event that changes our relation to the right, the holy, and the free— i.e., to the God from whom this wisdom came. It is because Christ is this sort of wisdom of God that he is also the power of God.[18]

Keck rightly asks about how people will know the message of Christ crucified as the power of God, and he points us in the right direction in appealing to a human experience of God's character. We need, however, a more robust answer that goes beyond talk of an "event" that changes our relation to God.

Keck seems to think that his talk of an "event" will save us from the doubt of skeptical worries. He remarks:

> For [Paul] the ex post facto thinker, the event [of God at work in the crucified and risen Christ] is a given, not a probability conceded or inferred, and as a given it admits no doubt about its actuality. Were it otherwise, the event would be an intriguing possibility but have no compelling power. At the same time, because "event" implies a tissue of meaning (and not a "naked fact"), [Paul] the ex post facto thinker does not assume that one predicates meaning of the given (an act of will as well as of cognition) but that one discerns meaning given with the event.[19]

---

16. Ibid., 153.

17. Ibid.

18. Leander Keck, "God the Other Who Acts Otherwise: An Exegetical Essay on 1 Cor 1:26–31," *Word & World* 16 (1996): 442.

19. Keck, "Paul as Thinker," *Interpretation* 47 (1993): 29.

The problem with this approach is its dubious claim that as a given event God's intervention in Christ "admits no doubt about its actuality." This claim is too strong, because one can have doubt—even plausible doubt—about what a given event is actually an event *of.* For instance, is it an event of God's intervention, or instead is it just an event of my hopeful postulation? The answer is not always easy, as ongoing controversy over the theological import of the New Testament story about Christ illustrates. At one point, Keck claims that "believing that God had raised Jesus from the dead was the determinative datum, the given"[20] for Paul, but this overlooks that such believing is subject to doubt and requires evidential support. As a result, we need a more resilient account.

We get a pointer in the right direction from Keck himself, even though he does not integrate it. He comments: "That intrusion [of God's new age in Christ] being the given event, the resulting new relation to God that the experience of the Spirit betokens and confirms (expressed in Romans 8:14–17 as being authorized to call God 'Abba') discloses dimensions of prior existence of which Paul had not been aware."[21] According to this pointer, the Spirit of God "betokens and confirms" the intervention, or self-manifestation, of God in Christ. This is indeed Paul's view, and it merits our careful attention. It suggests a way to join objective divine self-manifestation with personal assurance and evidence from God.

Paul himself offers the key suggestion in Romans 5:5: "Hope [in God] does not disappoint us, because God's love has been poured into our hearts through the Holy Spirit that has been given to us" (NRSV). Part of this removal of disappointment is the removal of cognitive or evidential disappointment (or shame) about the basis for hope in God, courtesy of a distinctive kind of personal assurance from God. Ernst Käsemann notes that "because for Paul Christ's death has concretely manifested the love of [i.e., from] God, the basis of Christian assurance lies in it. This is why the presence of the Spirit is described in [Romans] 5:5b as the presence of God's love."[22] Käsemann explains:

---

20. Ibid., 30.
21. Ibid., 31.
22. Käsemann, *Commentary on Romans*, 138.

[In Romans 5:5] the reference is to the encompassing power of God with a special orientation to [God's] being for us, as [Romans] 8:31ff. clearly indicates. . . . First, when God's love has seized us so totally and centrally, we no longer belong to ourselves; a change in existence has taken place. Secondly, since the Spirit is a down payment (Rom. 8:23, 2 Cor. 1:22), we have an "objective" pledge that our hope will not be confounded. Finally, when the Spirit who is given us makes us constantly sure of this love, we can praise God in the midst of earthly affliction as in [Romans] 8:37ff.[23]

In Paul's perspective, we need to allow *God* to supply not only redemption in Christ by divine grace (as an unearned gift) but also assurance of God's genuine self-manifestation to us. This assurance comes courtesy of God's Spirit (that is, God in self-manifesting action) but not just as a testimony. It comes by the Spirit's "pouring into our hearts" the same love from God that was self-manifested in the crucified and risen Christ. We need to make room, then, for *cognitive* grace in our being assured of God's reality and presence, just as we make room for grace in salvation.

The Spirit of God does bear witness to the reality of God's love for us, as Paul acknowledges in Romans 8:

> You did not receive a spirit of slavery to fall back into fear, but you have received a spirit of adoption. When we cry, "Abba! Father!" it is that very Spirit bearing witness with our spirit that we are children of God, and if children, then heirs, heirs of God and joint heirs with Christ—if, in fact, we suffer with him so that we may also be glorified with him." (Rom 8:15–17 NRSV)

No intervening speculative argument is needed for this witness; God alone is adequate to the task.

God's Spirit witnesses to receptive humans by sharing divine self-manifested character traits with them, such as God's righteous love. So it would be irrelevant to object that "talk is cheap," because we have much more than talk here. We have the divine self-manifestation and sharing of God's unique character. The claims of other gods cannot copy

---

23. Ibid., 135–36.

this righteous character, because those gods do not have it to share. One cannot share what one does not have. In this self-manifestation, God himself witnesses to the risen Christ as the unique representative of God, the one who proved God's righteous love on the cross for us.

We do well to note the close connection between the Spirit and *God in Christ*. Paul suggests part of the connection as follows: "No one can say, 'Jesus is Lord,' except by the Holy Spirit" (1 Cor 12:3). He has in mind the Jesus resurrected by God, and his talk of "saying" connotes "saying with an adequate basis," the basis provided by the Spirit of God. Käsemann adds:

> The Pauline doctrine of the Spirit is constitutively shaped by the fact that the apostle . . . is the first to relate it indissolubly to Christology. In the Spirit the risen Lord manifests his presence and lordship on earth. Conversely the absolute criterion of the divine Spirit is that he sets the community and its members in the discipleship of the Crucified, in the mutual service established thereby, and in the assault of grace on the world.[24]

The talk of "grace" here is talk of *God's* grace, and therefore the Spirit represents the character of God in promoting "the discipleship of the Crucified." So there is no conceptual circle that threatens. God's Spirit witnesses to the reality that Christ is God's unique agent, in agreement with God's character of righteous love.

Alexandra R. Brown comments on the revelatory and drawing function of God's Spirit for humans: "For Paul, the Spirit not only makes accessible true knowledge of God according to the cross but pulls the knower toward a new realm of existence, namely the lordship of Christ."[25] Paul himself mentions the revelatory function of the Spirit as follows: "We have received not the spirit of the world, but the Spirit that is from God, so that we may understand the gifts bestowed on us by God. And we speak of these things in words not taught by human wisdom but taught by the Spirit, interpreting spiritual things to those who are spiritual" (1 Cor 2:12–13 NRSV). I take Paul's use of "gifts" here broadly, to include whatever comes from God's grace, including the

---

24. Ibid., 213.
25. Brown, *The Cross and Human Transformation*, 124.

risen Christ himself and his work for us. In this perspective, knowledge of Christ's resurrection does not come by natural means, in keeping with 1 Corinthians 12:3. Because his work frees us from obstructive powers, however, the Spirit functions as not only revelatory but also liberating from spiritual and moral bondage. Hence Paul emphasizes freedom in connection with the benefits of Christ and God's Spirit (see Gal 5:1, 16–25).[26] Such freedom is part of the humanly experienced power of God on behalf of his people, and it aids in realizing the lordship of Christ for receptive humans.

Working by grace rather than human achievement, God provides assurance on his terms, courtesy of his Spirit. We may prefer more control in this area—perhaps by our own speculative arguments—but the option is not ours if God seeks to destroy human wisdom and its role for self-achievement and self-boasting. We should be open to God's effort to negate worldly epistemology when it comes to human knowledge of God, given that such epistemology is a branch—or at least an analogue—of worldly, human wisdom. The epistemology from God goes deeper, as we shall see, and it calls for human participation.

Participation and Natural Theology

Participation

Paul links knowing Christ, and by implication knowing God in Christ, with existential participation in the sufferings of Christ. He writes: "I want to know Christ and the power of his resurrection and the sharing of [=participating in] his sufferings by becoming like him in his death, if somehow I may attain the resurrection from the dead" (Phil 3:10–11 NRSV). In addition: "[We are] always carrying in the body the death of Jesus, so that the life of Jesus may also be made visible in our bodies. For while we live, we are always being given up to death for Jesus' sake, so that the life of Jesus may be made visible in our mortal flesh" (2 Cor 4:10–11 NRSV). Paul holds that in the crucified Christ (who is the risen Christ), humans can find God's wisdom and power instead of a worldly alternative. Human appropriation of this wisdom and power through faith in God, however, is demanding because it requires dying

---

26. Cf. J. Louis Martyn, "Epistemology at the Turn of the Ages," in *Theological Issues in the Letters of Paul* (Edinburgh: T&T Clark, 1997), 431–66.

to anti-God ways in order to live cooperatively with God in Christ, even as Christ cooperated with God in Gethsemane. It thus requires one's struggling against some of one's own tendencies—particularly selfish tendencies—in order to be conformed to Christ.

Paul endorses the inextricable connection between dying and rising with Christ as follows:

> We have been buried with him by baptism into death, so that, just as Christ was raised from the dead by the glory of the Father, so we too might walk in newness of life.... So you also must consider yourselves dead to sin and alive to God in Christ Jesus.... No longer present your members to sin as instruments of wickedness, but present yourselves to God as those who have been brought from death to life, and present your members to God as instruments of righteousness. (Rom 6:4, 11, 13 NRSV)

Paul here speaks of those who, having died with Christ, "have been brought from death to life," and he remarks that this is "just as Christ was raised from the dead by the glory of the Father." He does not have bodily resurrection in mind, of course, but talk of spiritual resurrection in the present time fits with Paul's statement. This theme is widely neglected in discussions of Paul, but it becomes explicit in later Pauline writings (see, e.g., Col 3:1). It is also important because, as Michael Gorman notes, "As an experience of the risen or resurrected Christ, co-crucifixion is not merely a metaphor but an apt description of an encounter with a living person whose presence transforms and animates believers (Gal. 2:20)."[27] One's rising now with Christ is thus experiential, courtesy of God's self-manifesting Spirit—the Spirit of the risen Christ—and it is anchored in the divine righteous love poured into one's spirit (Rom 5:5).

Only the Spirit of God enables us to apprehend God's presence in the cross of Christ. As Brown notes in the light of 1 Corinthians 2:10, "The wisdom of the cross Paul preaches finds its way into the heart only by the agency of God's Spirit who alone has the power to claim for God the hearts of 'those who love God' (1 Cor. 2:9)"[28] Even so,

---

27. Gorman, *Inhabiting the Cruciform God* (Grand Rapids: Eerdmans, 2009), 71.
28. Brown, *The Cross and Human Transformation*, 165.

the claiming of the Spirit is not coercive toward humans; it is sensitive to the volitional receptivity of human agents and thus does not thwart their being genuine agents. Following the pattern set by Abraham (Rom 4:16), a faith commitment of self-entrustment to God's work in Christ is needed as a free response to God's self-manifestation.[29] This kind of response does not earn or merit God's offer of Christ and his benefits, and therefore it fits with God's working by grace with humans (cf. Rom 4:4–5). This working by grace allows humans to be genuine agents and not pawns of God.

We can see the role of human weakness, or impotence, in relation to God's power. Paul remarks: "We have this treasure [of salvation from God in Christ] in clay jars, *so that* it may be made clear that this extraordinary power belongs to God and does not come from us" (2 Cor 4:7 NRSV; emphasis added).[30] According to Paul, the power and wisdom needed by humans must come from God because God alone has such power and wisdom for life. In a late letter, Paul describes the relevant power and wisdom as follows:

> We have not ceased praying for you and asking that you may be filled with the knowledge of God's will in all *spiritual wisdom* and understanding, so that you may lead lives worthy of the Lord, fully pleasing to him, as you bear fruit in every good work and as you grow in the knowledge of God. May you be made strong [i.e., empowered] with all the strength [or "power"; Gk.: *dynamis*] that comes from his glorious power, and may you be prepared to endure everything with patience, while joyfully giving thanks to the Father. (Col 1:9–12 NRSV; emphasis added)

Paul's "spiritual wisdom" is not mere knowledge that a claim is true; instead, it is directed toward "lead[ing] lives worthy of the Lord, fully pleasing to him." We now have a sharp contrast between "spiritual wisdom" and mere knowledge and even any kind of "human wisdom."

---

29. Cf. Charles H. Cosgrove, *The Cross and the Spirit* (Macon, GA: Mercer University Press, 1988), 176.

30. Cf. John Fitzgerald, *Cracks in an Earthen Vessel* (Atlanta: Scholars Press, 1988); Alexandra R. Brown, "The Gospel Takes Place: Paul's Theology of Power-in-Weakness in 2 Corinthians," *Interpretation* 52 (1998): 271–85; Timothy Savage, *Power through Weakness* (Cambridge: Cambridge University Press, 1996); Michael J. Gorman, *Cruciformity* (Grand Rapids: Eerdmans, 2001), 268–303.

Exceeding mere knowledge, spiritual wisdom *welcomes* God's power, including the power of *agapē*, for the sake of living a lasting good life, pleasing to God (or, "worthy of the Lord"). Such wisdom participates in God's character and work in Christ and hence cannot be reduced to armchair reflection or speculation. It therefore does not sit well with traditional speculative philosophy.

Paul anchors spiritual wisdom—not in an abstract or speculative principle or even in a Platonic Form—but instead in a personal agent who manifests God's power without defect. As suggested, he refers to "Christ the power of God and the wisdom of God" (1 Cor 1:24) and to "Christ Jesus, who has become for us wisdom from God . . . and redemption" (1 Cor 1:30). An immediate question concerns what particular features of the person of Jesus Christ constitute his being the power and the wisdom of God.

Paul's answer includes the following:

> Christ Jesus, who, though he was in the form of God, did not regard equality with God as something to be exploited, but emptied himself, taking the form of a slave, being born in human likeness. And being found in human form, he humbled himself and became obedient to the point of death—even death on a cross. (Phil 2:5b–8 NRSV)

A key feature is the willing conformity of Jesus to God's will, even when the result is self-sacrificial death. Paul introduces the idea of Jesus's *humble obedience* to God to capture this feature. This obedience differs from grudging obedience and even mere obedience. It ultimately welcomes God's perfect will—even if one is initially ambivalent and faces rigorous consequences—as in the case of Jesus in Gethsemane. In his conformity to God's character and will, Jesus exemplifies the power and wisdom of God as an agent humbly and reverently cooperating with God on the basis of God's wisdom and power, including the power of self-sacrificial *agapē*. We humans are called to participate in the same divine wisdom in the same way, as we participate in dying and rising with Christ. In doing so, we entrust ourselves to God and thereby exemplify faith in God. We then live as adopted children of God, with God as our Father. In this regard, "if anyone is in Christ, there is a new creation: everything old has passed away; see, everything has become new!" (2 Cor 5:17 NRSV).[31] Such new creation changes the standard for philosophy, at least in a Christian context.

Philosophers conformed to Christ are philosophers conformed to a new life of dying and rising with Christ in the power of self-sacrificial *agapē*. That point involves *philosophers* conformed to Christ, because human agents—rather than philosophical views—undergo the dying and rising in question. Going beyond philosophers, the conforming of philosophical *content* to Christ can take two forms. One form, "the strict-content form," entails philosophy that is explicitly Christian in substantive conceptual content, involving positive claims regarding Jesus Christ, the Spirit of Christ, reconciliation to God in Christ, inward transformation by Christ, and so on. This form will be significantly narrowing toward philosophy if one uses it to exclude all other forms of philosophy, but it need not be used in that exclusive manner. It can be combined with a different form of philosophy.

A second form of content conforming to Christ, which we may call "the kingdom-enhancement form," requires philosophy (whatever its substantive content) to *contribute positively* to a philosophy that (a) is Christian in substantive content, *and* (b) enhances God's redemptive kingdom under the good news of God in Christ and its divine love commands. In contributing positively in the manner indicated, this form does not require philosophy conformed to Christ to be explicitly Christian in substantive conceptual content. Such contributing can be genuine without itself offering explicitly Christian content, such as when a philosophical contribution illuminates an "I—Thou" interaction between humans and God without offering explicitly Christian content.

The relevant kingdom enhancement can contribute either to new human reconciliation to God or to deepened reconciliation with God, including a deepened appreciative understanding of God's redemptive ways. Given that the desired reconciliation is under divine *agapē* and its love commands, we may understand kingdom enhancement in terms of the expansion or the deepening of God's kingdom of *agapē*. Such kingdom enhancement depends on the power of divine *agapē*, which can exist and work apart from explicit Christian content. Otherwise, one

---

31. Cf. Moyer V. Hubbard, *New Creation in Paul's Letters and Thought* (Cambridge: Cambridge University Press, 2002).

might argue that the Spirit of God would be unable to prepare people in advance of their coming to consider and to receive Christian conceptual content. Even so, we may think of the relevant kingdom enhancement as being conformed to Christ—at least in a broad sense—if we accept the New Testament view that Christ is the focal point of the kingdom (see Matt 12:28; Mark 1:14–15; Luke 11:20; Col 1:13–14).

It would be unduly narrow, exclusive, and shortsighted to prohibit doing philosophy in the kingdom-enhancement form for the sake of just the strict-content form. In addition, such narrowness conflicts with the way various contributors of wisdom literature in the Old Testament engaged with, and borrowed from, non-Hebraic wisdom traditions. If God is the ultimate ground and sustainer of all wisdom, then genuine wisdom is valuable wherever it emerges—even outside the people or church of God. We should therefore not expect or advocate for an explicitly Christian ghetto with a monopoly on wisdom.

It does not follow either that "anything goes" in philosophy conformed to Christ, or that all philosophical truth or sound argument is intrinsically valuable or even worthy of human pursuit. The kingdom-enhancement requirement for philosophy conformed to Christ sets a definite boundary with this standard: it must enhance God's redemptive kingdom under the good news of God in Christ and its divine love commands. Mere truth acquisition—even for philosophical truth—does not meet this standard. Some philosophical truths contribute to kingdom enhancement; others (such as the metaphysics of celestial time travel for angels or demons) do not. That much is clear, even if some cases call for patience in careful discernment, and even if some cases are disputable.

We humans have finite resources, including finite time, in this life under the divine love commands, and therefore we should adopt a triage approach to the matters we pursue in philosophy conformed to Christ (as in Christian life generally). We should distinguish between (a) the philosophical questions we may engage, if only briefly, to find out their positive relevance or the lack thereof to kingdom enhancement, and (b) the questions we may pursue as a research focus in a Christian life as an evident means of kingdom enhancement. Any new question may be fair game for category (a), but (b) is more demanding. As a research focus, philosophy conformed to Christ (and Christian inquiry in general) should be attentive to (b) in a manner that is often neglected, owing perhaps to the dubious assumption that any philosophical inquiry or truth is intrinsically valuable or otherwise worthy of human pursuit. I find no good reason to accept the latter assumption, even if the field of options can raise some epistemic problems regarding which truths are actually kingdom enhancing.

Natural Theology

God in Christ is worthy of worship and hence altogether without moral defect. Otherwise, we would have a false god. This is an implication of the maximally exalted title "God." The speculative arguments of philosophy, found in traditional natural theology, will not take us to such a God, even if they yield lesser gods who fall short of worthiness of worship.[32] God's self-manifestation alone will take us there, courtesy of the divine character manifestation of God's Spirit, as identified in Romans 5:5.

I agree with Ethelbert Stauffer that "the word of the cross marks the end of all the false attempts which are summed up in the concept of natural theology."[33] It does so because it brings God near to humans in the power of the message of Christ crucified. It provides for a direct manifestation of God's righteous love, courtesy of God's Spirit, without any need for speculative arguments. An appeal to speculative philosophy here is akin to the mistake of certain opponents of Paul to seek to establish their own righteousness before God (Rom 10:3). The analogous mistake is to seek to establish one's own avenue to knowing God in direct conflict with the lesson of 1 Corinthians 1:21 and 2:4. Humans have this tendency to make room for self-credit, but God's self-manifestation has no need for it.

Speculative philosophy goes awry in not giving a primary and irreplaceable role to God's self-manifestation of his character—his righteous love—in the message of Christ crucified. This message enables God's presence and character to be confirmed and witnessed to by God's unique Spirit, with no need of speculative argument. It enables

---

32. For the details on this failure of traditional natural theology in connection with traditional arguments, see Paul K. Moser, *The Evidence for God* (Cambridge: Cambridge University Press, 2010), chapter 3.

33. Ethelbert Stauffer, *New Testament Theology*, trans. John Marsh (New York: Macmillan, 1955), 90.

198 • FOUR VIEWS ON CHRISTIANITY AND PHILOSOPHY

God himself to give the needed assurance to receptive humans by a self-manifestation of his unmatched character of righteous love. Hence, we see the abiding importance of this message in the New Testament. Speculative philosophy assumes that, at least for some people, God's self-manifestation in the message of the cross does not adequately witness to God's presence and reality. It thus goes speculative in search of different, natural sources of potential evidence for God. This is the big mistake of speculative philosophy and traditional natural theology. They thus have the same defect of worldly wisdom: they neglect God's unique and irreplaceable self-manifestation via the Spirit through the message of Christ crucified. It is here that God chooses to self-manifest paradigmatically in order to bring the highest honor to his crucified Son. Alternative human preferences will not change this. Just as we do not guide God's plans for creation, we do not manage God's plan for re-creation in Christ—including his plan for supplying evidence by self-manifestation via his Spirit.

The neglect in question obscures the immediacy or directness of evidence for God via God's Spirit in the message of the cross. Alluding to passages in Deuteronomy, Paul remarks:

> Do not say in your heart, "Who will ascend into heaven?" (that is, to bring Christ down) or "Who will descend into the abyss?" (that is, to bring Christ up from the dead). But what does it say? "The word is near you, on your lips and in your heart" (that is, the word of faith that we proclaim). (Rom 10:6–8 NRSV)

Speculative philosophy, including traditional natural theology, aims to find evidence of God's reality outside the self-manifestation of divine righteous love. Instead, it obscures the key role of God's self-manifestation with philosophical complexity and controversy. It leaves the matter obscure and controversial at best and falls short of the reality and power of a God of perfect love, the God in Christ.

We do not find the New Testament writers appealing to speculative arguments to offer evidence for God's reality or presence. In principle, Paul could have done so, but he acknowledges that God self-manifests instead with a personal witness, the witness of God's Spirit. It is implausible then for some writers to suggest that in Romans 1:18–20 Paul is suggesting an argument of natural theology based on creation. This is not natural theology at all because Paul reports that *God* has shown his reality to people: "For what can be known about God is plain to them, because God has shown it to them" (Rom 1:19 NRSV). God can show himself "through creation," but this would not entail that creation *by itself* shows or otherwise establishes God's reality. We do not therefore have a basis for an argument of natural theology here. Some people try to read such a basis into Romans 1, but Paul is clear: God himself is doing the showing of himself, and creation by itself is not. This lesson fits well with Paul's other acknowledgments of God's self-manifestation (e.g., Rom 10:20).

Clearly Paul uses arguments, but it does not follow that he uses speculative philosophy or arguments of natural theology. He also seeks to destroy certain arguments. "We destroy arguments and every proud obstacle raised up against the knowledge of God, and we take every thought captive to obey Christ" (2 Cor 10:4b–5). Destroying arguments, however, does not require any endorsement of speculative philosophy or arguments of natural theology. One can destroy arguments by identifying why they fail to deliver their promised conclusions. Many philosophers have contributed to doing this for the traditional arguments of natural theology. Such arguments thus become little more than an intellectual distraction. Paul offers a more resilient approach that takes seriously the evidential role of God's own Spirit in self-manifesting God to humans. He thus embraces cognitive grace and disowns cognitive merit before God.

A serious problem with the arguments of traditional natural theology is that they do not sit well with the recurring biblical theme that God is elusive and hides his existence from some people at times. God does not offer his existence as ever transparent, in part because some people are not ready to face his reality.[34] God does not force the matter of evidence of his reality, and we should not try to do so either, especially with arguments that fall short of a God worthy of worship. Even if one gets to the reality of a lesser god by some speculative argument (which is highly doubtful), one still would face the debilitating question of how

---

34. See Paul K. Moser, *The Elusive God* (Cambridge: Cambridge University Press, 2008) for relevant biblical passages; cf. Samuel Terrien, *The Elusive Presence*; Samuel Balentine, *The Hidden God* (Oxford: Oxford University Press, 1983); and Paul K. Moser, *The Severity of God* (Cambridge: Cambridge University Press, 2013).

one gets from the lesser god to the God worthy of worship. One will need some kind of account, and if one has such an account, it will be doubtful that one needs the original argument for the lesser god. In that case, the speculative argument in question would be dispensable. We then have no real need of it.

A proponent of an argument of natural theology might retreat to a distinction between "knowing that God exists" and "knowing God." The claim would be that the preferred argument supports the former but not necessarily the latter. This would be no surprise if "knowing God" requires some kind of direct personal interaction between a human and God. Clearly, a speculative argument of natural theology does not require any such interaction. Even so, it is unclear that God would want to separate the two kinds of knowing, because merely knowing that God exists could be accompanied by hate toward God. Such knowing thus would be very thin relative to God's desire to redeem people in a cooperative relationship with God. Some version of this concern perhaps underlies the following deflationary remark in James 2:19: "You believe that God is one; you do well. Even the demons believe—and shudder" (NRSV). Arguably, God would want to promote "knowing that God exists" only as it figures in "knowing God" in a cooperative manner. In other words, God would seek to be cognitively redemptive.

Perhaps much of speculative philosophy about God and natural theology stems from a failure to trust God's Spirit in an evidential role. Part of the problem is that we cannot predict whether God's Spirit will self-manifest God at a certain time. Jesus suggests this kind of inability in John's Gospel (see John 3:8), and I see no reason to try to overcome it with arguments that only create more problems for, and divert attention from, the genuine evidence for God. I recommend, then, that we consider anew the more fitting kind of evidence in divine self-manifestation. The latter evidence is experiential and not speculative, and it fits with God's unique character as a personal agent with perfect love for all concerned—even enemies. In that case, we are not talking about a god who falls short of worthiness of worship. Christian philosophy should fall in line with the character of a God worthy of worship. It should be conformed to the Christ who represents this God perfectly.

GRAHAM OPPY

Moser says that philosophy is the "love and pursuit of wisdom" (175), where wisdom is "knowledge that enables us to prioritize our values and valued things and to guide our plans and actions in ways that are good" (176). While that conception of philosophy has significant historical antecedents—as Moser himself observes—it fits very poorly with most actual philosophical practice, both ancient and modern. If, as I say, philosophy is the discipline that addresses questions for which we do not know how to produce—and perhaps cannot even imagine how to produce—agreed answers using agreed methods, then it is obvious that many, perhaps even most, philosophical questions have nothing to do with prioritizing values and valued things and guiding plans and actions in good ways.

Moser says that he favours an approach to the understanding of philosophy that has "normative value": "Not just *anything* can qualify as philosophy" (178). In one sense, it is true that, on my approach, not just anything can qualify as philosophy. In particular, any questions for which we do know how to produce agreed answers using agreed methods are not philosophical questions. Everyone agrees that regular questions in other disciplines—mathematics, physics, chemistry, biology, psychology, history, sociology, economics, literary theory, musicology, and so forth—are *not* philosophical questions. However, there may be a different sense in which, on my approach, anything at all can qualify as philosophy: *wherever* questions arise for which we do not know how to produce—and perhaps cannot even imagine how to produce—agreed answers using agreed methods, we are in the domain of philosophy. Each discipline shares a boundary with philosophy; at the boundary of any discipline, philosophical questions arise.

Perhaps Moser might concede that philosophy of mathematics, philosophy of physics, and philosophy of chemistry have more or less nothing to do with prioritizing our values and valued things and guiding our plans and actions in good ways, while nonetheless insisting that the subdisciplines that are proper to philosophy—logic, metaphysics, epistemology, ethics, aesthetics, metaphilosophy, history of philosophy, and so forth—are all about prioritizing our values and valued things and guiding our plans and actions in good ways. But we only need to think about the questions that are actually taken up in the subdisciplines that are proper to philosophy in order to realize that this, too, is incorrect. While there is something to be said for the view that ethics has a particular concern with prioritizing our values and valued things and guiding our plans and actions in good ways, it is obvious that logic, metaphysics, aesthetics, metaphilosophy, and history of philosophy do not have anything like that kind of concern.

Moser's primary topic is "Christian philosophy." In his view, Christian philosophy should be "conformed to God": "Its motive and content [should be] subjected fully to the good news of God in Christ" (176). It is not entirely clear what Moser takes to be the connection between philosophy and Christian philosophy. It may be that he is thinking that, properly so-called, all philosophy is Christian philosophy. Or it may be that he is thinking that Christian philosophy is one approach to—one branch or part of—philosophy properly so-called. If he is thinking that Christian philosophy is one branch or part of philosophy properly so-called, then it seems that there is not much here to pique the interest of a naturalist. While a naturalist may well wish to investigate questions about Christianity for which we do not know how to produce—and perhaps cannot even imagine how to produce— agreed answers using agreed methods, there is rather less to interest the naturalist in questions of that kind that arise in connection with an inquiry whose motive and content is subjected fully to the good news of God in Christ.

If Moser is thinking that, properly so-called, all philosophy is Christian philosophy, then there are things to argue about (and not just for those who are sympathetic to naturalism). It seems reasonably clear what it would be for a philosopher's *motive* to be subject fully to the good news of God in Christ: that philosopher's engagement in the pursuit of philosophy would have to sit happily with that philosopher's acceptance of the good news of God in Christ. After his "night of fire," Pascal mostly gave up mathematics, because he thought that being motivated to engage in mathematics was incompatible with being subjected fully to the good news of God in Christ. There are at least two different Pascalian concerns to distinguish here. One is *worldly vanity*: if one engages in mathematics in order to gain the approbation of other mathematicians, then one is engaging in mathematics for a reason that is inconsistent with subjecting oneself fully to the good news of God in Christ. Another is *cognitive focus*: if one engages in mathematics, then the time that one spends doing mathematics is not time that one spends subjecting oneself fully to the good news of God in Christ because it is time that is not spent contemplating or communicating the good news of God in Christ. What goes for mathematics goes equally for philosophy: if one is subject fully to the good news of God in Christ, then one won't engage in philosophy for reasons of worldly vanity, and one will not engage in philosophy at the expense of devoting sufficient time to contemplating and communicating the good news of God in Christ.

Even given these observations about what it would be for a philosopher's motive to be subject fully to the good news of God in Christ, it is still not entirely clear what it would be for the *content* of philosophy to be subjected fully to the good news of God in Christ. Moser recognizes two possibilities: (1) "Explicitly Christian ... substantive conceptual content"; and (2) a positive contribution to a philosophy that is "Christian in substantive content" and that "enhances God's redemptive kingdom under the good news of God in Christ" (195). While Moser says that it would be "unduly narrow, exclusive, and shortsighted" to insist solely on explicitly Christian substantive conceptual content, it is not very clear what he takes to fall under a positive contribution to a philosophy that is "Christian in substantive content" and that "enhances God's redemptive kingdom under the good news of God in Christ."

It is hard to see how, on any understanding of "positive contribution," discussion of translational embeddings in modal logics, or Woodin's Ω–conjecture, or λ–categorial languages, or the liar paradox, or the two-envelope problem, or unrestricted mereological composition, or a host of similar topics, makes any positive contribution to Christian substantive content that enhances God's redemptive kingdom under the good news of God in Christ. But, whether or not these things make a positive contribution to Christian substantive content that enhances

God's redemptive kingdom under the good news of God in Christ, they—and a million other things just like them—are unproblematically philosophical topics that philosophers have good reason to pursue. Moreover, I think that even most Christians would agree with this verdict: it requires a particularly severe cast of mind to suppose that God would object to our using our God-given capacities to pursue deep and interesting questions that arise within us as a result of our God-given natures.

It might seem reasonable to think that natural theology could contribute to Christian substantive content that enhances God's redemptive kingdom under the good news of God in Christ. Moser disagrees. He says that natural theology "obscures the key role of God's self-manifestation with philosophical complexity and controversy" (198). Further, he claims that (1) "we do not find the New Testament writers appealing to speculative arguments to offer evidence for God's reality or presence" (198); and (2) "the arguments of traditional natural theology . . . do not sit well with the recurring biblical theme that God is elusive and hides his existence from some people at times" (191).

All three of my fellow contributors to this volume discuss Romans 1:18–20. Moser says that it is implausible to claim that Paul here suggests "an argument of natural theology based on creation" (198). Citing Romans 1:19—"For what can be known about God is plain to them, because God has shown it to them"—he argues that this is not natural theology because it is reported that God shows his reality to his people. However, Romans 1:20 says: "Ever since the creation of the world his invisible nature, namely, his eternal power and deity, has been clearly perceived in the things that have been made" (RSV). This line seems to me to suggest—contrary to Moser's own claim—that "creation by itself shows or otherwise establishes God's reality" (199).

It is interesting to set McGrew's comments against Moser's:

> From time to time, some ardent Christians . . . have tried to deny that there is any actual natural theology in Scripture. . . . Calvin famously reads Romans 1 as referring not to natural theology but to the *sensus divinitatis*. . . . I can see no rational ground for taking this point of view, which seems to me to torture both the biblical text and the principles of sound historical investigation. (129)

Oliphint's view is much closer to Moser's:

> God has been speaking (nonverbally) "since the creation of the world".… That speech of God makes clear to everyone his "invisible qualities".… It is truth that comes, not by way of demonstration or proof, but solely through the ever-revealing activity of the God who made us. (81)

While Moser—along with Oliphint and McGrew—accepts that there is virtue in "destroying" objections to Christian belief, he does not accept that this activity is participation in speculative philosophy and natural theology. But many of the objections to Christian belief just are arguments that belong to speculative philosophy and, in particular, to natural theology (perhaps, as McGrew would have it, "in its broader forms" [129]). Consider logical arguments from evil, evidential arguments from evil, arguments from divine hiddenness, arguments from nonbelief, arguments from the incompatibility of divine attributes, and so forth. In order to "destroy" these arguments, there is no alternative but to engage with them: to question whether their conclusions are supported by their premises, to raise objections against their premises, and so on. If you ignore these arguments, or mock them, or quote Scripture at those who present them, then—whatever you may achieve in doing these things—you clearly will not have "destroyed" the arguments.

It is not clear why Moser thinks that the arguments of traditional natural theology do not sit well with the recurring biblical theme that God is elusive and hides his existence from some people at times. Even if there are arguments in traditional natural theology that are absolutely compelling, it is plainly the case that many people—including many Christians—have never encountered those absolutely compelling arguments. Moreover, even if there are arguments in traditional natural theology that are absolutely compelling, there is no guarantee that everyone who encounters one of those arguments will be compelled. Gödel's proof of his famous incompleteness theorem is absolutely compelling, yet many people are not so much as capable of following it. Given God's omnipotence and omniscience, it ought not to be so very difficult for him to hide from those who have never encountered the absolutely compelling arguments and those who, despite having encountered the absolutely compelling arguments, have failed to understand them.

Of course, one might be well disposed towards natural theology even if one does not think that there are arguments in traditional natural theology that are absolutely compelling. One might think that natural theology is a work in progress; eventually, there might be absolutely compelling arguments in natural theology, but that time is not yet upon us. Or one might think that, while natural theology does not yield absolutely compelling arguments, there is virtue in the less-than-absolutely compelling arguments that it delivers. Perhaps, for example, those less-than-compelling arguments serve, for some, as stepping-stones along the path to belief.

RESPONSE FROM THE COVENANT MODEL

K. SCOTT OLIPHINT

I read with much appreciation and interest Paul Moser's "conformation model" essay. If time and space allowed, I would want to probe more deeply into the meaning of some of his terms. In my read, however, and given my own meaning, there is a great deal with which a covenant model would be in agreement. He does a wonderful service in explaining to us just what true wisdom is, including *how* and *that* such wisdom has its focus only in Christ.

There are a few points in Moser's essay that I would want to explore, but space only allows for one. The others I will briefly mention.

First, though Moser doesn't pursue it, he seems to aver that the options available to us with respect to God's character are *either* that he is immutable and impassable (according to philosophical definitions), *or* that he is active and self-manifesting (177). I think Scripture allows us, even *requires* us, to recognize *both* that God is *actively* immutable (including impassable), and yet in his condescension (supremely in Christ) he is active and self-manifesting in the world.

Second, (and this will connect more directly with my more explorative response below), Moser rightly notes that we must recognize the close connection between the Spirit and Christ (190). That connection, however, is even closer than Moser allows in his essay. Since the day of Pentecost, wherein Christ himself baptizes the church with the Holy Spirit, the *function* of the Spirit is identical to the *function* of Christ. This is why the apostle Paul can argue that "the last Adam became a life-giving Spirit" (1 Cor 15:45 NRSV), and that, in speaking of Christ, he can say that "the Lord is the Spirit" (2 Cor 3:17). All this is to say that what the Spirit of God is doing *now*, and since Pentecost, including his *revelation* of himself, *Christ himself* is doing by, with, and through the Spirit.

In the remaining space that I have, I would like to explore with Moser his particular view of natural theology and its relationship to

God's revelation. In his essay, Moser is partial to terms like "event" and "self-manifestation" and "experiential." Such terms evoke my orthodox antennae and cause me to wonder if neoorthodoxy is lurking nearby.[1] Perhaps, but perhaps not. There is certainly an orthodox way to use such terms.

Whether by virtue of neoorthodoxy or not, there is a lacuna in Moser's discussion of natural theology that I would like to explore with him. First, we need to highlight some of his salient points on natural theology:

> Speculative human arguments in natural theology, including such arguments for God's existence, ignore or neglect the importance of God's unique self-manifestation of redemptive power in Christ, that is, the divine power of righteous love (see Rom 3:21–26).... Such arguments call attention to human reasoners in their speculative reasoning skills, as if God's self-manifestation is somehow deficient, unreal, dubious, shameful, or embarrassing. (184)

This is exactly right. Speculative attempts at natural theology have explicitly denied God's clear revelation of himself and thus have their focus in human reasoning, as if such reasoning is, in itself, up to the task. But sin's effects preclude such a focus. So also rightly Moser:

> The speculative arguments of philosophy, found in traditional natural theology, will not take us to such a God, even if they yield lesser gods who fall short of worthiness of worship. (197)

So far, so good. Then Moser proposes that

> the relevant evidence of God's self-manifestation needs a basis in human experience if it is to be evidence of God for a human person. God can self-manifest in an objective event, but this will have interpersonal evidential significance for a human person only if the person apprehends the event somehow in his or her experience. (186)

---

1. *Neoorthodoxy* is "a 20th-century development in theology, which is 'orthodox' inasmuch as it emphasizes key themes of Reformed theology, but 'neo-', *i.e.* 'new', inasmuch as it has taken serious account of contemporary cultural and theological developments. It originated with continental theologians: Barth, Brunner, Bultmann and Friedrich Gogarten. . . . It was in no sense an organized movement, and precise definitions or boundaries are impossible" (Sinclair B. Ferguson, David F. Wright, and J. I. Packer, eds., *New Dictionary of Theology* [Downers Grove, IL: InterVarsity Press, 1988], 456).

With respect to this point, it is best to follow the reasoning of the apostle Paul in Romans 1:18ff. Moser is aware of this passage, of course, and of the illicit uses to which it has been put in the service of speculative natural theology. Concerning this passage, Moser says, "God can show himself 'through creation,' but this would not entail that creation by itself shows or otherwise establishes God's reality" (199).

Perhaps a closer look at the apostle's argument can help clarify what God is up to in his revelation in and through creation.

The general topic of discussion in Romans 1:18–3:20, as introduced by the apostle, is the wrath of God. In introducing this topic, the apostle wants to make clear that everyone, both Jew and Greek, falls under the wrath of God by virtue of our sinfulness (cf. Rom 3:9). Only by this recognition of universal sinfulness will we be able properly to understand and make sense of the righteousness that is found in Christ alone and that is ours through faith by way of imputation (Rom 3:21ff.).

So, says the apostle Paul, "The wrath of God is being revealed from heaven against all the godlessness and wickedness of people, who suppress the truth by their wickedness" (Rom 1:18). Two ideas are introduced in this verse that are going to need further explanation. What might the apostle mean by "truth," and what does "suppress" refer to? Paul first further defines what he means by "truth":

> For what can be known about God is plain to them, because God has shown it to them. For his invisible attributes, namely, his eternal power and divine nature, have been clearly perceived, ever since the creation of the world, in the things that have been made. So they are without excuse. (Rom 1:19–20 ESV)

The "truth" to which Paul refers is the truth about God. Specifically, it is the truth concerning God's "eternal power and divine nature (*theiotēs*)." As Moser rightly notes, this passage is *not* a call for speculative natural theology; Scripture is clear that it is *God* who is the actor here. He is the one revealing and ensuring that those to whom his revelation is given "clearly perceive" what is revealed. So clearly do they perceive it that such perception, as it entails the possession of truth, renders each of us "without excuse" (*anapologētous*) before God.

To Moser's point above, this revelation of God, because it is *God* who is revealing, is *clear*, not ambiguous, and it gets through to each and every one of God's human creatures. God's revelation in and through creation, as it reaches into the recesses of the human heart, is the basis upon which none of us will be excused before the judgment seat of God.

What then, I wonder, does Moser mean when he says that this revelation of God "would not entail that creation by itself shows or otherwise establishes God's reality"? It depends. Taken one way, it could mean that creation *by itself* does not show God's reality. If taken this way, then I would agree.

But the apostle's argument clearly indicates that there is no such thing as creation "by itself." Rather, the point of Paul's argument in Romans is that *creation itself just is God revealing*. This revelation that God gives supplies all people everywhere "since the creation of the world" with *true knowledge of God*. To Moser's point in his essay, the apostle is not arguing that all people simply know *that there is a god*. Paul is explicit as he summarizes the effect of God's revelation that it results in our "knowing God" (*gnontes ton theon*, v. 21; my translation). The true knowledge that all people possess is *personal* knowledge. It is knowledge of God's eternal power and deity, and it is sufficient to render us all inexcusable.

The apostle Paul goes on to explain what he means when he says that we all, in our sins, "suppress" the truth that God gives and reveals. It means that we do "not honor him as God or give thanks to him" (v. 21 ESV). Instead, we become futile in our thinking, and our senseless minds are darkened. *This point* accounts, in part, for the need for philosophy that conforms to Christ. Any other philosophy originates from the slimy swamp of suppression in which all of us, apart from Christ, swim. Of course, as Moser notes, there can be "kingdom enhancements" in philosophies that are bound by sinful suppression. The slimy swamp of suppression will, inadvertently and occasionally, bubble up with some formal truth. But such *formal* truth can only be "kingdom enhancing" when supplied with the *material* of a philosophy according to Christ.

Another centrally relevant aspect of our suppression of the truth according to Paul is that in claiming to be wise, we become fools (v. 22). This, I think, is Scripture's explicit judgment on any and every philosophy that proceeds according to the principles of this world. When Paul denotes those who "claim to be wise," he is likely referring to those who claim to be "lovers" (*philo-*) of "wisdom" (*sophia*). Speculative or worldly philosophy, therefore, is a practice that claims to love wisdom, but by virtue of its constant, intractable, and sinful suppression of the truth, it moves inexorably toward foolishness.

The sum of suppression, therefore, according to Scripture is that human beings—all of us as long as we are apart from Christ—are immersed in utter and radical *self-deception*. We deceive ourselves when we think that we can understand our world, ourselves, or *whether or not God exists* according to our own human resources. We deceive ourselves into thinking that such things are subject in the first place to our analysis rather than to God's interpretation, and that we have—in and of ourselves—the intellectual resources available to understand them.

Speaking of which, Scripture's analysis in Romans 1 has something to say also to the so-called "hiddenness of God" problem. Moser broaches it this way:

A serious problem with the arguments of traditional natural theology is that they do not sit well with the recurring biblical theme that God is elusive and hides his existence from some people at times. (199)

There is of course clear biblical teaching that God's special revelation is given according to his own sovereign purposes (see, e.g., Matt 11:25–27). Often, however, the notion of God's "hiddenness" is used as an excuse not to believe in him. Some have wanted to say that *if* God exists and *if* he is good, then surely he would make himself clearly known. Since he has not done so, he must not exist.

The argument of the apostle in Romans 1:18ff., however, is that God *has* made himself clearly known to each and every person, always and everywhere, and continues to do so. Not only so, but the clear revelation that God gives and is giving is itself "clearly perceived." As is the case with all objections against God's existence, the problem is *not* that God has not provided clear evidence of his existence but rather that the clear revelation of God that is clearly perceived is constantly, intractably, and culpably suppressed in unrighteousness.

The foundation, therefore, for any and every "conformation model" of Christianity and philosophy must be the universal, infallible, clear, and dynamic revelation of God in and through creation. Such revelation means that we all begin our self-conscious lives as *knowers*, knowers of the true God and of creation as the means to that knowledge. The good news of the gospel comes to those who know God. When effectual, it "meets" those who know God with hearts and minds that are forever changed—regenerated—so that Christ can be the center of all thinking, including of philosophy.

There are two other points that cannot be pursued here, but which are central to Scripture's discussion and to Moser's concerns. First, this revelation of God in and through creation is effectual from the beginning of creation because it comes through the Son of God, the second person of the Trinity.[2] This point has deep and profound redemptive implications for God's general revelation.

Second, we must recognize that any experiential self-manifestation of God will necessarily have its ground in God's revelation. It will have its universal ground in God's general revelation in and through creation. It will have its Christian ground in *both* God's general *and* his special revelation. Apart from these two modes of God's revelation, there is no ground available for experience, nor can there be real content given to God's self-manifestation.

---

2. For exegetical support of this, see K. Scott Oliphint, "Bavinck's Realism, the Logos Principle and Sola Scriptura," *WTJ* 72.2 (2010): 359–90.

RESPONSE FROM THE CONVERGENCE MODEL

TIMOTHY MCGREW

Over the course of about a decade, Paul Moser has been developing and articulating a distinctive approach to the rationality of religious belief, an approach that stresses the individual's relationship with God via a divine self-disclosure. He criticizes alternative approaches, whether they ground that rationality in traditional natural theology or in historical evidence, as not just limited or inadequate but positively contrary to Scripture. It is tempting to classify his position as a nonevidential approach akin to fideism. But Moser would, I think, reject this suggestion. He is trying instead to bring about a reorientation of the notion of evidence itself, since the concepts of evidence that most philosophers (at least) bring to the discussion seem to him to be arbitrarily narrow and to close off avenues of knowledge that can arise through personal experience.

But Moser does more than gesture toward ineffable experience, in three ways. He seems to be arguing that the experiential epistemology of his model is normative for Christians; he sets up his self-disclosure model in direct opposition to more traditional forms of philosophical reasoning; and he tries to draw support for his position from the letters of the apostle Paul. On all three points, if I am understanding him properly, we have very serious disagreements.

A few words will have to suffice on the matter of religious experience. I have little to say about religious experiences that swing free of the more traditional kinds of evidence. I am not personally subject to such experiences, but I do not think I am in a strong position to object to the idea that God might disclose himself in a private, self-authenticating way. Some people—including eminent philosophers like Alvin Plantinga—claim to have had such experiences, and I have no reason to doubt their sincerity. And every individual is responsible to the evidence he has, whether others share that evidence or not.

But to the extent that my circle of acquaintances is representative, many serious self-professing Christians do not have such experiences. Indeed, Moser seems to realize this point, as on p. 199 he refers to

> the recurring biblical theme that God is elusive and hides his existence from some people at times. God does not offer his existence as ever transparent, in part because some people are not ready to face his reality.

My own response would be that there is no particular reason for God to disclose himself in an extraordinary and private way to those for whom the public evidence is available and sufficient. But Moser consistently deprecates such evidence, claiming, in fact, that

> speculative philosophy assumes that, at least for some people, God's self-manifestation in the message of the cross does not adequately witness to God's presence and reality. (198)

There is at least an apparent tension between these two quotations. If Moser thinks that God hides his existence from some people at times, in what sense does God's self-manifestation in the message of the cross witness adequately to his presence and reality to them, at those times?

The opposition between "speculative philosophy" and Moser's model is at the heart of our second disagreement. There are several meanings of the word "speculative," two of which are important here. On the one hand, the term can mean *abstract*, *theoretical*, or *academic*; on the other, it can mean *doubtful*, *precarious*, *based on inadequate evidence*. Beyond question, some of the arguments of natural theology are speculative in the first sense. But there is no logical connection between that sense and the latter sense.

Whether *all* such arguments are philosophically defective is a significant point of contention in contemporary philosophy of religion. Moser clearly wants to dismiss the lot of them, saying that God does not desire

> the speculative arguments of philosophers, or anything else that puffs up humans. God has the power to self-manifest his righteous and gracious character in Christ's death and resurrection without relying on human achievement and pride. (184)

It is difficult to read this expression without concluding that Moser thinks all "speculative" arguments for God's existence puff up humans, a reading that receives support from his odd comments about "cognitive shame" in the same context (185). He is entitled to his opinion on the matter. But I cannot see any compelling line of reasoning from the nature of such arguments to the conclusion that they are intrinsically defective or that their use is inherently prideful.

In the same vein, Moser writes that spiritual wisdom

> participates in God's character and work in Christ and hence cannot be reduced to armchair reflection or speculation. It therefore does not sit well with traditional speculative philosophy. (194)

Presumably, failure to "sit well" is supposed to be some kind of problem. But if so, I am not sure what it is, since nothing relevant seems to follow from the failure of reduction. My love for my wife cannot be reduced to my washing the dishes after dinner. But the act of washing the dishes "sits" perfectly well with my loving her.

My third disagreement with Moser arises from what I can only describe as his repeated and sometimes extraordinary misreadings of Paul. This disagreement is critical, because Moser offers, in this essay, nothing else in support of his views. Five passages quoted by Moser will illustrate the magnitude of our disagreement. First, on p. 182, Moser quotes a portion of 1 Corinthians 1:17, from a chapter in which Paul is chiding the Corinthian Christians for their pettiness in forming factions based on individual personalities:

> For Christ did not send me to baptize but to proclaim the gospel, and not with eloquent wisdom, so that the cross of Christ might not be emptied of its power. (NRSV)

Paul is likely here referring to the reputation of Apollos, described in Acts 18 as an eloquent man, who had worked with the Christians in Corinth after Paul's departure from that city. But Moser's interpretation goes in an entirely different direction:

> Here we have a stark contrast between God's wisdom in the cross of Christ and the wisdom of the world, which is the kind of wisdom God seeks to destroy. Christian philosophers should attend to this important contrast.

Why should Christian philosophers need to attend to this contrast any more than others? Apparently, it is because they are more prone, as a group, to prefer the latter kind of wisdom to the former. How so? Moser's interpretation of a second passage offers a clue. On p. 184 he mentions Paul's quotation of Isaiah 65:1 in Romans 10:20:

Then Isaiah is so bold as to say,

> "I have been found by those who did not seek me;
> I have shown myself to those who did not ask for me."
> (NRSV)

In context, Paul is referring to the extension of God's grace to the gentiles. But Moser leaps from the fact that God showed himself to the gentiles who did not seek him to the remarkable conclusion that it is wrong to give arguments for the existence of God, an activity that he says "call[s] attention to human reasoners in their speculative reasoning skills" and reflects a need "to mitigate any cognitive shame with speculative arguments from philosophy."

I am deeply puzzled by the mismatch between this text and the moral Moser wishes to draw. Nothing that Paul says here implies anything, favorable or unfavorable, about philosophical arguments for God's existence. As for the suggestion that the arguments themselves call attention to human reasoners, perhaps in the hands of some people they do. But the same might be said with as much or more justice of some people who pride themselves on their criticisms of such arguments.

A third Pauline passage that Moser cites is Galatians 6:14–15:

> May I never boast of anything except the cross of our Lord Jesus Christ, by which the world has been crucified to me, and I to the world. For neither circumcision nor uncircumcision is anything; but a new creation is everything! (NRSV)

Moser contrasts this work of God with "human achievement and pride," which is perfectly true so long as one remembers that Paul brings this up in his controversy with the Judaizers in the early Christian community. But in that case, it is very difficult to see how giving good public reasons for belief in God ought, as such, to fall into the category of "human achievement and pride." Again, almost anything can be done in a wrong spirit or from improper motives. But why think that philosophy of religion is a field more likely to "puff up humans" than other intellectual fields?

Moser appeals to Paul a fourth time on p. 197, where he claims that an appeal to what he calls "speculative philosophy" is

> akin to the mistake of certain opponents of Paul to seek to establish their own righteousness before God (Rom 10:3). The analogous mistake is to seek to establish one's own avenue to knowing God in direct conflict with the lesson of 1 Corinthians 1:21 and 2:4.

Here are those two verses, with 2:5 added for context:

> For since, in the wisdom of God, the world did not know God through wisdom, God decided, through the foolishness of our proclamation, to save those who believe. . . . My speech and my proclamation were not with plausible words of wisdom, but with a demonstration of the Spirit and of power, so that your faith might rest not on human wisdom but on the power of God. (NRSV)

Paul is describing the approach he himself took with the Corinthians, but the contrast he draws throughout these chapters is not with clear thinking and public evidence but rather with mere persuasive rhetoric and philosophical ostentation. Pagan philosophy is indeed deprecated, but not because it is philosophy. The problem, according to Paul, is that through that sort of wisdom the world did not know God (1 Cor 1:21). The specific truths of the gospel can be known only by special revelation, and that disseminated through preaching. But special revelation can be attested (and in the New Testament is frequently attested) by historical evidence such as signs and wonders. To draw attention to the need for special revelation is not to criticize evidence. There is no reason why Paul's criticism of inadequate philosophy should be turned into an indictment of philosophical arguments that do point to the existence and nature of God.

Perhaps the strangest interpretation of all is the one Moser puts upon Paul's words in 2 Corinthians 10:4b–5:

218 • FOUR VIEWS ON CHRISTIANITY AND PHILOSOPHY

We destroy arguments and every proud obstacle raised up against the knowledge of God, and we take every thought captive to obey Christ. (NRSV)

The plain meaning of this sentence is that Christians destroy arguments and obstacles raised up *against* the knowledge of God. By a sort of hermeneutical alchemy, Moser transmutes this passage into a mandate for destroying arguments designed to *promote* the knowledge of God. "Destroying arguments," he assures us,

does not require any endorsement of speculative philosophy or arguments of natural theology. One can destroy arguments by identifying why they fail to deliver their promised conclusions. Many philosophers have contributed to doing this for the traditional arguments of natural theology.

This interpretation stands Paul's plain meaning on its head. I want to express myself carefully here to forestall a possible misunderstanding. I certainly grant that criticizing what one views as flawed arguments for the existence of God need not be, in and of itself, a wrong or prideful thing. But those are absolutely not the sort of arguments that Paul here speaks of destroying.

Despite the fact that Moser and I are both devout Christians and analytically trained philosophers, a vast gulf separates us. I am well aware that the approach I favor is exactly the sort of position he is most fervently concerned to reject. I would be relieved to learn that he is not saying what I take him to be saying and that I have misunderstood him. But I fear that I have not.

PAUL K. MOSER

The present exchange illustrates the typical inadequacy of convincing people by appeals to "clarity," "public reasons for belief," or "the Bible." Often what is not adequately clear to one person is sufficiently clear to another person, and the "public reasons" for one person are doubtful for another person, even relative to the latter's evidence. In addition, the Bible admits of various interpretations of many of its themes, thus resisting its use for excluding positions in many cases. Fortunately, one's having good grounds for a position does not depend on convincing others of one's position.

To Oppy

I see no reason to accept Oppy's view of philosophy as "the discipline that addresses questions for which we do not know how to produce . . . agreed answers using agreed methods" (201). Aristotle was doing important philosophy, specifically epistemology, in the *Posterior Analytics* when he showed that inferential knowledge depends on noninferential knowledge, and many epistemologists have followed suit, extending his argument to elucidate the structure of justification and knowledge. No discipline attracts *full* agreement among humans, but disagreement does not by itself challenge reasonableness on a position. I would not bother with philosophy at all if it had the kind of cognitive deficiency alleged by Oppy. The history of philosophy does not share his pessimism about the questions of philosophy.

Oppy fails to see that on my portrait of philosophy we can accommodate such disciplines as the philosophy of mathematics and the philosophy of physics as integral means to a larger end of philosophy as the love and pursuit of wisdom. The wisdom in question is of the kind immortalized by Plato and Aristotle, and it includes knowledge that enables us to prioritize our values and valued things and guide our plans and actions in ways that are good. In the aforementioned disciplines, we gain significant knowledge that illuminates some things in a manner that aids us in prioritizing those things. We can extend the term "philosophy" to them, courtesy of their special, integral role in the broader project of philosophy as just characterized. The sciences typically proceed at a less general level of explanation, without the kind of prioritizing in question, and thus differ from philosophy as traditionally understood.

Regarding Christian philosophy, Oppy remarks that "it requires a particularly severe cast of mind to suppose that God would object to our using our God-given capacities to pursue deep and interesting questions that arise within us as a result of our God-given natures" (204). This claim is too vague to assess, and it is unclear what "deep and interesting questions" are at issue. A key question is: *How* are we to pursue the questions that arise within us? God, being morally perfect, would care about this, even if we do not. Will we pursue them to the neglect or the disadvantage of other people? Will we thereby exclude ourselves from obeying the divine love commands? How we pursue questions is not an ethically neutral matter, as if God would not care. In any case, I have not excluded any "deep and interesting questions" from Christian philosophy, so long as they are pursued in keeping with the love commands and contribute to the Christian calling of God in Christ. We do not need a complete list of what would thus contribute to use my criterion, just as we do not need a full list of vegetables to recommend that people eat more vegetables.

Oppy puts in a word for natural theology in the New Testament. He remarks: "Romans 1:20 . . . seems to me to suggest . . . that 'creation by itself shows or otherwise establishes God's reality'" (204). Perhaps it does seem to him this way, but the reality is that the apostle Paul contradicts the position suggested. Paul does not say or even suggest, contrary to Oppy, that "creation by itself shows or otherwise establishes God's reality." Instead, he says that "what can be known about God is plain to them, because *God* has shown it to them" (Rom 1:19 NRSV). Paul does not suggest that creation by itself shows this. God does the showing, in Paul's account.

We should not confuse the finding of flaws in the arguments of speculative philosophy and natural theology with one's *doing* speculative philosophy or natural theology. One can, and sometimes should, engage such arguments, but it does not follow that one is undertaking speculative philosophy or natural theology. Oppy seems to miss this distinction. In addition, he fails to see that a redemptive personal God would be elusive in a way that the premises and conclusions of arguments are not. People can fail to comprehend arguments, but that does not entail that the arguments are elusive *in the way God is*. God is *purposively elusive* toward humans for redemptive ends; arguments are not. God intentionally bobs and weaves in many interactions with humans; arguments do not.

It does not help to suggest that "perhaps . . . those less-than-compelling arguments [of natural theology] serve, for some, as stepping-stones along the path to belief" (206). Perhaps, but perhaps not, too. It is unclear what kind of "stepping-stone" Oppy has in mind. Merely psychological? If the arguments in question (notably, Oppy does not offer one) do not cogently conclude with a God worthy of worship (as I have argued), they do not conclude with the Jewish-Christian God. In that case, they will not be crucial or adequate "stepping-stones" that lead to that God. As for lesser gods, we have no reason to think they are "stepping-stones" to the Jewish-Christian God; in fact, they are typically impediments, nothing more than diversions.

To Oliphint

Even if Oliphint and I agree on the absence of natural theology in Romans 1, I do not share his Calvinist reading of that chapter. He holds that "all of us as long as we are apart from Christ . . . are immersed in utter and radical *self-deception*. We deceive ourselves when we think that we can understand our world, ourselves, or *whether or not God exists* according to our own human resources" (211). This seems too strong. I do not see Jesus allowing for such a severe position in the parable of the sower (Mark 4:14–20) or in his comment on Nathanael (John 1:47). We must not let systematic theology distort our understanding of God in Christ.

Oliphint claims: "Paul is explicit as he summarizes the effect of God's revelation that it results in our 'knowing God'. . . . The true knowledge that all people possess is *personal* knowledge. It is knowledge of God's eternal power and deity, and it is sufficient to render us all inexcusable" (210). This position runs afoul of various remarks by the apostle Paul. For instance, Paul speaks of "the Gentiles who do not know God" (1 Thess 4:5 NRSV), and elsewhere he refers more generally to "those who do not know God" (2 Thess 1:8). We also find Jesus saying: "Righteous Father, the world does not know you, but I know you" (John 17:25; cf. Hosea 4:1; John 14:17). In the same vein, 1 John 4:8 states: "Whoever does not love does not know God, for God is love." Once again, we must not let systematic theology distort our understanding of God in Christ. Paul is not making in Romans 1 the kind of sweeping statement alleged by Oliphint; otherwise, he would contradict himself and Jesus.

It is misleading for Oliphint to claim: "Any experiential self-manifestation of God will necessarily have its ground in God's revelation. It will have its universal ground in God's general revelation in and through creation" (212). The self-manifestation of God *is* a key feature of God's revelation; it does not have or need a "ground" in God's revelation, let alone a ground in creation. God, as *sui generis* in being worthy of worship, provides God's own ground. So, as the Bible teaches, God swears by himself for God's authenticity (see Hebrews 6:13).

To McGrew

McGrew notes that "a vast gulf separates us" (218), but he does not get the gulf right. He alleges that according to my position "it is wrong to give arguments for the existence of God" (216). I have tried to correct this serious misunderstanding (most recently in *Philosophia Christi* 17.2 [2015], 385–96), because I myself defend (in *The Elusive God*) an argument for God's existence from a first-person perspective.[1] My objection is against the kind of arguments found in speculative philosophy and natural theology. In addition, my position requires undefeated evidence for reasonable belief in God's existence. I reject, however, the common confusion of evidence and argument. I contend that the kind of foundational evidence offered by God is not an argument but is something more existentially and morally profound, in keeping with Romans 5:5.

---

1. Paul K. Moser, "New Testament Apologetics, Arguments, and the End of Christian Apologetics as We Know It," *Philosophia Christi* 17.2 (2015): 385–96; and Paul K. Moser, *The Elusive God* (New York: Cambridge University Press, 2008).

My argument from a first-person perspective and its corresponding evidence base differ from what McGrew calls "good public reasons for belief in God" (216). I deny that the God of the Bible, who is elusive and hides at times, gives such public reasons to all people. In addition, I deny that the familiar arguments of natural theology yield such public reasons, at least if we have the Jewish-Christian God in mind. The key problem is that those arguments do not yield a God worthy of worship, even if they should happen to yield a lesser god.[2] In addition, if they bring one to a lesser god, a big question remains: How is one going to get to a God worthy of worship, the Jewish-Christian God? McGrew and other friends of natural theology fail to explain here, and this is a big omission for a Christian philosophy. In addition, if they turn to a special intervention from God (say, of the sort I acknowledge), then the natural-theology step becomes dispensable. I have contended that it is indeed dispensable and is foreign to the teaching of the New Testament. It is remarkable that McGrew fails to give the "good public reasons for belief in God" that he prizes. I doubt that he has any to give that will bear on all rational inquirers. In any case, it is unconvincing to affirm the existence of such reasons without supplying them.

McGrew misses the point of my exegesis of Paul. The key is in this remark from Paul: "My speech and my proclamation were not with plausible words of wisdom, but with a demonstration of the Spirit and of power, so that your faith might rest not on human wisdom but on the power of God" (1 Cor 2:4–5 NRSV). Paul is not making a contrast just between exalted rhetoric or pagan philosophy and truths of the gospel. Instead, he is drawing a sharp contrast with any "plausible words of wisdom" and the "power" of God. That power is the divine foundation of not only the life of Jesus but also the earliest movement and message generated by Jesus. The gospel truths describe that power, and that power is, at heart, the power of God in Christ.

The apostle Paul's epistemology puts the power of God in Christ, including the power of *divine love*, front and center, and hence differs from the norm in contemporary Christian philosophy and apologetics. Here's one clear statement: "Hope [in God] does not disappoint us,

---

2. See Paul K. Moser, *The Evidence for God* (New York: Cambridge University Press, 2010), chapter 3.

because God's love [*agapē*] has been poured into our hearts through the Holy Spirit that has been given to us" (Rom 5:5 NRSV). This foundational experience of God's love enables and grounds what Paul thinks of as *being* a child of God and as *being witnessed to* by God. He writes: "All who are led by the Spirit of God are children of God. For you did not receive a spirit of slavery to fall back into fear, but you have received a spirit of adoption. When we cry, 'Abba! Father!' it is that very Spirit bearing witness with our spirit that we are children of God" (Rom 8:14–16 NRSV). The idea of "witness" here is crucial to Paul's epistemology. It is a witness that brings evidence of God's reality and moral character, in divine love being "poured into" the hearts of those receptive to God. No natural theology is needed here, and "public reasons" are not to the point. Relevant public evidence will have to accommodate the foundational role of this evidence.

McGrew misses the heart of Paul's epistemology anchored in *agapē* experiences, both in theory and, by his own report, in his life. He remarks: "I am not personally subject to such experiences" (213). This is a very serious matter for a Christian, because, as Paul indicates, it corresponds to whether one is led by God's Spirit. Many people lack the experiences in question, but Christian hope and faith in God depend on such experiences according to the apostle Paul. A Christian philosophy must not neglect this lesson. Instead, it must give it a central role, and the result will be a profound transformation of "Christian philosophy" as currently practiced.

CONCLUSION

PAUL M. GOULD & RICHARD BRIAN DAVIS

You've read the debate. You've carefully weighed each contributor's argument and counterargument. Now what? What ought you to *think*—especially if you are a beginner in philosophy or new to Christianity? Which view, if any, of the four defended in this volume is closest to the truth? As should now be clear, no easy answers to these questions are forthcoming. In theoretical matters, as in life, there is freedom to choose, for good or for ill. Instead of listing reasons why you ought to pick view X instead of view Y, in this conclusion we propose to explore and make explicit themes that are percolating just beneath the surface of the debate, themes which point to key aspects of a life well lived as a Christian and as a philosopher.

We begin with lessons from philosophy to Christianity. First, *the mind matters*. As Aristotle noted long ago, man is a rational animal. He is more than that but not less. Part of what it means to flourish as a human being includes employing one's mind in the service of truth. The Christian has ample motivation for developing the mind. In fact, for the Christian, the proper use of the mind is part of what it means to love God (Matt 22:37–39). It is part of what it means to be a follower of Jesus. Jesus is smart, as Dallas Willard reminds us, and those who follow him should develop intellectual virtue.[1]

The idea that Christians are called to love God with their minds might come to some as a shock. Setting aside those who teach and write for a living, Christians are not generally known as intellectuals. Anti-intellectualism rules the day and runs rampant in the church. In this YouTube and Twitter age, maintaining focus to follow a line of thought or an argument to its conclusion proves difficult. For this reason alone, you should be applauded for making it this far in the book! Difficult as it may be, faithfulness to Christ demands we develop our minds. And

---

1. Dallas Willard, *The Divine Conspiracy* (New York: HarperCollins, 1998), 93–95.

this takes effort. Wonder and curiosity, properly followed will lead, we believe, to Christ "in whom are hidden all the treasures of wisdom and knowledge" (Col 2:3).

Secondly, *ideas matter.* Philosophers, theologians, cultural critics, and historians have made this point time and time again.[2] Ideas move us to action. They can liberate, and they can shackle. Some are life-giving, and some can be deadly. An *idea* is a thought, a constituent of our mental life that guides behavior and governs discussion with others. We think *with* them, but don't always thing *about* them. But, as Socrates famously puts it, "The unexamined life is not worth living" (*Apology* 38a).[3] In other words, we *ought* to examine our lives and the beliefs that form the rails on which we live in order to align our lives with reality.[4]

Consider, for example, our idea of God. What you think about God matters a great deal. As one theologian aptly put it, "What comes into our minds when we think about God is the most important thing about us."[5] This is because our lives are partly shaped by what we think great. We run to that which we love. We long for that which we think beautiful. Part of the spiritual malaise within the church—and within a secular culture where unbelief is now possible—results from a low conception of God. Philosophy can help—pointing out error, redirecting when headed in the wrong direction, and, if we let it, awakening our sense of awe and wonder of the world, a world which echoes everywhere of the divine.

Finally, we end with a lesson from Christianity to philosophy: *philosophy without Christ is existentially unfulfilling.* The apostle Paul calls such philosophies "hollow and deceptive" (Col 2:8). Young Augustine, after reading Cicero's *Hortensius*, determined to become a truth seeker and realized, even as a nonbeliever, that any philosophy that fails to mention Christ falls short of the whole truth. He notes, "Any book which lacked this name [i.e., Christ], however well written or polished or true, could

---

2. See, e.g., Richard Weaver, *Ideas Have Consequences* (Chicago: University of Chicago Press, 1984); R. C. Sproul, *The Consequence of Ideas* (Wheaton, IL: Crossway, 2009); James Davison Hunter, *To Change the World: The Irony, Tragedy, and Possibility of Christianity in the Late Modern World* (Oxford: Oxford University Press, 2010).

3. Plato, *Five Dialogues*, trans. G. M. A. Grube (Indianapolis: Hackett, 1981), 41.

4. J. P. Moreland, *Love Your God with All Your Mind* (Colorado Springs, CO: NavPress, 2012), 86.

5. A. W. Tozer, *The Knowledge of the Holy* (New York: HarperCollins, 1961), 1.

not entirely grip me."[6] The famous philosopher and mathematician Blaise Pascal reminds us that the God of Christianity is a *living* God, a God who is, as C. S. Lewis puts it, "Approaching at an infinite speed."[7] In a piece of parchment found sewn into Pascal's clothing after his death in 1662 were recorded these words, which he seems to have carried with him at all times:

> The year of grace 1654. Monday, 23 November, feast of Saint Clement. . . . From about half past ten in the evening until half past midnight. Fire. "God of Abraham, God of Isaac, God of Jacob," not of philosophers and scholars. Certainty, certainty, heartfelt, joy, peace. God of Jesus Christ. God of Jesus Christ. My God and your God. . . . Let me never be cut off from him! He can only be kept by the ways taught in the Gospel. Sweet and total renunciation. Total submission to Jesus Christ and my director. Everlasting joy in return for one day's effort on earth. *I will not forget thy word.* Amen.[8]

The God of Christianity is alive. Moreover, he actively pursues us even as we run. He wills our good, and our good is to love him. And to love him, we must know him, and if we know him, our response should be to fall flat on our face in worship.[9] Christianity offers something that no philosophy on its own provides: a story that is true to the way the world *is* and true to how the world *ought* to be. It offers us Jesus Christ and with him forgiveness for sins, wholeness, and true happiness.

In closing, we submit the words of the great statesman Charles Malik, who along with Eleanor Roosevelt was one of the chief architects of the 1948 Universal Declaration of Human Rights. While Malik is best known as the Lebanese statesman and ambassador to the United Nations, he was first and foremost a Christian. What is lesser known is that he was also a Harvard-educated philosopher. Reflecting on the discipline of philosophy as it is often experienced, he writes as follows:

> The fact that philosophical systems historically knock each other out was clearly seen by Kant and Hegel, who nevertheless were

---

6. Augustine, *Confessions* 3.4 (Chadwick).

7. C. S. Lewis, *Miracles* (New York: Touchstone, 1996), 125.

8. Blaise Pascal, "In Memorial," in *Pensées*, trans. A. J. Krailsheimer (Harmondsworth, UK: Penguin, 1995), 285–86.

9. C. S. Lewis, *The Problem of Pain* (New York: HarperCollins, 1996), 46.

themselves sucked into the immanent process of the history of philosophy and could not liberate themselves into genuine transcendence. They simply succeeded in depositing themselves as links in an endless chain of thought. . . . [But they kick] against the enclosing cage of reason. These men are not to be taken very seriously. . . . What an incredible jolt your whole being undergoes when you come to the Bible or attend the Divine Liturgy or have an intimate personal chat with a friend after reading or lecturing on the sublimest philosophy—that of Plato or Aristotle or Kant or Hegel! The philosophers are worth nothing so far as being and existence are concerned compared to one passage from the word of God—a Psalm or chapter from Paul or the Gospels—or a genuine moment of living and free communication with a friend. This existential jolt is the most terrible experience I know in my life. Supposing you really know what David or Paul or Jesus Christ is talking about so far as your own living-dying existence is concerned—how can you then take any of the philosophers seriously?[10]

That Malik took philosophy seriously is clear, attested by his many years of teaching philosophy at institutions of learning such as Harvard, The Catholic University of America, and the American University of Beirut. What is also clear is that he believed an encounter with the living God is the fitting object of all human longing. Philosophy can and does point and prod us toward the divine, but in the end all strategies fail. In the end we must, one and all, fall on our knees, lay down our objections, and worship the "God who made the world and everything in it" (Acts 17:24).

---

10. Charles Malik, *The Wonder of Being* (Waco, TX: Word Books, 1974), 34–35, as quoted in John North, "Reflections from the Humanities," in *The Two Tasks of the Christian Scholar: Redeeming the Soul, Redeeming the Mind*, ed. William Lane Craig & Paul M. Gould (Wheaton, IL: Crossway, 2007), 171–72.

BIBLIOGRAPHY

Adams, William. *An Essay in Answer to Mr. Hume's Essay on Miracles.* 3rd ed. London: B. White, 1767.

Aeschylus. *The Oresteia.* Translated by Robert Fagles. New York: Penguin, 1979.

Aquinas, Thomas. *Summa contra Gentiles.* Translated by Anton C. Pegis. Notre Dame: University of Notre Dame Press, 1975.

Aristotle. *Metaphysics.* Edited by W. D. Ross. Oxford: Clarendon, 1924.

Atran, Scott, and Ara Norenzayan. "Religion's Evolutionary Landscape: Counterintuition, Commitment, Compassion, Communion." *Behavioral and Brain Sciences* 27.6 (2004): 713–30.

Augustine. *Confessions.* Translated by Henry Chadwick. Oxford: Oxford University Press, 2008.

Balentine, Samuel. *The Hidden God.* Oxford: Oxford University Press, 1983.

Balfour, Arthur James. *The Foundations of Belief.* 8th ed. New York: Longmans, Green and Co., 1918.

Barr, James. *Biblical Faith and Natural Theology.* Oxford: Clarendon Press, 1993.

Bavinck, Herman. *Reformed Dogmatics: God and Creation.* Edited by John Bolt. Translated by John Vriend. Vol. 2 of *Reformed Dogmatics.* Grand Rapids: Baker Academic, 2004.

Blunt, John James. *Undesigned Coincidences.* New York: Robert Carter & Brothers, 1855.

Brown, Alexandra R. "Apocalyptic Transformation in Paul's Discourse on the Cross." *Word & World* 16 (1996): 427–36.

———. *The Cross and Human Transformation.* Minneapolis: Fortress, 1995.

———. "The Gospel Takes Place: Paul's Theology of Power-in-Weakness in 2 Corinthians." *Interpretation* 52 (1998): 271–85.

Butler, Joseph. *The Analogy of Religion.* New York: E. P. Dutton & Co. Inc., 1906.

Calvin, John. *Institutes of the Christian Religion.* Edited by John T. McNeill. Translated by Ford Lewis Battles. Vol. 1. The Library of Christian Classics. Louisville: Westminster John Knox, 2011.

Campbell, George. *A Dissertation on Miracles.* Edinburgh: A. Kincaid & J. Bell, 1762.

Chalmers, Thomas. *The Evidence and Authority of the Christian Revelation.* 4th ed. Edinburgh: William Blackwood, 1817.

Cosgrove, Charles H. *The Cross and the Spirit.* Macon, GA: Mercer University Press, 1988.

Dawkins, Richard. *The God Delusion.* New York: First Mariners Books, 2008.

Derrida, Jacques. *Of Grammatology.* Translated by Gayatri Chakravorty Spivak. Baltimore: John Hopkins University Press, 1976.

Douglas, John. *The Criterion.* 4th ed. Oxford: Oxford University Press, 1832.

Earman, John. *Hume's Abject Failure.* Oxford: Oxford University Press, 2000.

Ehrman, Bart. *Jesus, Interrupted.* New York: HarperOne, 2010.

———. *The New Testament: A Historical Introduction to the Early Christian Writings.* 2nd ed. New York: Oxford University Press, 2000.

Farmer, Herbert H. *Towards Belief in God.* London: Macmillan, 1943.

———. *The World and God.* London: Nisbet, 1935.

Ferguson, Sinclair B., David F. Wright, and J. I. Packer, eds. *New Dictionary of Theology.* Downers Grove, IL: InterVarsity Press, 1988.

Fitzgerald, John T. *Cracks in an Earthen Vessel.* Atlanta: Scholars Press, 1988.

Fitzmyer, Joseph. *First Corinthians.* AB 32. New Haven: Yale University Press, 2008.

———. *Romans.* AB 33. New York: Doubleday, 1993.

Forbes, Archibald. "Napoleon the Third at Sedan." *The Nineteenth Century* 31 (1892): 419–32.

Gibbon, Edward. *History of the Decline and Fall of the Roman Empire, Volume 1.* London: W. Strahan, 1776.

Gilson, Etienne. *History of Christian Philosophy in the Middle Ages.* New York: Random House, 1955.

Gorman, Michael J. *Cruciformity.* Grand Rapids: Eerdmans, 2001.

———. *Inhabiting the Cruciform God.* Grand Rapids: Eerdmans, 2009.

Hedley, Douglas. "Forms of Reflection, Imagination, and the Love of Wisdom." *Metaphilosophy* 43.1–2 (2012): 112–24.

Hemer, Colin. *The Book of Acts in the Setting of Hellenistic History.* WUNT 49. Tübingen: Mohr Siebeck, 1989.

Heschel, Abraham. *God in Search of Man: A Philosophy of Judaism.* New York: Jewish Publication Society of America, 1955.

———. *The Prophets.* New York: Harper & Row, 1962.

Hubbard, Moyer V. *New Creation in Paul's Letters and Thought.* Cambridge: Cambridge University Press, 2002.

Hunter, James Davison. *To Change the World: The Irony, Tragedy, and Possibility of Christianity in the Late Modern World.* Oxford: Oxford University Press, 2010.

Inwagen, Peter van. *Metaphysics.* 2nd ed. Dimensions of Philosophy Series. Boulder: Westview, 2002.

Joad, C. E. M. *The Recovery of Belief.* London: Faber and Faber, 1952.

Käsemann, Ernst. *Commentary on Romans.* Translated by G. W. Bromiley. Grand Rapids: Eerdmans, 1980.

———. "'The Righteousness of God' in Paul." Pages 168–82 in *New Testament Questions of Today.* Translated by W. J. Montague. London: SCM, 1969.

———. "The Righteousness of God in Paul." Pages 15–26 in *On Being a Disciple of the Crucified Nazarene.* Translated by R. A. Harrisville. Grand Rapids: Eerdmans, 2010.

Keck, Leander. "Biblical Preaching as Divine Wisdom." Pages 137–56 in *A New Look at Preaching.* Edited by John Burke. Wilmington, DE: Michael Glazier, 1983.

———. "God the Other Who Acts Otherwise: An Exegetical Essay on 1 Cor 1:26–31." *Word & World* 16 (1996): 437–43.

———. *Paul and His Letters.* 2nd ed. Philadelphia: Fortress, 1988.

———. "Paul as Thinker." *Interpretation* 47 (1993): 27–38.

———. *Romans.* Nashville: Abingdon, 2005.

Kyburg, Henry. "The Justification of Induction." *The Journal of Philosophy* 53 (1956): 394–400.

Leathes, Stanley. *The Religion of the Christ.* 2nd ed. New York: Pott, Young, and Co., 1876.

Leftow, Brian. "Jesus and Aquinas." Pages 124–46 in *Jesus and Philosophy: New Essays*. Edited by Paul K. Moser. Cambridge: Cambridge University Press, 2009.

Lenski, R. C. H. *The Interpretation of the Acts of the Apostles*. Minneapolis: Augsburg, 1961.

Lewis, C. S. *Mere Christianity*. New York: HarperOne, 2007.

———. *Miracles*. New York: Touchstone, 1996.

———. *The Problem of Pain*. New York: HarperCollins, 1996.

Malik, Charles. *A Christian Critique of the University*. Waterloo, CA: North Waterloo Academic Press, 1987.

———. *The Wonder of Being*. Waco, TX: Word Books, 1974.

Marshall, David. *The Truth about Jesus and the "Lost Gospels."* Eugene, OR: Harvest House, 2007.

Martyn, J. Louis. "Epistemology at the Turn of the Ages." Pages 89–110 in *Theological Issues in the Letters of Paul*. Edinburgh: T&T Clark, 1997.

———. *Galatians*. AB 33A. New York: Doubleday, 1997.

McGrew, Timothy. "The Argument from Miracles." Pages 593–662 in *The Blackwell Companion to Natural Theology*. Edited by William Lane Craig and J. P. Moreland. New York: Blackwell, 2009.

———. "A Defense of Strong Foundationalism." In *The Theory of Knowledge: Classic and Contemporary Readings*. 2nd ed. Edited by Louis Pojman. Belmont, CA: Wadsworth, 1998.

———. "Direct Inference and the Problem of Induction." *The Monist* 84 (2001): 153–78.

———. *The Foundations of Knowledge*. Lanham, MD: Littlefield Adams, 1995.

———. "Scientific Progress, Relativism, and Self-Refutation." *Electronic Journal of Analytic Philosophy* 2 (1994).

McGrew, Timothy, and John DePoe. "Natural Theology and the Uses of Argument." *Philosophia Christi* 15 (2013): 299–309.

McGrew, Timothy, and Lydia McGrew. *Internalism and Epistemology: The Architecture of Reason*. New York: Routledge, 2007.

Moreland, J. P. *Love Your God with All Your Mind*. Colorado Springs, CO: NavPress, 2012.

Moser, Paul K. *The Elusive God*. New York: Cambridge University Press, 2008.

———. *The Evidence for God*. New York: Cambridge University Press, 2010.

———. "God without Argument." Pages 69–83 in *Is Faith in God Reasonable?* Edited by Corey Miller and Paul Gould. New York: Routledge, 2014.

———. "Introduction: Jesus and Philosophy." Pages 1–23 in *Jesus and Philosophy: New Essays*. Edited by Paul K. Moser. Cambridge: Cambridge University Press, 2009.

———. *Knowledge and Evidence*. Cambridge: Cambridge University Press, 1989.

———. "New Testament Apologetics, Arguments, and the End of Christian Apologetics as We Know It." *Philosophia Christi* 17.2 (2015): 385–96.

———. *The Severity of God*. Cambridge: Cambridge University Press, 2013.

Muller, Richard A. *Post-Reformation Reformed Dogmatics: The Rise and Development of Reformed Orthodoxy; Volume 1: Prolegomena to Theology*. 2nd ed. Grand Rapids: Baker Academic, 2003.

North, John. "Reflections from the Humanities." Pages 155–75 in *The Two Tasks of the Christian Scholar: Redeeming the Soul, Redeeming the Mind*. Edited by William Lane Craig and Paul M. Gould. Wheaton, IL: Crossway, 2007.

Oliphint, K. Scott. "Bavinck's Realism, the Logos Principle and Sola Scriptura." *WTJ* 72 (2010): 359–90.

———. *Covenantal Apologetics: Principles and Practice in Defense of our Faith*. Wheaton, IL: Crossway, 2013.

Oppy, Graham. *Arguing about Gods*. Cambridge: Cambridge University Press, 2006.

———. *The Best Argument against God*. New York: Palgrave-Macmillan, 2013.

———. "Ultimate Naturalistic Causal Explanations." Pages 46–63 in *The Puzzle of Existence*. Edited by Tyron Goldschmidt. New York: Routledge, 2013.

Owen, John. *The Works of John Owen*. Edited by William H. Goold. Edinburgh: T&T Clark, n.d.

Paley, William. *Horae Paulinae*. London: SPCK, 1877.

———. *A View of the Evidences of Christianity.* London: John W. Parker and Son, 1859.

Pascal, Blaise. "In Memorial." Pages 285–86 in *Pensées.* Translated by A. J. Krailsheimer. Harmondsworth, UK: Penguin, 1995.

Plantinga, Alvin, and James F. Sennett. *The Analytic Theist: A Collection of Alvin Plantinga's Work in Philosophy of Religion.* Grand Rapids: Eerdmans, 1998.

Plato. *Apology.* Translated by Hugh Tredennick. London: Penguin, 1959.

———. *Five Dialogues.* Translated by G. M. A. Grube. Indianapolis: Hackett, 1981.

———. *The Laws of Plato.* Translated by A. E. Taylor. London: J. M. Dent & Sons, 1934.

Plessis-Mornay, Philippe du. *A Worke Concerning the Trunesse of Christian Religion, Written in French: Against Atheists, Epicures, Paynims, Iewes, Mahumetists, and Other Infidels.* Translated by Sir Philip Sidney Knight and Arthur Golding. London: George Potter, 1604.

Prestige, G. L. *God in Patristic Thought.* London: William Heinneman Ltd., 1936.

Reppert, Victor. *C. S. Lewis's Dangerous Idea.* Downers Grove, IL: InterVarsity Press, 2003.

Reynolds, John Mark. *When Athens Met Jerusalem.* Downers Grove, IL: InterVarsity Press, 2009.

Rist, John. "Faith and Reason." Pages 26–39 in *The Cambridge Companion to Augustine.* Edited by Eleonore Stump and Norman Kretzmann. Cambridge: Cambridge University Press, 2001.

Robertson, A. T. *A Commentary on the Gospel according to Matthew.* New York: Macmillan, 1911.

Russell, Bertrand. *The Problems of Philosophy.* Oxford: Oxford University Press, 1997.

Savage, Timothy. *Power through Weakness.* Cambridge: Cambridge University Press, 1996.

Scroggs, Robin. *Christology in Paul and John.* Philadelphia: Fortress, 1988.

Smith, James K. A. "Who's Afraid of Postmodernism? A Response to the 'Biola School.'" Pages 215–28 in *Christianity and the Postmodern Turn: Six Views.* Edited by Myron B. Penner. Grand Rapids: Brazos, 2005.

Sproul, R. C. *The Consequence of Ideas.* Wheaton, IL: Crossway, 2009.

Stark, Herman E. "Philosophy as Wonder." *Dialogue and Universalism* 1–2 (2005): 133–40.

Stauffer, Ethelbert. *New Testament Theology*. Translated by John Marsh. New York: Macmillan, 1955.

Stoker, Hendrik G. "Reconnoitering the Theory of Knowledge of Professor Dr. Cornelius Van Til." Pages 25–71 in *Jerusalem and Athens: Critical Discussions on the Philosophy and Apologetics of Cornelius Van Til*. Edited by E. R. Geehan. Phillipsburg, NJ: P&R, 1977.

Stove, David C. "Part IX of Hume's Dialogues." *The Philosophical Quarterly* 28 (1978): 300–309.

———. *The Rationality of Induction*. Oxford: Oxford University Press, 1986.

Swinburne, Richard. *The Existence of God*. 2nd ed. Oxford: Oxford University Press, 2004.

Terrien, Samuel. *The Elusive Presence*. San Francisco: Harper & Row, 1978.

Tozer, A. W. *The Knowledge of the Holy*. New York: HarperCollins, 1961.

Turretin, Francis. *Institutes of Elenctic Theology*. Edited by James T. Dennison Jr. 3 vols. Phillipsburg, NJ: P&R, 1994.

Van Til, Cornelius. *Common Grace and the Gospel*. Edited by K. Scott Oliphint. Phillipsburg, NJ: P&R, 2015.

———. *In Defense of the Faith, Volume IV: Christian-Theistic Evidences*. Phillipsburg, NJ: P&R, 1978.

Vos, Geerhardus. *Reformed Dogmatics*. Edited by Richard B. Gaffin. Translated by Annemie Godbehere et al. Vol. 1. Bellingham, WA: Lexham, 2012–14.

Weaver, Richard. *Ideas Have Consequences*. Chicago: University of Chicago Press, 1984.

Willard, Dallas. *The Divine Conspiracy*. New York: HarperCollins, 1998.

Williams, Donald. *The Ground of Induction*. New York: Russell & Russell, 1963.

Witherington III, Ben. *The Acts of the Apostles: A Socio-Rhetorical Commentary*. Grand Rapids: Eerdmans, 1998.

Wood, Allen. "Philosophy—What Is to Be Done?" *Topoi* 25 (2006): 133–36.

NAME INDEX

SCRIPTURE INDEX